D1478319

Myth, Ritual, and Kingship in Buganda

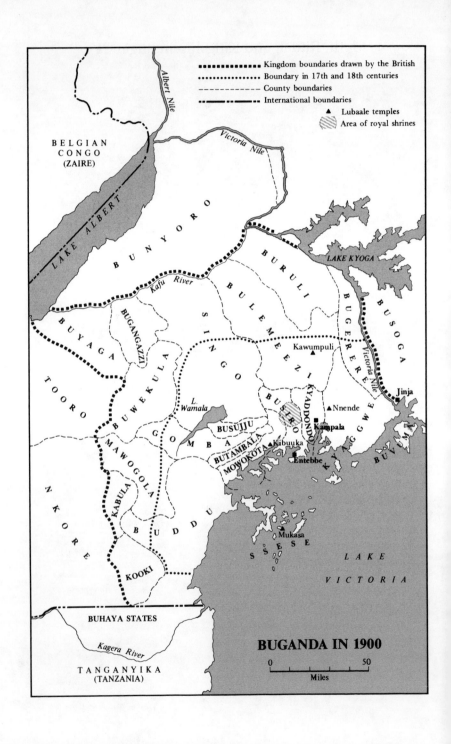

BUGANDA IN 1900

Kingdom boundaries drawn by the British
Boundary in 17th and 18th centuries
County boundaries
International boundaries
▲ Lubaale temples
▨ Area of royal shrines

0   50
Miles

BELGIAN
CONGO
(ZAIRE)

Albert Nile

Victoria Nile

LAKE ALBERT

B U N Y O R O

LAKE KYOGA

B U R U L I

Kafu River

B U L E M E E Z I

BUGANGAZZI

BUYAGA

S I N G O

BUGERERE

BUSOGA

Victoria Nile

Jinja

TOORO

B U W E K U L A

L. Wamala

BUSIRO

KYADDONDO

Kawumpuli ▲

▲ Nnende

Kampala ■

G O M B A

BUSUJJU

BUTAMBALA

MOWOKOTA

Kibuuka ●

Entebbe ●

K Y A G G W E

BUVUMA

N K O R E

M A W O G O L A

KABULA

B U D D U

● Kibuuka

▲ Mukasa

S S E S E

LAKE
VICTORIA

KOOKI

BUHAYA STATES

Kagera River

T A N G A N Y I K A
(TANZANIA)

MYTH, RITUAL, AND KINGSHIP IN BUGANDA

Benjamin C. Ray

New York   Oxford
OXFORD UNIVERSITY PRESS
1991

Oxford University Press

Oxford   New York   Toronto
Delhi   Bombay   Calcutta   Madras   Karachi
Petaling Jaya   Singapore   Hong Kong   Tokyo
Nairobi   Dar es Salaam   Cape Town
Melbourne   Auckland

and associated companies in
Berlin   Ibadan

Copyright © 1991 by Benjamin C. Ray

Published by Oxford University Press, Inc.,
200 Madison Avenue, New York, New York 10016

Oxford is a registered trademark of Oxford University Press

Library of Congress Cataloging-in-Publication Data
Ray, Benjamin C., 1940–
Myth, ritual, and kingship in Buganda /
by Benjamin C. Ray.
p.   cm.
Includes bibliographical references.
ISBN 0-19-506436-4
1. Ganda (African people)--Kings and rulers.
2. Ganda (African people)—Rites and ceremonies.
I. Title.
DT433.245.G35R39   1991
306.6′996896395706761—dc20
90-7127

9   8   7   6   5   4   3   2   1
Printed in the United States of America

To the Memory of
Ssaabalangira Paul M. Lukongwa

Acknowledgments

This study, which has taken a number of years to complete, owes a great deal to the help of others. I am indebted first of all to the two academic institutions with which I have been associated and to two granting agencies. A sabbatical leave from Princeton University and a Study Fellowship from the American Council of Learned Societies made it possible for me to visit Uganda in 1972. In 1976, a grant from the Stewart Lectureship Fund at Princeton University gave me time to begin translating Luganda texts and to write up field notes. A fellowship from the National Endowment for the Humanities the following year provided additional opportunity to translate texts and begin working on the manuscript. Part of the final stage of writing was supported by a summer grant from the University of Virginia in 1980.

A number of people have also given most valuable assistance. Dr. John Mbiti, the former head of the Department of Religious Studies at Makerere University, invited me to visit Uganda in 1972 and to join the department as a visiting professor. Professor Peter Rigby, then head of the Department of Sociology at Makerere, kindly helped to secure housing and obtain research permission from the National Research Council. For the constant support that professors Mbiti and Rigby extended to me and my family during our stay, I am most grateful. I was also fortunate in finding George Kijjambo, who served as both a competent translator and a helpful colleague in our discussions with the officials at the royal shrines. Hamo Sassoon, then Conservator of Antiquities, took a lively interest in my fieldwork and, under somewhat trying circumstances, helped to prepare my research report for publication in the *Uganda Journal* (1972).

Later, as I began to consider the possibility of writing more extensively about the rituals of the kingship, Professor John Rowe encouraged me to proceed, and generously provided access to his large collection of Luganda publications and manuscripts. Margaret C. Fallers also kindly permitted me to use materials from the ethnographic files and manuscript collection of her late husband, Professor Lloyd A. Fallers, a former director of the East African Institute of Social Research (now the Makerere Institute of Social Research). I am also indebted to the late Audrey I. Richards, another former director of the institute, who allowed me to look over her field notes on Ganda clans and certain officials at the royal shrines. In 1976, by good fortune I happened to meet Dr. Robert Ackerman, then beginning work on his biographical study of Sir James G. Frazer, who drew my attention to Frazer's extensive correspondence with the Reverend John Roscoe. Trinity College Library graciously provided copies of letters from Frazer and Roscoe. The University Museum of Archaeology and Ethnology at Cambridge was most helpful in allowing me to delve into Roscoe's enthnographic collection from Uganda, now kept in storage, and to photograph selected items. While I worked on a first draft of the manuscript in Oxford, Professor Rodney Needham and Dr. R. Godfrey Lienhardt provided me with colleagueship and a place to work at the Institute of Social Anthropology, for which I am most grateful. I also wish to acknowledge the help of S. Byekwaso Mayanja, then a student at Bristol, who translated some difficult portions of the newsletter *Munno* and other antiquated Luganda texts.

In the course of writing, I have benefited greatly from the comments and advice of a number of scholars who have read all or part of the manuscript: Robert Ackerman, Hoyt S. Alverson, John Baines, Tom Beidelman, Catherine M. Coles, David Henige, Ivan Karp, Semakula Kiwanuka, Godfrey Lienhardt, Charles H. Long, Aloysius M. Lugira, Joseph Miller, Helen K. Nabasuta, John Orley, Hans H. Penner, and Fred B. Welbourn. Stylistically, the manuscript has also benefited from the careful copy-editing of Tracy Fessenden and Gail Weiss. I am, of course, responsible for any of the inadequacies of style and content that remain. Over the years, my family has endured the research and writing of this book with great patience and understanding, and for this I am deeply appreciative.

For permission to reproduce manuscript material and copyrighted matter, I wish to thank the following sources: the Master and Fellows of Trinity College, Cambridge, for the use of quotations from the letters of James G. Frazer and John Roscoe; Pillans and Wilson for the use of the illustration "Speke and Grant at King Mtesa's Levee" from *Journal of the Discovery of the Source of the Nile* by John Hanning Speke; Frank Cass & Co. Ltd. for the use of the diagram "Plan of Mutesa's Capital" from *The Baganda* by John Roscoe; Indiana University Press for the use of my essay "Myth, Death, and Ontology in Buganda" from *Explorations in African Systems of Thought*, edited by Ivan Karp and Charles S. Bird, in slightly revised form as Chapter 2; and the University of Chicago Press for the use in Chapter 5 of portions of my essay "Sacred Space and Royal Shrines in Buganda" from *History of Religions*.

Finally, I wish to express my deepest appreciation to the Ganda officials who made this study possible, especially the late Ssaabalangira (Head of the Princes) Paul M. Lukongwa. Without his endorsement and active support, my fieldwork would have been entirely unproductive. I am also indebted to several princesses, prime ministers, bearers, and other officials associated with the royal shrines, especially those at Bumera, Bulondo, Kaliti, and Wamala, where most of my work was conducted. Their generous help consisted of many hours of conversation, ceremonial preparations, and ritual activity. To the memory of Ssaabalangira Lukongwa this book is gratefully dedicated.

Contents

Myth, Ritual, and Kingship in Buganda

Ethnography and the History of Religions

Ethnography is an interpretive enterprise, one that is intimately bound up with the perspective of the investigator and the circumstances in which the fieldwork is carried out. I was led to this conclusion in the course of doing fieldwork in Buganda, and it has persuaded me to reflect critically on my perspective as a historian of religions and upon the perspectives that have informed earlier anthropological studies of Buganda. I wish to begin, therefore, by explaining how and under what circumstances I conducted the ethnography on which this study is partly based, why I have chosen to concentrate on the mythic and ritual aspects of the kingship, and in what ways this study draws on some of the central concepts of the history of religions.

Ethnography

I arrived in Kampala, the capital of Uganda, in March 1972, with the intention of studying ritual among the Baganda.[1] The Baganda, who live in Kampala and the surrounding area, developed the most powerful kingdom in the Lake Victoria region. Situated in the rolling hills and swampy valleys along the northwestern shore of Lake Victoria, the kingdom of Buganda originated in the fourteenth century through the unification of clans under a paramount leader called the Kabaka. By the nineteenth century, the Kabaka had gained substantial superiority over the once-powerful clan chiefs. In 1900, after a drawn-out civil war between Christian and Muslim factions, Buganda came under British rule as part of the Protectorate of Uganda. When Uganda gained its independence in 1962,

Buganda retained its status as a traditional kingdom within Uganda, together with the other traditional kingdoms of Bunyoro, Toro, and Ankole (Nkore); in 1967, these kingdoms were abolished. Today, as in the past, Buganda's subsistence economy consists of small-scale peasant farming (the main crop being several varieties of bananas), livestock raising (goats and chickens), small-scale cattle herding, in addition to fishing along the lake shore and hunting in the forests. There were no markets in precolonial times, and long-distance trade with the coast was restricted to royal trafficking in ivory, slaves, guns, cloth, and beads. Precolonial Buganda was a predatory state and regularly extracted cattle and slaves from its weaker neighbors, principally Bunyoro and Bugosa, through periodic raids, and tribute in the form of cattle and craft goods from Nkore and other neighboring societies.

Intense Western contact since the late nineteenth century has made the Baganda perhaps the most researched people in East Africa, and the literature in English, French, and Luganda is considerable.[2] In searching about for a ritual institution that might not have been covered, I picked up the newly translated edition of Sir Apolo Kaggwa's noted historical work *The Kings of Buganda* ([1901] 1971). At the back of this book is a list of all the extant royal shrines, including instructions on how to find them. The shrines had been an important feature of the kingship, and virtually nothing had been written about them. Because ritual was the central matrix of cultural expression in a society whose means of communication was, until recently, fundamentally oral, I decided that a study of the ceremonies at the shrines might yield additional insight into Buganda's impressive and already well-examined institution of kingship.

An earlier attempt to study the shrines had failed for political reasons. In 1959, the historian Roland Oliver visited most of the shrines, but the hostile attitude of the attendants prevented him from entering them and examining their contents (Oliver 1959). Instead, he wrote an important article on the historical significance of the shrines and compiled the accurate list that appears in Kaggwa's book.[3]

The resistance to Oliver's inquiries was understandable, although the situation was more complex than his reference to "the prevailing state of xenophobia" would suggest. In 1953, the British protectorate government sent the king of Buganda, Kabaka Edward Frederick Mutesa II ("King Freddie"),[4] into exile in England for refusing to approve the government's plan to abolish Buganda's special status within the proposed state of Uganda. The Kabaka remained steadfast, and the British were forced to concede.[5] When the Kabaka returned to Buganda two years later, he received a hero's welcome and immediately became the focus of Ganda resistance to British rule. As Uganda prepared for national elections and independence in 1962, Ganda royalists formed their own political party, the Kabaka Yekka, or King Alone, and they made the Kabaka's throne the party emblem.[6] Thus the kingship became the focus of royalist political ambitions. When Oliver visited the shrines in 1959, he brought along a personal representative of the Head of the Princes (*Ssaabalangira*) and carried a letter from the prime minister (*Katikkiro*) of the Buganda government. But the local attendants still objected to his inquiries. As part of the kingship, the shrines had obviously become symbols of Ganda nationalism and resistance to colonialism.

By 1972, the political climate had changed radically and the kingship had been abolished. In 1967, Milton Obote, the prime minister of Uganda, with the help of his army general Idi Amin, forcefully expelled the Kabaka from his palace, and Mutesa immediately fled to England.[7] Obote then abolished the kingdom of Buganda together with the other traditional kingdoms of Bunyoro, Toro, and Nkore. This action dismantled the federalist structure of the national government. Obote himself took over the office of president of Uganda, which Mutesa had held, and declared Uganda to be a republic. Two years later, Mutesa died in London.[8] In January 1971, General Idi Amin, having consolidated his power within the armed forces, overthrew Obote when he was out of the country. Amin, who was from the northern Kakwa people, was immediately hailed by the Baganda as their liberator. But he was also known to have led the attack on the Kabaka's palace, and he needed to gain solid Ganda support, for the Baganda are the largest and most politically powerful ethnic group in Uganda. As a gesture to the Baganda, Amin called for the return of Mutesa's body from England and arranged for its burial in the great royal shrine at Kasubi, where the last three Kabakas were entombed. Amin also cleverly turned the ceremonies surrounding this event into a state occasion. In doing so, he not only won over the Baganda, but also demonstrated effectively to the rest of the nation that his regime was recognized by the many foreign governments (most notably Great Britain) whose ambassadors attended the ceremonies for the Kabaka. Even though Amin reaffirmed the abolition of the traditional kingdoms, Ganda hopes ran high for the restoration of the Kabakaship.[9]

In March 1972, the shrine attendants, whom Obote's soldiers had driven away, began to return. At the Kasubi shrine near Kampala, the sound of drums could be heard once again at the time of the appearance of the new moon, and ceremonies also started up at the outlying shrines in the countryside. I began to visit the shrines, having obtained authorization from the National Research Council and from the Ministry of Culture.

Only later did I discover that the shrines fell under the immediate jurisdiction of the Ssaabalangira. At that time, the holder of this office was the stern and venerable Prince Paul Lukongwa. Eventually, I called on Prince Lukongwa at his house, and there I met an angry man. My work had been reported to him, and he intended to have me arrested for conducting unauthorized research. After receiving a lengthy scolding, I explained my purpose in halting Luganda and apologized for my mistake, expecting the worst. The prince then suddenly smiled. He said that after hearing me speak in Luganda he decided to adopt the attitude of a father who chastizes and forgives a disobedient child. He not only consented to my work, but enthusiastically endorsed it and secured the cooperation of the other officials associated with the shrines.

Further language study enabled me to initiate conversations and ask simple questions, although I always relied on the help of an interpreter. From the beginning of our contact the shrine officials were clearly in charge. They regarded our conversations as opportunities for instructing an outsider, and they wished to provide me with the most accurate information. Usually I spoke with several people at a time, and we always met inside the shrines or within their precincts. If the shrine officials were uncertain about an important matter, a discussion ensued in order to clarify different views. Ultimately, the views of royalty were considered authoritative and were always followed. When I wished to clarify my understanding, I would repeat in my own words what I was told, and I often made mistakes. In these situations, I felt that my tape recorder was intrusive, and it seemed better simply to take notes on the points that I understood and that were regarded as conclusive.

Although the results of these group interviews were objective, I wish to emphasize that I was part of the process of articulating Ganda ideas, and that my questions largely set the lines of discussion. This is not to say that another person operating in the same fashion would have arrived at a different set of facts. The special terminology associated with the shrines articulated the basic ritual framework, and the group interviews, coupled with my participation in the ceremonies, provided me with a solid ethnographic footing. But another investigator might well have brought a different interpretive perspective to this work. I was not just collecting "facts," but also trying to ascertain how the Baganda understood them.

Such a task necessarily involves the perspective of the investigator (Geertz 1983b). While interpretation and explanation must make use of the actor's views, the integrative perspective that the ethnographer develops — the way he or she sees the parts in terms of the whole and the whole in terms of the parts—is intrinsic to the account that he or she ultimately presents.[10]

Consider the following example. Only one person, the Katikkiro at Ssuuna's shrine, was able to explain why the inner sanctum of the shrines, where the spirits of the royal ancestors dwelled, was called the "forest" (*kibira*). He pointed out that it had to do with Kintu, the legendary founder of the kingship, who is said to have disappeared into a forest grove at Magonga, now a sacred site where his spirit lives. For this reason, the shrines of Kintu's successors contain special sanctuaries called "forests" where their spirits dwell. Another inquirer might not have persisted with this question or might have discounted the explanation of a single informant, although other Baganda found it perfectly acceptable. To me, it showed that the story of Kintu's disappearance had become a mythic paradigm and that the shrines were conceived as symbolic replicas of the Kintu myth. When the Kabakas died, they were not said to have died but to have "disappeared," and their spirits were believed to take up residence in the "forests" of their shrines. Thus the "forest" sanctuary enabled Kintu's successors to repeat his original transcendence of time, allowing them to communicate with the world of the living from generation to generation.

Consider another example. The political and administrative structure of the kingship may be described perfectly well without referring to the shrines, as most anthropologists and historians have done. But the mythic and ritual dimension of the kingship cannot. The shrines constituted its sacred center, the focus of dynastic myth, history, and ritual. This became evident only in the course of visiting the shrines, listening to dynastic histories, attending rituals, and seeing the relationship of the shrines to one another and to Mutesa I's last capital. The royal shrines were the missing sacred dimension of the kingship.

In an important sense, then, ethnography must be recognized as a work of the imagination because of the ethnographer's way of selecting, perceiving, and representing his or her subject matter (Geertz 1988: 140). But at the same time, ethnographers cannot be overly subjective or imaginative lest they obscure the very cultural phenomena they seek to render accessible.

Mircea Eliade, commenting on the limitations of nineteenth-century studies of India, especially of India's religions, has remarked that "the analysis of a foreign culture principally reveals what was sought in it or what the seeker was already prepared to discover" (1969: xiii). This is an important ethnographic (and hermeneutical) truism, and Eliade's critical use of it suggests that it cuts two ways. First, it draws attention to the obvious fact that ethnography consists of the ethnographer's descriptions, not those of the described; second, it suggests that ethnography must be self-critical in its attempt to represent the described, lest it reflect only the imagination of the describer (cf. Geertz 1988: 145).[11]

Ethnographers, of course, are in a position to minimize their own bias and subjectivity by directly interrogating their sources. Knowing that some scholars had looked on the Kabakas of Buganda as divine kings and priestly figures, I asked repeatedly about their ritual powers and their relationship to the fertility of the land. I was told that such questions were based on a mistaken assumption: neither the king nor the royal ancestors had any special ritual powers, nor was the king divine (that is, a deity or *lubaale*); he was an ordinary person. However, as I reflected on the matter, the Kabaka seemed to possess a certain sacredness, for he was Buganda's supreme symbol of order and meaning. But I was incapable of discussing this idea in Luganda because there is no term for the "sacred" in this sense. My thinking about this matter developed only later in the course of writing this book.

Ethnography for me was a series of dialogues that at some points were simply factual; at others, more perspectival. I was conscious of asking questions that had not occurred to my informants before, and while these were sometimes misconceived, at other times they were mutually intriguing. Ethnography was also a matter of attending rituals, helping with the preparations, and joining in the songs. The Baganda were fully aware of the purpose of my inquiries, and together we articulated the information that they knew would appear in published form. This was important. Most of my informants had read Apolo Kaggwa's books on the history of the kingship, and they wished to see further work on the subject. For this reason, they were willing to answer my questions, and they were especially concerned that I get the basic facts right.

Our relationship involved an important moral dimension as well, the reality of which was symbolized by the gifts we exchanged. I helped to fund ceremonies, made presents of photographs, and served as a rural taxi driver. (I paid no one but my research assistant.) The Baganda in turn gave me presents of chickens, plantains, and peanuts; and, most important, they gave me their time. In attending ceremonies at the shrines, I was not just an observer but an acknowledged participant in the world of Ganda values. The most routine indication of my involvement was my placing of coins in the offering baskets at the shrines and my chewing of dried coffee berries proffered in return. Most research sessions began this way because most took place within the shrines where this etiquette was observed.

Such personal involvement, of course, directly affects the outcome of the field experience and cannot be separated from it. For me, it was not just a matter of empathy with my informants; there was also the element of moral trust, for the increasingly violent political circumstances involved some personal risk. Had I been unwilling to become personally involved with the Baganda, or they with me, the results would have been quite different. Indeed, my experience was shaped by this progressively mutual involvement. Before I received the endorsement of the Ssaabalangira, my inquiries proceeded at a superficial level and would have remained there but for his commitment to the project. Thereafter, I was not simply an "observer" collecting objective "facts," a perspective that anthropologists now recognize to be a simplistic distortion of actual fieldwork situations; I was a participant whose work was highly valued by the Baganda. To be sure, I obtained what can be called facts. But more important, I obtained some comprehension of their meaning in the Ganda context, and in this process I myself was morally and intellectually involved.

I visited the twenty-three shrines that were still standing and spoke with most of the attendants. I returned to some of the shrines repeatedly for interviews over a period of four months, and I attended four ceremonies. Two were held especially for my benefit, and I initiated one by providing the funds for the beer. In a small way, I was therefore part of the revival of the shrines that was occurring at this time. Surprisingly, I gained the least information from the central shrine at Kasubi. There were no royal mediums at this shrine, and apart from dancing and singing songs at the time of the new moon, no mediumship rites had been performed there for some time, and the attendants had no knowledge of them. Most of my interviews took place at the shrines in the Kaliti area, about fourteen miles west of Kampala, largely because of the influence of the Ssaabalangira who lived there. The ceremonies I attended were also held at these shrines.

In September 1972, the political situation in Uganda began to deteriorate dramatically. Idi Amin's mass expulsion of the Uganda Asians made the presence of all foreigners suspect in the eyes of the military, and roadblocks were set up outside the capital. I realized that it would not be long before my regular travels into the countryside to visit Ganda royalty, who supported the return of the kingship, would be noticed, putting both myself and them at risk. So I stopped work and prepared a report for the Uganda Society (Ray 1972). After a lengthy and rewarding conversation at his country estate in Ssingo, the Ssaabalangira and I concluded that further work would be unwise. Amid increasing violence, I decided to leave the country several months sooner than originally planned.

Later, I read through the large body of ethnography published in Luganda to see if anything further might be done on the royal rituals. Historians and anthropologists had already exploited the Luganda sources but had given little attention to the rituals of the kingship. This was not for want of information. The Luganda accounts contained detailed descriptions of the installation ceremonies, funerary rites, royal symbolism, myths of origins, regicide, human sacrifice, and lunar ritual—all classic subjects in the study of African kingship. Indeed, by drawing on some of this literature that had been translated into English, the Swedish ethnologist Tor Irstam placed the kingship of Buganda at the center of a comparative study of divine kingship in Africa (*The King of Ganda* [1944] 1970). According to Irstam, who followed the theories of Sir James George Frazer in *The Golden Bough* (1911–1915), the king of Buganda was the high priest of a fundamentally ritualistic institution. Here Irstam was embellishing on the pioneering ethnography of Buganda written by Frazer's disciple, the missionary anthropologist John Roscoe. Roscoe's book *The Baganda* (1911) had already cast the kingship in a Frazerian mold. Yet this view, which was accepted by other European ethnologists (Baumann, Westermann, and Thurnwald 1940; Lagercrantz 1944), was flatly rejected by British anthropologists who worked in Buganda in the 1930s and 1950s. As they saw it, the king was a secular leader of a fundamentally political and bureaucratic monarchy. This was also the view of Buganda's foremost historian, the British-trained Semakula Kiwanuka, who has written that the kings "were the political and military leaders of their people and that was all" (1971a: 101).

Clearly, there was an important problem here. Both Frazer's emphasis on ritual symbolism, which shaped Roscoe's ethnography, and the subsequent shift in British anthropology to the study of social and political structures had led to significant distortions. One represented the kingship as an archaic magical system; the other, as a proto-bureaucratic one. In different ways, both avoided examining Ganda conceptions of the kingship.

Of the four anthropologists who worked in Buganda in the 1930s and 1950s—Lucy Mair, Martin Southwold, Audrey Richards, and Lloyd Fallers—it was Richards who saw more clearly than the others that the Kabaka was a symbolic figure as well as a political one, although she did not examine the mythic and ritual foundations of his office (1964: 274–288).

A major development in the study of African kingship was E. E. Evans-Pritchard's attack on Frazer's interpretation of Shilluk regicide, one of Frazer's primary examples. In reexamining the Shilluk ethnography, Evans-Pritchard argued that the king "must be in society and yet stand outside it and this is only possible if his office is raised to a mystical plane. It is the kingship not the king who is divine" ([1948] 1962: 210). This, he believed, was characteristic of "kingship everywhere and at all times." Evans-Pritchard's interpretation, while acknowledging the Frazerian divinity of the king, had the effect of reducing it to a mere political construct. Although in other contexts Evans-Pritchard allowed African gods an independent status, he held the divinity of kings to be a reflection of their political role as unifiers of segmented interests. Hence, he concluded that it was the kingship, not the king, that was divine. Other Africanists, such as Meyer Fortes and Audrey Richards, carried forward this perspective and showed how African royal rituals transformed persons into offices.

A second major development within the African context was the anthropologist Thomas Beidelman's attempt to show how rituals transformed the Swazi king into a "royal monster," something entirely beyond conventional Swazi social categories, but essential to the supernatural powers of his office (1966). While accepting that the king must transcend various group interests in order to unify his people, Beidelman's cultural analysis argued (explicitly against Max Gluckman [1960] and implicitly against Evans-Pritchard) that his ritual role stood on its own as an independent symbolic function within Swazi cosmology. It could not be reduced to the political role of his office. Here, Beidelman took a step beyond Michael Young, who was unable to resolve the apparent conflict between symbolic and political explanations of regicide, Frazer's "why" and Evans-Pritchard's "how" (Vaughn 1980), in the case of the Jukun (Young 1966). Beidelman was able to show that explanations of ritual symbolism depend first on the meanings and values assigned within a particular culture, for it is these that give ritual symbols their psychological force and sociopolitical efficacy. In such cases, political, psychological, and other explanations can only supplement; they cannot supplant the semantic configuration of any symbolic value system. Thus the scholar is required, as Young believed, to make the (then) "unfashionable" choice of explaining kingship in essentially symbolic terms.

This development converges with the more recent Weberian perspective proposed by Edward Shils (1975) and Clifford Geertz (1983a). This view takes the argument one step further by claiming that it is the cultural form of central authority that gives it its power. Kings are charismatic and sacred by virtue of their intimate relation to symbolism of the "center" as symbols of total order, meaning, and power. That is, in addition to their political function kingships possess an overriding symbolic function: the creation and maintenance of order, power, and prosperity. From this vantage point, all kings are sacred in the sense that they are pivotal symbols of meaning and value, regardless of the degree to which they are styled as gods. Hence, the study of divine kingship is no longer a matter of examining kings according to universal "traits" that define their divinity or ritual roles. Instead, it is a question of determining how in each instance the king symbolizes a society's ultimate values of authority, legitimacy, and prosperity. It is no longer a quasi-religious inquiry into a king's "divine" attributes, but a semiotic investigation into the king's symbolic and ideological features and how they are communicated. Since these features are categorically different from ordinary human attributes, because they pertain to the "totality" of things, they necessarily belong in the sphere of the sacred.

History of Religions

As a historian of religions, I thought it possible to bring a perspective of this kind to the Ganda materials. Given the rich symbolic significance of the royal shrines, I wanted to examine further the mythic and ritual dimensions of the Kabakaship, and to interpret them in the wider context of the social, political, and historical aspects of the nineteenth-century kingship. There is no doubt that the kingship was the central institution of nineteenth-century Buganda and that it was saturated with mythic images, ritual action, and sacred symbols. Even though the kings may be correctly regarded as secular figures, they also possessed the sacredness of central authority and ultimate power, what Geertz has called the "inherent sacredness of sovereign power" (1983a: 122). Any attempt to gain a fuller understanding of the kingship in terms of its own forms of expression therefore had to take its myths, rituals, and symbolic acts of power as the primary points of departure.

In saying this, however, I must emphasize that the history of religions does not endorse a single method of analysis that need only be applied to the study of the Ganda kingship. There is, in fact, a major division between historians of religions who study religion as an expression of the sacred or Ultimate Reality and those who study religion without making any assumptions about its metaphysical grounds or object. The first approach, also known as the phenomenology of religion, has been called a "hermeneutics of faith" by the philosopher Paul Ricoeur (1970: 28) because it commits the investigator to an affirmation of the existence of a transcendent sacred (cf. Smart 1973; Wiebe 1984; Penner 1986a). Jonathan Smith has called the second approach, which is fundamentally historical and humanistic, the "humanistic mode within the secular academy" (1982: 103) because it does not involve metaphysical assumptions.

The two approaches constitute fundamentally different perspectives on the study of religion. The history of religions has tried to embrace both, and this has entailed some ambiguity. An ambiguity of this kind appears in the manifesto signed by many members of the International Association for the History of Religions at the Tenth Congress, held at Marburg in 1960. Its central statement reads:

> The common ground on which students of religion *qua* students of religion meet is the realization that the awareness of the numinous or the experience of transcendence (where these happen to exist in religions) are — whatever else they may be — undoubtedly empirical facts of human existence and history, to be studied like all human facts, by the appropriate methods. (quoted in Penner 1986a: 173)

This statement has been interpreted in different ways. Hans Penner has argued that it is a quasi-theological assertion that the numinous is an empirical fact (1986a), a reading that commits the history of religions to Ricoeur's hermeneutics of faith. It can also be read, according to Donald Wiebe, as a statement that establishes the history of religions as an objective, scientific study (1984: 407), a reading that is neutral about the existence of the numinous or transcendence as such.

The question is not which reading is right, but which is appropriate to the history of religions. In connection with the first, the hermeneutics of faith, Ricoeur refers to such scholars as Rudolf Otto ([1910] 1963), Gerhardus van der Leeuw ([1932] 1963), and Mircea Eliade (1959). Their phenomenological method, he points out, possesses only an "apparent neutrality" because it is aimed at achieving a "postcritical faith" (1970: 28). By contrast, the second approach follows the *epoché*, the bracketing of assumptions about the existence of transcendence or absolute reality. "The *epoché*," says Ricoeur, "requires that I participate in the reality of the religious object, but in a neutralized mode; that I believe with the believer, but without positing absolutely the object of this belief" (1970: 29). For this reason, Ricoeur notes, "the scientist as such can and must practice this method." The *epoché* is appropriate to the history of religions because its foundations in the Enlightenment commits it to the principles of reason, not those of faith. Its goal is the intelligibility and understanding of religious phenomena, not the discovery of "a new tidings of the Word," as Ricoeur puts it (1970: 29).

Nevertheless, there exists, despite these differences, a widely shared methodological paradigm, which includes four basic components: (1) a description of particular symbolic forms (mythic themes, ritual acts, symbolic objects) as defined expressions of sacred realities; (2) an elucidation of such forms as parts within a whole, as elements within a structure of meaning that defines a religious or cosmological system; (3) a historical contextualization of these symbolic forms, noting their change and transformation over time; and (4) the comparative study of such forms for the purpose of understanding their historical uniqueness and their generically religious character. This holistic, comparative, and historical approach to the interpretation of religious phenomena is the most characteristic feature of the history of religions; it is found in the best work of such diverse scholars as Mircea Eliade, Jonathan Smith, and Wendy Doniger O'Flaherty.

Such a method is not unique to the history of religions and does not rest on exclusive epistemological grounds. A version of it can be found in the work of such anthropologists as Clifford Geertz and Victor Turner. Its central concern with religion as a historical and human phenomenon locates the history of religions firmly within humanistic studies and ties it closely to the social sciences, especially anthropology and history (Smith 1982: 102; Smart 1985).

Essential to the history of religions is the view that "religion" and the related terms "myth," "ritual," and the "sacred" are irreducible categories of human experience and that they formulate and express ultimate values, the most comprehensive notions about the transcendent order of things. A society's myths articulate its place in the world and the conceptual foundations of its major institutions. Ritual, it is often said, speaks in the subjunctive mood (Turner 1982: 82ff.). It attempts to transform our experience of the world as it is into the world as it meaningfully should be, fusing the imagined and the real in a unified vision that creates an overall meaning (Geertz 1973: 112–13). Although the Ganda kingship was not itself a religious institution, it was Buganda's most important cultural institution — its symbolic and ritual center. Its myths, rituals, and symbols formulated Buganda's world view and expressed its ultimate foundations. Although the Kabaka of Buganda was not a god or a priest, he did possess the sacredness of central authority, for he both represented and maintained the ultimate order of things.

Attention to the meanings of the word "religion" and of such related terms as "myth," "ritual," and "sacred" is therefore necessary. This task must take seriously the fact that these terms possess a variety of meanings that cannot be reduced to an essential one. Since the several meanings of each word often bear only a familial resemblance to one another, the subject matters they designate possess no clear boundaries and, conversely, no central essence or structure (Alston 1967; Smart 1973). Thus a definition of religion or myth or ritual will necessarily be perspectival and interpretive of the subject as a whole, a lens through which to view it; and such lenses always stand in need of justification.

Concerning "religion," the most useful definitions will be those that are broadly conceived, embracing the typical features of a religion but not necessarily the elements of all religions, and that allow some significant overlap with other cultural phenomena that resemble religions. Least helpful will be definitions constructed around an assumed "object" of religious experience – God, the Sacred, or Ultimate Reality. Most helpful will be those that conceive of religion as a humanly constructed system of meaning, based on notions of transcendent realities, that gives ultimate value to the experiences of life through mythic and ritual forms. The spiritual objects of religious experience – the gods, spirits, demons, powers – are only parts of the wider religious whole, whose purpose is to articulate an ultimately meaningful universe. Religion, from this point of view, is a distinctive mode of human creativity that gives ultimate meaning to life and provides human beings with their place and destiny in the universe. Broad definitions, without clear boundaries, will entail a convergence of methods and approaches associated with such other disciplines as anthropology, psychology, and philosophy.

This is a very different way of looking at the history of religions than phenomenologists such as Otto, van der Leeuw, Wach, and Eliade have proposed. From their point of view, the concept of the Sacred, together with its correlatives, the "numinous" (Otto), "Power" (van der Leeuw), and "Ultimate Reality" (Wach), is the essential metaphysical fulcrum. Throughout its career in the history of religions, the Sacred has served as the uninterpreted ontological given, both the presumed source of religious experience and the a priori on which the history of religions as an academic discipline was grounded.[12]

Once the "sacred" is detached from its metaphysical footing, it ceases to be a reified concept that is imposed on the data. Instead, it becomes a category of interpretation that is evaluated in terms of its analytic usefulness, as in any other academic discipline. Detached from any ontological grounds, the "sacred" must receive its definition partly in terms of the various religious systems to which it is applied. The primary task then becomes one of interpreting the structure of meanings that particular systems contain as expressions of the sacred.[13]

Thus in reference to the kingship of Buganda, the term "sacred" has to be used with care. Devoid of divinity or any mystical powers, the Kabakas were largely secular figures. They were not sacred in a substantive sense but possessed Shils's sacredness of the social "center" (1975: 3–10); they were sacred in an iconic or a symbolic sense. The Kabakas were, in Shils's terms, the "center of the order of symbols of values and beliefs," and their actions defined what was "ultimate and irreducible" in Ganda society. In the nineteenth century, the Kabakas also exercised the most awesome power over life and death. For this reason, they were sometimes said to be "gods (*lubaale*) on earth," not because of their divinity but because of their supreme rank and power.

The generic character of religion, myth, and ritual also entails that the history of religions be conceived as a comparative enterprise. On this point, it must be noted that the history of religions has not developed a particular method. Since my purpose in this study will be to examine the myths and rituals of Buganda as much as possible in their own terms, I have undertaken to make only a few comparisons with other societies. Nevertheless, I have made use of general theories and analytic concepts, for they permit more generic understandings by placing the particular phenomena within the wider context of the study of myth, ritual, and symbolism. In this sense, my analyses are implicitly comparative, which, as Smith reminds us, is "*the* method of scholarship" (1971: 68).

I have used such theories and concepts heuristically in order to establish a framework of interpretation. Although universal religious "structures" may exist, I believe that all formulations of them must still be regarded as theoretical constructs that remain open to critical investigation. *Homo religiosus*, which historians of religions sometimes speak of as a sort of universal being, is of course an abstraction. Indeed, historians of religions often suppose that ethnographic texts are addressed to *Homo religiosus* or mankind in general and wish to interpret them in this fashion. But such texts are rarely so intended, and attempts to interpret them in this way are hardly credible, especially when the interpreter lacks knowledge of the language of the text in question. Here, too, I have not presented the elements of Ganda myth, ritual, and kingship as belonging to a wider comparative scheme or system, either a morphological one, such as Eliade's idealist system of archetypes, or a structuralist one, such as Claude Lévi-Strauss's system of binary oppositions. While there is nothing misconceived about comparative studies that seek to demonstrate the existence of universal religious forms — indeed, such studies are necessary for any theoretical advance — this work has the opposite purpose: understanding and explaining the particulars of Ganda myths and rituals in their own historical context.[14]

Myth, Ritual, and Kingship in Buganda

In the past, historians of religions have sometimes treated ethnographic accounts as if they represented the unmediated voice of "primitive" religious experience. Rarely have historians of religions examined the ethnographer's perspective or the way in which information was collected or, for that matter, the point of view of the informants. Even more rarely have historians of religions learned the languages of nonliterate societies and engaged in ethnographic studies. My task here is not the sociological one of showing how the general structure of Ganda society relates to the grander features of the monarchy. Several excellent studies of this nature written by social anthropologists and political scientists already exist (Mair 1934; Apter 1961; Southwold 1961; Fallers 1964). Rather, I intend to focus on the myths and rituals of the kingship and elucidate their history and meaning as symbolic forms within the wider cosmology and political order. Part of this task will involve a critique of previous ethnographic and historical studies, as well as critical consideration of certain general theories of myth and ritual.

In Chapter 1, I show how deeply the anthropological theories of the great comparativist Sir James George Frazer guided his disciple, the missionary anthropologist John Roscoe, whose fieldwork laid the foundations of Ganda ethnography. Although Frazer believed in separating "facts" from "theories," one of the burdens of this chapter, which draws on the unpublished correspondence between Frazer and Roscoe, is to demonstrate how closely fact and theory were related in Roscoe's account of the Ganda kingship. A close examination of Roscoe's ethnography reveals its thoroughly Frazerian perspective. Indeed, Roscoe's ethnographic accounts of Buganda's neighbors, the kingdoms of Bunyoro and Nkore, seem to have helped Frazer overcome his doubts about the theories presented in *The Golden Bough*, especially his theory of divine kingship. Buganda, however, was not a Frazerian divine kingship, nor was it a sacral kingship based on an ancient Near Eastern ritual pattern, as Irstam and others imagined. Nevertheless, it was redolent with mythic imagery, ritual actions, and symbolic objects, which were of little concern to later anthropologists. As the central symbol of national order, power, and vitality, the king, too, possessed a certain charismatic quality, Shils's and Geertz's "sacredness of the center." This is something that Frazer's theistic notion of kings as god-men badly distorted, for there are forms of sacredness other than divinity.

For the historian of religions, considerations of text and context must be at the forefront of any discussion of mythology in nonliterate societies. In Chapter 2, "The Story of Kintu: Myth, Death, and Ontology," I examine the creation myth of the Baganda. This profound story, first recorded by the White Fathers in 1882, is one of the masterpieces of the African mythical heritage. Unfortunately, it has never attracted the attention of anthropologists or historians of religions. The study of creation myths has been important to historians of religions because such myths often explain in a society's own terms its foundations in the sacred acts of supernatural beings. Most historians of religions follow Eliade's often useful theory that creation myths establish sacred archetypes or paradigms that are repeated in rituals and expressed in temples, palaces, and domestic architecture.

But all too often, this is where the analysis stops. Historians of religions have failed to treat myths among nonliterate peoples as historically conditioned texts that reflect sociopolitical change, such as colonial rule and the coming of Christianity (cf. Smith 1982). Perhaps because historians of religions have considered such myths to be expressions of primordial time, they have often viewed them as timeless documents, immune to historical change. This, of course, is hardly the case in societies whose myths are not fixed in written form. It was not the case in Buganda, even after the creation story was written down. The several versions of the myth, some influenced by Christianity, enhance our understanding of the myth as a whole. Indeed, new versions of the Kintu myth helped to integrate Christian ideas into the Ganda understanding of the world. By transforming their own cosmogony along Christian lines, some Baganda sought to transform their traditional value system.

Historians of religions usually classify creation myths as sacred narratives because they relate the deeds of supernatural beings and are connected to ritual acts (Eliade 1963: 18–20; Pettazzoni 1967: 15–17). The Ganda myth clearly qualifies as a sacred narrative in these respects, but its significance is fundamentally philosophical, not ritualistic. It is not a story that is repeated in ritual; rather, it presents a perspective on the meaning of death in Ganda life. Since the myth concerns the actions of characters who are related as husband, wife, father-in-law, and mother's brother, interpretation of the story requires an understanding of these key relationships in Ganda social structure. Unfortunately, some historians of religions so dread social scientific reductionism that they have cut themselves off from other disciplines, such as anthropology, and thus they have failed to see the relevance of social relations for the interpretation of mythic narratives. My analysis, which makes use of structuralist methods, is an attempt to interpret the myth in its own terms as a story about the meaning of death in Ganda society.

The close ties between myth and ritual are examined in Chapter 3, "Myth, Ritual and History: The Origins of the Kingship." For the most part, anthropologists and historians have treated the oral traditions about the founding of the kingship as quasi-historical accounts. However, when I listened to these traditions at the royal shrines, and read published accounts of them in Luganda, it became apparent to me that the events described were substantially the same as those performed in the installation ceremonies. These ceremonies comprised a three-phase ritual sequence, each phase reenacting one or more of the deeds of the first four kings. To historians of religions, the ritual enactment of founding deeds is a familiar phenomenon. Such enactments both explain and justify the world by "reproducing" mythically established models of it. A society reestablishes itself at critical moments by repeating the deeds on which it was originally founded. This was especially important in Buganda. When the king died, the kingship temporarily ceased to exist and had to be institutionally reestablished by the new king, who performed the deeds of the founder kings. By enacting the ideal order of myth expressed in the deeds of the founders, the chosen prince reestablished the kingship and became the new king. These acts, it turns out, were themselves based on ritual models. Thus the Baganda, who are often credited with a thoroughly historical perspective on the past, fashioned their origin traditions on a ritual model, which became the true foundation of the kingship. The founding traditions were but historical metaphors of ritual realities.

For the most part, historians of religions have fixed their attention on ritual as an expression of sacred realities, such as mythic paradigms and ecstatic experiences. In Buganda, royal ritual also expressed important sociopolitical realities. Indeed, ritual forms and political structures were closely related, and a genuine phenomenology of ritual should examine this relationship. Chapter 4, "The King's Four Bodies: Ritual Change, 1856–1971," examines the royal ritual matrix in order to shed light on the Ganda theory of kingship. Royal ritual was, of course, the focus of Frazer's *The Golden Bough*. Instead of Frazer's misguided pursuit of ritual magic, I follow the lead of the historian Ernst Kantorowicz's masterly work, *The King's Two Bodies* (1957). My purpose is to show how the installation rites and the ritual symbols of the king's person, both in life and in death, expressed the Ganda theory of the monarchy and its changing character over time. Within the royal shrine, the jawbone relic, Twin, and spirit medium represented the immortal person of the king, and collectively the shrines kept alive the eternal nature of the kingship despite the death of kings. Here I am concerned with structures of meaning rather than structures of power. At the same time, I am interested in how the two interact, how royal ceremonial both expressed and shaped political change in Buganda. To borrow David Cannadine's apt phrasing of the matter, I try to show both "the working of ceremonial *in* society" and "the working of society *through* ritual" (Cannadine and Price 1987: 14).

Chapter 5, "The Royal Shrines," is inspired by Eliade's concept of the sacred center, a concept that Smith points out owes its origins to Eliade's studies of ancient Near Eastern kingship (Smith 1987: 122). The boundaries of the kingdom were maintained by both military and ritual action, and the royal capital was laid out as a microcosm of the kingdom. Located some distance from the capital were the shrines of the royal ancestors. These large, cone-shaped buildings, approximately one for each of the thirty-three kings, were the centers of dynastic myth, history, and ritual. Ignored by colonial anthropologists, perhaps because they played no important political role in the colonial era, the shrines were closely linked to the throne of the nineteenth-century kingdom. Indeed, the two were so closely related that the kingship must be seen as a dualistic institution consisting of separate but complementary components: the living king and the royal ancestor spirits. The two parts were spatially separate but intimately joined through ritual ties.

However, as the spiritual component of the kingship, the shrines were not its primary "reality," nor was the secular, bureaucratic administration located in the capital somehow "nonreal," to use terms by which Eliade has contrasted the sacred and the profane. In Bantu-speaking Africa, the sacred realm of the spirits and the profane world of human beings are equally real. Rituals both maintained the separation of the sacred and profane and facilitated communication between them. The shrines provided a model of this conception; their symbolic architecture both joined together and kept apart the realms of the living and the dead kings. As sacred centers, the shrines were an "opening" to the "other" world of the ancestors, conjoining past kings to the present through sacred relics and mediumship rites, thus keeping alive the eternal nature of the kingship.

Two of the most puzzling and significant features of the eighteenth- and nineteenth-century kingship are the practices of regicide and human sacrifice. Both were, of course, central to Frazer's theory of divine kingship. But the kings of Buganda were not divine. They were not killed when they became old or ill, nor were their subjects killed in order to "strengthen" them through ritual death. Chapter 6, "Regicide and Ritual Homicide," seeks to answer the following question: If regicide and ritual homicide were not practiced for the sake of a Frazerian kingship, what was their purpose? Regicide, it turns out, was a purely political act with no ceremonial purpose. It did, however, find its justification in the origin myth of the kingship, a myth that tells about Kintu's killing of a tyrannical ruler, and every act of regicide was an implicit enactment of this myth. As for the king's killing of his subjects, the sources indicate that people were killed for a variety of reasons: as ritual scapegoats, as offerings to the ancestors, as sacrificial victims of the installation rites, as convicted criminals, and as expressions of the king's power. The frequent and some-times large-scale acts of homicide were somehow fundamental to the political and ritual life of the kingship. Previous explanations have not, however, been satisfactory. A careful examination of the evidence shows that whenever the king killed his subjects, the essence of his authority, as defined in the installation rites, was expressed, and the order of the realm thereby reasserted. Whatever the context, the king's killing of his subjects was a display of royal power and vitality, and consequently a most power-ful expression of national order and well-being.

The final chapter, "Buganda and Ancient Egypt: Speculation and Evi-dence," takes up an old and intriguing question: the relation between ancient Egypt and tropical Africa. In 1911, the well-known Egyptologist E. A. Wallis Budge advanced the claim that the roots of Egyptian religion lay in sub-Saharan Africa. Among the evidence he cited were certain features of the kingship of Buganda, based on early travelers' accounts (Budge 1911). In the same year, the anthropologist Charles G. Seligman used the ethnography of Roscoe, among others, to argue that the ancient Egyptians, as a Hamitic people, shared deep cultural ties with East Afri-ca, especially the institution of divine kingship. This notion had a deep impact on both Egyptologists and historians of Africa. Seligman also claimed that certain Egyptian rites and symbols had been transmitted up the Nile River to the kingdoms of Buganda and Bunyoro. Much of this discussion, including its racial element, has been revived today in the context of the African and African-American critique of Egyptian stud-ies. The racial issue aside, the important question is: Is there any evidence of specific cultural bonds or historical connections between ancient Egypt and sub-Saharan Africa, especially among the kingdoms around Lake Victoria? This question poses a challenge to the historian of reli-gions who has observed the rites and symbols of Buganda's royal shrines.

1

Early Ethnography and Theory:
The Influence of Frazer

Buganda was a well-organized state in the nineteenth century; it was the dominant power among the smaller kingdoms and chiefdom societies around the northern and western shores of Lake Victoria. A decade before Britain established protectorate rule in 1894, many of Buganda's leaders were literate in Arabic or Luganda, and they possessed an articulate sense of their kingdom's political history and cultural integrity. In 1897, a group of Christian chiefs drew on British support when they overthrew their wayward king Mwanga II. The British in turn enlisted these same chiefs to administer the Uganda Agreement of 1900 when the protectorate government was reestablished over Buganda and its neighboring kingdoms and ethnic groups.[1] Although British overrule curtailed some of the powers of the Kabakaship, the Kabaka and his chiefs retained control over most of their own affairs. Far from suffering a sense of inferiority, the Ganda leaders saw themselves as virtually equal partners with the British in governing Buganda. Islam and Christianity had also spread rapidly among the leaders in Buganda, and these religions were closely tied to literacy. Indeed, one way of saying that someone was a Muslim or a Christian was to say that he "read" (*kusoma*) that religion. Literacy and the printing press were exploited by the leaders as instruments of administration and of cultural self-expression. Thus it was that Sir Apolo Kaggwa (1869–1927), a convert of the Church Missionary Society (CMS) who was the Katikkiro and first regent of the kingdom,[2] published five volumes of historical and ethnographic work between 1901 and 1921. His *Basekabaka be Buganda* (The Kings of Buganda), published in 1901, was the first indigenous history of a sub-Saharan society written in an African language. Six years later, Kaggwa published an ethnographic book, *Empisa za Baganda* (The Customs of the Baganda). These two volumes were immediately recognized as authoritative works, and they stimulated other Baganda to write their own historical and ethnographic accounts.

The impetus behind Kaggwa's ethnography was the fieldwork of the Reverend John Roscoe (1861–1932), a missionary with the CMS in Buganda and a disciple of Sir James G. Frazer (1854–1941). Under Frazer's tutelage, Roscoe wrote *The Baganda* in 1911. Roscoe was greatly indebted to Kaggwa, who supplied him with knowledgeable informants, even as he himself drew heavily on Roscoe's interviews for his own ethnography. Following the systematic outline in Frazer's ethnographic *Questions* ([1887] 1889) and utilizing the informants provided by Kaggwa, Roscoe produced an anthropological classic.

Taken together, the writings of Roscoe and Kaggwa constituted a unique, two-dimensional picture of late-nineteenth-century Buganda, indigenously described in Kaggwa's Luganda works and systematically presented in Roscoe's ethnography, written according to Frazer's ethnographic and theoretical scheme. Later students of Buganda, both Ganda and European alike, have been indebted to these works. Some have extended and deepened the original lines of inquiry; others have opened up new ones. All have taken Roscoe and Kaggwa as important points of departure.

Roscoe's work, however, has not been closely examined, nor have Frazer's theories been considered in light of Roscoe's and Kaggwa's ethnographies.[3] It will therefore be important to investigate the relationship among all three men and their works, and especially to estimate the nature and extent of Frazer's influence. The relationship between Frazer and Roscoe as revealed in their letters also brings to light an important and thus far unexamined episode in the history of anthropology.[4] Moreover, Frazer's theory of divine kingship, although seriously flawed and largely rejected by later anthropologists, still remains a major document in the study of kingship. As Gillian Feeley-Harnik has pointed out, Frazer's questions concerning indigenous conceptions of "power, legitimacy, and prosperity," as expressed in myth and ritual, have again come to the fore (1985). Thus Clifford Geertz, in affirming the "inherent sacredness of sovereign power," argues that we should look for "the vast universality of the will of kings . . . in the same place we look for that of gods: in the rites and images through which it is exerted" (1983a: 124). The elucidation of the rites and images of kingship was Frazer's project in *The Golden Bough*, and it became the project of Roscoe, Frazer's most devoted ethnographic disciple, in *The Baganda*.

Frazer and Roscoe

Before the publication of Roscoe's book, a good deal had been written about Buganda by travelers, missionaries, and colonial officials, beginning with John Hanning Speke's *Journal of the Discovery of the Source of the Nile* (1863). Speke, in quest of the source of the Nile River, was the first European to arrive in Buganda (1862). He was later joined by his traveling companion, James A. Grant, and stayed at the capital of Mutesa I for a period of four and a half months. Speke, who was unable to converse in Luganda, was constantly distracted by worries about accomplishing his mission. Nevertheless, his observations about Mutesa and daily life at the capital were remarkably accurate. After an interval of thirteen years, other European visitors followed. The next to write extensively about Buganda was the explorer Henry M. Stanley in *Through the Dark Continent* (1878). Stanley, who sought to confirm Speke's discovery of the Nile's source, spent three months in Mutesa's capital at Rubega. His description of the mature Mutesa I was very favorable, and in a famous letter to the *Daily Telegraph*, written from Buganda in 1875, Stanley called on British missionaries to go to Uganda and convert the enlightened king and his people. The missionaries and colonial officers who followed Speke and Stanley sometimes wrote substantial accounts of their own experiences, but none wrote in any significant detail about the kingship or the religious system.[5]

By the turn of the century, an informal ethnographic practice had developed. From the beginning, Mutesa I and his successor Mwanga II controlled all relationships between Buganda and the outside world, and they required all foreigners, Arabs and Europeans alike, to reside at the capital under their supervision. Published accounts of precolonial Buganda were therefore written primarily on the basis of conversations with these two kings and their chiefs, which gave the works a distinctly royal bias. The Baganda also took pride in their own language, and although Swahili was initially used as an intermediary language, it was not widely known. Thus anyone attempting to do ethnographic research in Buganda had both to master Luganda and to obtain the cooperation and assistance of the royal authorities who lived at the capital.

Roscoe had been in the CMS in Buganda for several years before he became acquainted with Frazer. Frazer notes that they met in the late 1890s ([1935] 1968: 73); perhaps it was in late 1896 when Roscoe was home on leave in Cambridge.[6] Roscoe was thirty-five years old at the time and Frazer forty-two. From the outset, their relationship was one of master and disciple. In 1889, Frazer published a pamphlet, *Questions on the Manners, Customs, Religion, Superstitions, &c. of Uncivilized or Semi-Civilized Peoples*. He sent the pamphlet to missionaries and colonial officials around the world for the purpose of obtaining firsthand information. Evidently, Roscoe received a copy because soon after he returned to Buganda in 1898 he began sending Frazer letters containing descriptions of Ganda customs, organized according to the categories of *Questions*. In 1901, Frazer compiled from excerpts from Roscoe's letters an article entitled "Notes on the Manners and Customs of the Baganda," and published it under Roscoe's name (Roscoe 1901).

It is uncertain just how Roscoe went about collecting information at this early stage. He seems to have interviewed people at random in the course of his duties, hoping — sometimes in vain — to have his notes verified by chiefs with whom he was acquainted. At the outset, Roscoe was disheartened. He told Frazer that if he had begun work earlier, "we should have been able to get old people who would have given reasons for some of the customs; now I may question twenty people without getting the point I require" (1901: 117). Roscoe attributed part of the problem to the imposition of colonial rule and to the falling away of traditional practices. Significantly, he did not mention the destructive effects of Christianity on traditional life, particularly on ritual practices, nor did he indicate the reluctance of older Baganda to speak openly to missionaries. Roscoe laid some of the blame on the Baganda: "It is most remarkable how soon they forget their old customs, and how little they know of the reasons for the things they do." He also questioned their reliability: "Even the people I think I can trust often mislead me through carelessness, or allow some important thing to pass over and thus give me the wrong impressions" (1901: 117).

At this time, Roscoe was perhaps insufficiently aware of the hierarchical organization of Ganda society and of the specialized nature of knowledge associated with certain social, political, and ritual roles. As anyone who has done fieldwork in Buganda discovers, ordinary people do not always know the reasons behind every ritual practice; and even when they do, they are sometimes reluctant to speak about matters that concern priests and royal officials.

A few surviving pages in one of Roscoe's early notebooks (n.d.) contain information, apparently collected at different times, under the headings — specified in Frazer's *Questions* — "Birth," "Birth (adoption)," and "Birth (baptism)." The notes from these pages appear almost verbatim in the first of Roscoe's articles edited by Frazer.

Soon after these notes were published, Roscoe apparently foresaw the possibility of collecting more extensive information in collaboration with

Apolo Kaggwa. When on leave in 1902, Roscoe expanded the material in his earlier article into a longer study in order "to clear away much surface matter and prepare the way for more detailed work" (1902). In this connection, he mentioned that Kaggwa had already been of assistance. Thus he may have had in mind the prospect of further collaboration leading to a book-length study.

Kaggwa's publication of *Basekabaka* in 1901 demonstrated his considerable qualifications. Although he was the product of the royal court of the 1880s and acquainted with some of its history, he had taken the trouble to interview a number of knowledgeable officials and members of the royalty in order to record the oral traditions of the kingship. As Katikkiro of Buganda and first regent of the young king Daudi Chwa II, Kaggwa was virtually the ruler of the country, and he was uniquely placed to summon almost anyone to help with his project. In 1897, Kaggwa finished the manuscript of *Basekabaka*, which was published in England in 1901 with the help of the CMS missionary Ernest Miller. Less than a year later, Kaggwa published a collection of folktales, *Engero za Baganda* (Folktales of the Baganda). He also began collecting materials for history of his own (Grasshopper) clan, which he completed in 1904 (Rowe 1969).

Kaggwa's keen interest in history and his success in obtaining expert informants were precisely what Roscoe needed. Following Frazer's direction, Roscoe wished to record the practices of the immediate past, many of which had already fallen into disuse or had been deliberately discontinued, even during Mutesa's reign. Hence, it was necessary for Roscoe to interview older authorities who could recall the religious and political institutions of the past. Such people were of considerable social stature, and only someone in Kaggwa's position could recruit them for Roscoe's purpose.

Kaggwa's visit to England for the coronation of Edward VII in August 1902 probably enhanced the prospects for collaboration. During his visit, Kaggwa spent several days in Cambridge, and one evening after dinner he went with Roscoe to call on Frazer, and they had coffee together (Mukasa 1904: 121). Unfortunately, there is no record of their conversation, but it would seem likely that Roscoe mentioned to Frazer his intent to work with Kaggwa on a comprehensive study. The project eventually got under way when Roscoe and Kaggwa returned to Buganda at the end of the year.

For several years, Roscoe had use of a room in Kaggwa's large, two-story house, and the Katikkiro arranged for informants to meet Roscoe for interviews in the evening hours when he was free from his teaching duties. This arrangement seems to have worked well for both men. In acknowledging his debt to Kaggwa, Roscoe wrote in the preface to *The Baganda* that

> he [Kaggwa] spared no pains to bring old people whom I should otherwise
> have failed to see, and who would have refused to give information to an
> Englishman, had not Sir Apolo induced them to do so. Often Sir Apolo
> had men carried sixty and sometimes a hundred miles, and entertained
> them for several weeks at a time that I might have opportunities for seeing
> and questioning them, and writing out their accounts. Through Sir Apolo's
> kindness, too, I have been able to see priests and mediums from most of the
> old temples, and the principal men from each clan. . . . Again, medicine-
> men versed in past customs have been brought to me and warned to speak
> the truth and to hide nothing. In addition to this Sir Apolo himself has not
> only placed his large store of knowledge at my disposal, but has been ever
> ready to prosecute the most careful enquiry into any difficulty that arose in
> the path of investigation. (1911: x–xi; cf. 1921: 173)[7]

Roscoe took notes in English, while Kaggwa or his secretary took notes
in Luganda.[8] During the course of their work, Roscoe is said to have
encouraged Kaggwa "to write in Luganda what he himself was writing in
English" — that is, a comprehensive ethnography of the Baganda (Kiwanuka 1971b: xxvi). This Kaggwa did, and the result was *Empisa za
Baganda*, published in 1907 and enlarged in 1911. Kaggwa's book was the
first African-language ethnography written by an African author. The
second book to emerge from the collaboration was *Ebika bya Baganda*
(The Clans of the Baganda), published in 1912. This small work dealt
briefly with the history of some thirty Ganda clans. Although Kaggwa's
writings were remarkably objective, they also had an implicit political
motive: to justify the exceptional degree of political autonomy that was
claimed by the Baganda, by describing the long history of the kingship
and its complex institutional characteristics — a "charter" for Kaggwa and
his group of ruling chiefs (Wrigley 1965: 21; Rowe 1967: 165). Thus
Kaggwa devoted his first book, *Basekabaka be Buganda*, entirely to dynastic history and almost half of his ethnography to the rites and institutions of the Kabakaship. Since the kingship lay at the center of Frazer's
and Roscoe's interests, Kaggwa's royalist perspective was well suited to
Roscoe's ethnographic needs.

Frazer was immediately impressed with Roscoe's ethnographic work.
Roscoe, who had originally studied to be a civil engineer, later trained for
missionary work at the Church Missionary College in London (Haddon
1933). Like other missionaries in Buganda, Roscoe became fluent in
Luganda and taught school in that language as principal of the Theological School at Mmengo in Kampala.[9] But unlike his CMS colleagues,

Roscoe also developed a serious interest in the traditional religion and culture. Most important, from Frazer's point of view, Roscoe devoted himself to the method of ethnographic inquiry prescribed by Frazer's *Questions*. Indeed, in a letter to Roscoe, written in 1907, Frazer acknowledged that he "regarded your [Roscoe's] testimony to the usefulness of my Questions as by far the most valuable and weighty I have ever received" (12 May 1907). During the year 1907, the two men got to know each other through afternoon walks that were part of Frazer's routine. Roscoe even did Frazer the favor of making a catalog of his large personal library, a job that Frazer described as "immense" (19 July 1907).[10] Two years later, Frazer began to incorporate large amounts of material from Roscoe's extensive field notes into his *Totemism and Exogamy* (1910), and he looked forward to the time when Roscoe himself would publish a full-scale study of the Baganda.

Because of ill health and differences with the mission board, Roscoe left the CMS in 1909. He returned to Cambridge and immediately set about writing up his field notes. The work took him less than a year. During this time, he served as a curate at Holy Trinity Church in Cambridge. He also gave lectures in the Department of Anthropology and was awarded an honorary master's degree by St. John's College for his contributions to the ethnography of Uganda. In 1912, he was presented by the university to the rectory of Ovington near Thetford, Norfolk, a country parish with a small population and moderate endowment. As soon as he finished his manuscript, he turned it over to Frazer, who recommended it to Macmillan for publication. Later Frazer read through the proofs, making corrections and suggesting minor editorial changes, including the title, *The Baganda: An Account of Their Native Customs and Beliefs*, which Roscoe accepted. Afterward, Frazer congratulated Roscoe for "having produced a most valuable and perfectly original work, which should keep your name green as long as people take any interest in the old African customs and religion" (1 March 1911).

For Frazer, the publication of *The Baganda* was the fruit of a deeply satisfying personal and professional relationship. He wrote to Roscoe, "to think that I have had however such a small share in contributing to the production of such a book is one of the greatest gratifications of my life" (15 November 1911). Frazer believed in the intrinsic value of what he called ethnographic "facts," and he consequently valued the writing of ethnography more highly than his own theoretical endeavors. "Your work," he told Roscoe, "is likely to be much more permanent than mine; for facts remain when theories are obsolete and forgotten" (15 November 1911). So impressed was Frazer that he asked his friend the Lord Advocate about the possibility of obtaining a royal honor for Roscoe (15 November 1911), but one was never granted.

Soon after the publication of *The Baganda*, Frazer began to look for funds to send Roscoe back to Uganda on an ethnographic mission. The idea was for Roscoe to visit the kingdoms of Bunyoro and Nkore, where he had done some previous work, in order to undertake more detailed research. Roscoe also wanted to become acquainted with the pastoral societies of northeastern Uganda, the Karamajong and Galla. While Frazer solicited funds, Roscoe busied himself with writing a book about his previous work among the Banyoro, Bagesu, and Bakene (*The Northern Bantu* 1915). Frazer read the proofs and drafted part of the preface, in which he made a special appeal for money. Roscoe then turned his hand to writing a popular account of his missionary work in Tanganyika and Uganda (*Twenty-five Years in East Africa* 1921). After failing to obtain funds from either the Carnegie Trust or the Colonial Office, Frazer succeeded in persuading a wealthy Glasgow distiller, Sir Peter Mackie, to support the project. Mackie put up the money (£3,500), and Frazer arranged for the Royal Society to oversee it. Upon Frazer's recommendation, the project was officially titled "The Mackie Ethnological Expedition to Central Africa." The plan called for Roscoe to hire a botanist and a photographer, but neither could be found in Mombasa or Kampala, so the expedition became a solo effort by Roscoe.

During the approximately eleven months Roscoe spent in the field (September 1919–July 1920), Frazer sent letters of advice and encouragement. He was especially concerned that Roscoe make copies of his field notes in triplicate for safety's sake and that he send copies home. Frazer was also anxious that Roscoe, who was fifty-eight at the time, conserve his strength, lest he fall ill and jeopardize the mission. Frazer even tried to prompt Roscoe by letter on certain ethnographic questions. For example, after listening to an impressive series of lectures by Bronislaw Malinowski at the London School of Economics, Frazer wrote: "Find out all you can about the economic system of your natives, their modes of production and distribution, whether individual or communal" (28 May 1920). While reading a book about burial practices, he urged: "Keep your eyes open for all such practices [as the mutilation of corpses to disable the ghost], also the abandonment of the house, village or camp after death, the destruction of the property of the dead and the motives for it etc." (28 May 1920). As soon as copies of Roscoe's notes arrived, Frazer pored over them and wrote occasional comments to Roscoe. Sometimes he was puzzled by what he found: "The marriage customs you describe [among the Banyoro] are very curious and interesting, particularly the intercourse of the bridegroom with the bride's maternal aunt on the wedding night. I don't yet see what to make of it" (28 May 1920).

Frazer prepared lengthy summaries of Roscoe's notes for *Man* and the *Geographical Journal*. For the sake of publicity, he also sent letters to the *Times* containing excerpts from Roscoe's work. One of the letters, published near the end of Roscoe's expedition, was the subject of a satirical column in *Punch*. The article, "Bettering the Banyoros," poked fun at British society and professional anthropology. It began by referring to the impending return of Roscoe's expedition "to the adjoining Noxas tribe whose manners and customs are of extraordinary interest," especially the dance fads called the Ognat, the Tortskof, and Zaj. The column ended by spoofing Frazer's theory of divine kingship:

> [T]he ruler of the country was chosen from . . . the powerful Renim clan, who devote themselves intermittently to the task of providing the country with fuel. The chieftain wields great power and is regarded with reverence by his followers, but is in turn expected to devote himself entirely to their interests, and if he fails to satisfy is replaced by a more energetic leader. (29 September 1920: 256)

Poor Frazer seems to have missed the joke (the key words were spelled backward), and he reported to Roscoe that the article made "some heavy fun about the Banyoro!" (12 October 1920). Nevertheless, the *Punch* column shows that Frazer's theories were well known among the educated public. The reports in the *Times* also suggest that anthropology associated with Frazer's name was considered a subject of interest to its upper-class readers.

Apart from the publicity, Frazer was stimulated by reading through and editing Roscoe's field notes. He seems to have taken vicarious pleasure in Roscoe's fieldwork and to have regarded the publication of Roscoe's ethnography as a joint enterprise. "How grand it will be," he wrote to Roscoe, who was still in the field, "when all your materials are collected and it only remains for us together to give them in the clearest and best form to the world" (31 January 1920). Indeed, Frazer gleaned some of the most interesting material from Roscoe's notes and published it before Roscoe had the chance.

This was unusual. There was no urgency about Roscoe's findings, and Frazer's summaries were hardly useful to the research scholar. But for the pedantic Frazer, publishing someone else's ethnographic notes was as close to fieldwork as he could or would get. Frazer seems to have relished the role. Although he published occasionally in anthropological journals, he was absent from the anthropological conference circuit of his day. He trained no students, and a Frazerian establishment in anthropology never developed. Indeed, his work, especially *The Golden Bough*, was generally rejected by professional anthropologists. But at this time in British scholarship, it was possible for prominent scholars to present their views over the heads of fellow specialists, straight to the educated public (Leach 1966: 570). By publishing reports of Roscoe's fieldwork in both *Man* and the *Times*, Frazer seems to have been trying to have it both ways: to present original ethnography to his professional colleagues and to promote his style of comparative anthropology to the wider public.

When Roscoe returned home in November 1920, he was surprised to find himself the subject of newspaper publicity. The enterprising Sir Peter Mackie sent reporters from the *Times* and the *Daily Mail* to interview Roscoe in order to publicize the results of the expedition. When Frazer, who was in Paris at the time, learned of the first report that appeared in the *Daily Mail*, he was appalled. He wrote a pointed letter to Roscoe saying he was sorry that such a "low and vulgar" paper had published an article that he feared would cheapen the scientific nature of the expedition (23 November 1920).

Frazer's fears were not unfounded. The *Daily Mail* ran five articles in four consecutive issues that hailed Roscoe's work with sensational headlines. For example: "East Africa 2000 B.C.: Explorer's Romantic Finds: Tribe Who Eat Their Dead"; "Cannibal Morals: Queer Secrets of East Africa: Drugged Babies: Wives on Loan"; "Mr. Roscoe's Triumph: African Cannibals' Friend" (20, 22, 23, 24 November 1920). The reports, written by Sir Beech Thomas, depicted Roscoe as a modest but talented country parson, fluent in three African languages, who braved the sometimes wild and "cannibalistic" natives and charmed them out of valuable ethnographic data. According to the lead article, "a journey richer in discovery of tribal customs and superstitions has never been made before." The report referred to photographs of "strange and grim ceremonies," "fetishes, implements and instruments going back to 2000 B.C.," and accounts of "the inner secrets of tribal religion and custom." As for scientific discoveries, readers were promised startling results. Roscoe's work, according to the paper, would show that the forebears of the Israelites had migrated up the Nile, that new light would be shed on the origins of the laws and customs of the Old Testament, and that the cattle-herding area of East Africa could be developed into a meat-packing site, rivaling the stockyards of Chicago!

Roscoe found these reports distasteful and wrote to Frazer that the *Daily Mail* had "muddled up what I said and woven a fine story much of which was not in my mind but which is so much claptrap for the popular mind" (25 November 1920). Roscoe was right; the articles clearly expressed what the contemporary British public expected to glean from anthropological reports about Africa: superstition, exotica, and opportunities for capitalism. Frazer was forgiving, but still annoyed, and replied that such reports were "always possible in the case of oral interviews, as a consequence of stupidity or deliberate exaggeration (not to say fraud) of the interviewer" (27 November 1920).

More appealing to Frazer was the prospect of a series of articles in the glossy, upper-class *Illustrated London News* (5, 12, 19 March; 2 April 1921), describing the royal rituals of Bunyoro. Roscoe wrote the text and supplied copies of photographs from which an artist worked up large composite drawings. The drawings were accompanied by somewhat lurid captions, stressing the more sinister aspects of the rites. The artist, an acquaintance of Frazer's, chose as the subject of one of his sketches an appropriately Frazerian scene. It showed a man seated on a throne giving presents to his courtiers. The caption read: "Destined to Be Strangled After a Week's 'Reign': A Make-Believe King 'Reincarnating' a Dead King" (12 March 1921: 338–39). The drawing, however, was a complete mock-up. Roscoe never photographed such a ceremony, and the custom had long since been discontinued. But for Frazer it was a unique example of "a [mock] king who is definitely said to act as the representative of the late king" (28 May 1920). Many of the other royal rites that Roscoe photographed and described in Bunyoro had also been abandoned and were performed solely for his benefit under the supervision of the missionary-educated king (Roscoe 1923: ix).

Due perhaps to the publicity surrounding Roscoe's work, for which Frazer was in large part responsible, Roscoe was asked to preach before the king and queen at Sandringham in January 1921. Afterward, Roscoe's college newsletter reported that he "was most graciously received and entertained by their Majesties, who shewed the utmost interest in his adventures and discoveries and in the future of Central Africa" (*The Eagle* 1922: 71). Later, the king told the colonial secretary, Winston Churchill, that he should consult with Roscoe about African affairs. This delighted the professionally minded Frazer, who wrote: "Really, my dear Roscoe, you are making anthropology hum, as they say" (21 January 1921).

Roscoe worked rapidly on writing up his field notes and on cataloging the dozens of artifacts and photographic plates that he had brought back for the Archaeological and Ethnological Museum at Cambridge. Within four years he had written four volumes on the expedition. The first, *The Soul of Central Africa* (1922), presented a general account of his work and travels; the remaining three, *The Bakitara or Banyoro* (1923), *The Banyankole* (1923), and *The Bageshu and Other Tribes of the Uganda Protectorate* (1924), contained the ethnographic record of the expedition. Frazer happily read through all the proofs and found them to be a "great stimulus and encouragement" to his own work (9 September 1924). When the last of the volumes appeared, he sent Roscoe a brief note of congratulation on "your great work." Later, he wrote more fully:

> No other inquirer, so far as I know, has ever done so much for African ethnography as you have done. Your seven volumes . . . will be anthropological classics for all future time and a lasting monument of your indefatigable zeal and ability. For myself, I am happy and proud to be able to reckon you among my best friends. (8 July 1923)

In 1923, Roscoe gave the second lecture in the newly founded Frazer Lecture series at Cambridge. He chose to speak on the cultural history of the Lake Region of East Africa. Unfortunately, he had nothing new to add to the subject, apart from some illustrative examples drawn from his own field material. He adhered to the then-current "Hamitic" hypothesis, which had been enlarged and developed by Charles G. Seligman, another disciple of Frazer. According to Seligman, the cultural history of the Interlacustrine area was to be understood in terms of the migration of three separate races into the region, the last being the Hamitic pastoralists who supposedly introduced the institution of divine kingship. Appropriately enough, Roscoe suggested that the process of cultural evolution reached its peak with the partially Hamitic Baganda, "among whom the greatest progress has been made." Convinced of the moral justification of colonialism, Roscoe concluded his talk by lauding the benefits of British rule, saying that it was "to the British that we must give the credit for the great and lasting reforms in this region" ([1924b] 1932: 46).

The Frazer Lecture was Roscoe's last publication. For a time he hoped that Frazer might again be able to obtain funds for another expedition, this time to study the pastoral peoples of northeastern Uganda and northern Kenya, about whom little was then known. One of Roscoe's theories was that gold- and iron-working originated in this area, spread into ancient Egypt, and thence into the Mediterranean world (16 January 1925; 19 January 1925). But this venture did not come to pass. In 1928, Roscoe suffered a thrombosis from which he never completely recovered (Roscoe, 3 January 1928). He died on December 2, 1932, at his parish at Ovington at the age of seventy-one.[11]

Roscoe's Fieldwork

At the beginning of his Frazer Lecture, Roscoe wrote: "I am proud to call myself a disciple of Sir James, to whose inspiration I owe my first love for this important branch of study" ([1924b] 1932: 25). Roscoe's discipleship involved, as we have seen, not only a commitment to fieldwork, but a commitment to doing it Frazer's way. Fundamental to Frazer's method was the separation of ethnography and theory. Referring to Roscoe, Frazer wrote:

> [F]or him it was enough to record the facts; he did not attempt to explain them by his own or other people's theories. Still less did he fall into the trap, into which too many field anthropologists have tumbled, by comparing his African facts with facts raked together from all ends of the earth: all such explanations and comparisons he rightly left to be elaborated by comparative anthropologists at home working in libraries on the reports filed by ethnologists like himself. ([1935] 1968: 77)

In Frazer's view, anthropology involved two distinct tasks, the collection of facts and the construction of theories, and these were to be carried out by different persons. As performers of these separate tasks, Frazer and Roscoe complemented each other and thus fulfilled Frazer's idea of proper anthropological method.

Of course, it was impossible for Roscoe not to be influenced by his mentor's theories. As already noted, his fieldwork was fundamentally shaped by Frazer's ethnographic outline in *Questions*. For Frazer to deny that Roscoe's fieldwork was tainted by "other people's theories," when his materials were collected and written up from beginning to end according to *Questions*, was simply naive.[12] To be sure, Roscoe managed to avoid the obvious importation of Frazer's (or anyone else's) theories into his material. Yet both he and Frazer seem to have been unaware of the more subtle fact that Roscoe's ethnography was essentially shaped by the theoretical concerns that underlay Frazer's work.

In *Questions*, Frazer directed the ethnographer primarily to the intellectual and symbolic aspects of culture, especially religious belief and ritual, which Frazer regarded as the central features of primitive society. The second edition of this pamphlet contained 507 questions, some with multiple parts, and they clustered thickly around such topics as totemism, magical acts, rites of passage, and scapegoats. In addition to listing the questions to be asked, Frazer advised ethnographers to keep the informant talking and to record everything. Absolute objectivity was the rule. "It is very important," wrote Frazer, "that he [the ethnographer] should as far as possible avoid the use of leading questions" (1907: 7). The ethnographer was also to avoid introducing his own analytical observations. According to Frazer,

> the best way is commonly to start the savage talking on some topic of interest, say on birth or death customs, to let him run on till he has exhausted himself, and then to jog his memory by asking about points which

he has either imperfectly explained or entirely omitted. In this way the enquirer may obtain a considerable body of information on the subject of inquiry . . . he will [also] find it useful to keep a printed set of questions beside him for reference in order to refresh his own memory as to the important points. . . . Further, the information obtained from one man should be tested by examining other and independent witnesses. (1907: 8)

For Frazer, detail was all-important. "General answers to the Questions are of little value. . . . No facts should be neglected as too trivial. . . . Let him [the ethnographer] accordingly put down everything" (1907: 7). But nowhere does Frazer tell the ethnographer to observe how beliefs and rites functioned in a living social context.

Ironically, of course, Frazer himself had never visited a non-European country or conducted an ethnographic interview. Indeed, when asked by William James about the natives he had actually known, Frazer reportedly exclaimed, "But heaven forbid!" (Downie 1970: 27).[13] Frazer had to rely on the testimony of others about the value of his fieldwork method, and he relied principally on Roscoe. Thus he assured prospective users of *Questions* that its "practical success in [Roscoe's] hands is a sufficient proof of the soundness of the principle" (1907: 10).

One may ask, however, why Frazer felt the need to publish *Questions* when a larger and more complete list of ethnographic questions, titled *Notes and Queries on Anthropology*, already existed. This book-length manual, originally compiled by the British Association for the Advancement of Science in 1874, was expanded and revised in 1892 and periodically thereafter. Frazer seems to have thought that a pamphlet-size list that could be sent free of charge all over the world would produce more results. Moreover, he instructed ethnologists to send reports directly to him or to the curator of the Archaeological and Ethnological Museum at Cambridge, where he would have access to them. By contrast, *Notes and Queries* was written under the auspices of the Anthropological Institute, and reports and papers that made use of the guide were to be sent to the institute for publication in its journal. Without deliberately appearing to do so, Frazer seems to have set himself up to compete with the Anthropological Institute in the collection of ethnographic information. In this way, he evidently hoped not only to stimulate ethnography, but also, perhaps, to gain some direct influence over its production and interpretation.

Frazer held that scientific thought should proceed from the general to the particular, a process he called particularization: "[W]e start from a general idea consisting of a very few qualities, and proceed downwards through genera, sub-genera, species, sub-species, etc., at every step adding to the number of diverse qualities" (quoted in Ackerman 1987: 48).

He understood anthropology to be a science of the evolution of culture, which proceeded deductively from general theories to individual facts and comparisons. Any particular society was a kind of laboratory specimen that could be examined for the purpose of classifying its cultural facts under general theories. Contained in *Questions* is the view that a primitive society consists of a collection of more or less universal institutions and customs, such as totemism, kinship relationships, birth ceremonies, puberty rites, government, priesthood, and so on, each having a general set of traits that were exhibited in specific social and ritual settings. The task of the ethnographer was to describe the local institutions well enough so that the theorist could pick out the salient constants and variables and interpret them according to theories about the origin and evolution of social institutions. Frazer thought it best for the theorist to formulate the questions to be asked in the field, for only the theorist possessed the broader perspective by which the facts were ultimately to be classified and explained.

From Frazer's point of view, much of the natives' own interpretations and explanations of life could be ignored, because local conceptions contained erroneous assumptions and ad hoc rationalizations. Indeed, Frazer stood in an adversarial relationship to the sources he used. He was convinced that his own explanations of primitive customs were superior to those of the natives, because his were based on comparative theories and rational principles, whereas theirs were based on local beliefs and mistaken notions of causality. Thus Frazer believed that he understood the intentions and motives of the natives better than they did. Frazer's readers shared this view, hence the effectiveness of Frazer's broadly ironic tone throughout his work (Ackerman 1987: 66). Nor did it matter whether the recorded beliefs and practices were still extant. Dead or alive, all ethnographic facts were part of the great process of cultural evolution that was the anthropologist's laboratory. Frazer was most anxious that the past, untainted by Western influence, be recorded so that it would not be lost to "science."

Following Frazer's method, Roscoe collected most of his materials from formal interviews conducted at Kaggwa's house. His procedure may be inferred from a copy of one of his field notebooks, dated March through July 1906 (Roscoe and Kaggwa 1906).[14] The notebook records some thirty interviews, mainly with royal officials, concerning a set of related topics: clan chiefship, land tenure, taxation, inheritance and succession, princes, naming rites, and legal practices. In each case, Roscoe listed the name, religious affiliation (Protestant, Catholic, or Muslim), clan membership, and clan or royal office held by the informant. He seems to have started the interview by asking the informant to describe a certain institution or practice as it had existed in the precolonial era – that is, during the reign of Mutesa I (1856-1884) or Mwanga II (1884-1887). The informant proceeded with his description until his knowledge was exhausted; then the interview ended or was resumed by the introduction of another, usually related, subject, and the informant continued until he told all that he knew. Some interviews were brief and required only one page of notes; others were more extensive. Because Roscoe covered the same topics with different informants, he received ample confirmation of the main points. He also seems to have "put down everything," virtually verbatim, as Frazer advised. He does not appear to have interrupted his informants by asking for further explanations, especially about ritual practices, perhaps because of Frazer's warning against the use of "leading questions." The notes also indicate that Roscoe did not stick slavishly to Frazer's *Questions*, but used them only as a general guide to subject areas and topics of inquiry.

In 1911, the Belgian anthropologist Arnold van Gennep published in France a satire on Frazer's *Questions* – "The Questionnaire: Or, Ethnographic Enquiries" ([1911] 1967). It is the story of a bumbling French anthropologist who takes Frazer's *Questions* to the field. He returns with a collection of contradictory answers to his queries, and wins the Grand Prix for the "renovation of scientific ethnography." Van Gennep's satire was aimed at Frazer's presumption that the questionnaire method was adequate to the demands of the field. In van Gennep's view, ethnography was an empirical science analogous to biology and should be based on the direct observation of social customs in their environment. Although van Gennep knew that the questionnaire method was admired by the anthropological establishment, he appears to have regarded it as fundamentally ill-conceived, merely a display of methodical investigation without observational foundation (Belmont 1979). Frazer, to be sure, insisted that anthropology should be based on "strict observation" (1931: 244), but what he chiefly meant by this was the acquisition of informants' accounts. Nowhere in *Questions* did he advise the ethnographer to observe the customs that his informants described. Instead, he told the fieldworker to test his information by questioning other informants: "If they all agree in substance, the enquirer may feel satisfied that he has got the truth" ([1887] 1889: 7). This is precisely the flaw that van Gennep exposed to ridicule: without observational foundation in living social contexts, the questionnaire method could lead to perfect nonsense.[15]

To this charge, Roscoe's work is partly vulnerable, despite his excellent linguistic ability and long acquaintance with the Baganda. Roscoe's use

of Frazer's *Questions* produced thorough and detailed accounts, but they
were subject to some major limitations. In the case of rituals that were no
longer performed, Roscoe obviously had to rely on informants. But in the
case of rituals that were still extant, such as marriage ceremonies and
funerary rites, Roscoe's accounts are, unfortunately, not derived from
actual contexts of performance. Although he obtained detailed descriptions, they tend to be formalized and abstract and present only the informants' point of view; they are generally lacking in sociological context
and devoid of analytic perspective. This is true even of Roscoe's own
firsthand accounts. For example, in describing the ceremonies at the royal
shrines, Roscoe writes that the mediums of the royal spirits were possessed for as long as an hour, spoke in a voice of the deceased king, held
"interviews" with people, and delivered messages to the crowd (1907b,
1921: 151). But he does not describe the content of the messages or the
questions that were put to the royal spirits. Nor does he say when, why,
or for whom the ceremonies were performed, or even what they were
called.[16]

In these respects we have only to compare Roscoe's work with more
recent studies of the same phenomena, such as Lucy Mair's accounts of
birth, marriage, and funerary rites (Mair 1934); John Orley's and Peter
Rigby's accounts of lubaale divination and healing (Orley 1970; Rigby
1973); and this writer's descriptions of the royal shrines (Ray 1972,
1977a). In each of these studies, the ethnographer's observational and
analytic perspective, which Frazer wished to deny, elicits the important
sociological and symbolic features of the materials. By comparison, Roscoe's ethnography is basically a summary of informants' accounts offered
to the armchair theorist for further explanation, as Frazer's method pre-
scribed.

Nevertheless, it should not be assumed that Roscoe's interviews produced unreliable results. On the contrary, we are in the unusual position
of being able to check virtually every detail of Roscoe's Ganda ethnography against Kaggwa's publications. The agreement is remarkable, as other scholars have recognized (Mandelbaum 1934: 7; Rowe 1967; Kiwanuka
1971b: xxvii). In some instances — for example, descriptions of royal
ritual — the concordance is so close as to suggest that Roscoe and Kaggwa
obtained their information from the same individuals. The few discrepancies are minor. It is apparent that Roscoe sometimes got certain details
wrong, such as titles. This is understandable, since his notes are written in
English, which means that he had to translate while writing down informants' accounts. The discrepancies also confirm that Roscoe did not copy
material from Kaggwa's already published *Empisa* (1907); had he done

so, he would have corrected his mistakes. The odd fact seems to be that he did not consult *Empisa* at all, or if he did, that he considered his notes more reliable than Kaggwa's. Sometimes Roscoe drew on material that he gathered from other sources, perhaps before he began to work with Kaggwa's informants. These enabled him to provide more information about certain ritual subjects — for example, the killings at the time of the installation of the king. Unfortunately, even though Kaggwa's accounts are generally more extensive and detailed, they are subject to the same limitations as Roscoe's because they derive from the same interview context and exhibit the same formality. *Empisa* is so thoroughly impersonal, in accordance with Frazer's method, that one would never guess that Kaggwa was a member of the society that he is describing!

As already noted, Roscoe wrote up his ethnography according to the subject headings of Frazer's *Questions*, which cast his accounts in a distinctly Frazerian mold. Most of the chapter titles of *The Baganda, The Bakitara or Banyoro*, and *The Banyankole* were taken directly from the topic headings of *Questions* and follow the same order. Because *Questions* dealt far more thoroughly with the intellectual and ceremonial aspects of traditional life than with the social and political, this imbalance is reflected in Roscoe's work. It is especially apparent in his failure to consider Buganda's complex political, economic, and legal systems; these subjects had to await the work of later anthropologists and historians. Instead, Roscoe dealt most fully with the ritual practices associated with birth, marriage, death, the installation of kings, royal shrines, ritual homicide, scapegoats, the gods, and sympathetic magic. Nevertheless, Roscoe's picture of the Baganda was as well rounded as he could make it, even though it necessarily bore a close resemblance to the master portrait of primitive culture drawn in *The Golden Bough*.

Divine Kingship in Buganda?

In an important sense, then, Frazer's ideas about anthropology directly shaped Roscoe's findings. Frazer's theory of divine kingship also influenced Roscoe's work, although less directly. Roscoe did not say that the Kabakas of Buganda were divine kings, and he tried to balance his account of the ritual features of the kingship with a description of the king's secular, political role. Instead of speculating about the origins and early development of the kingship, a major emphasis of Frazer's theory, Roscoe summarized Ganda oral tradition on the subject, as recorded in Kaggwa's work. But, as we have seen, Roscoe was deeply influenced by his mentor's theories, and he thus gave a distinctly Frazerian view of the Kabakaship.

Earlier, I noted that Frazer's treatment of kingship can be seen as a general inquiry into indigenous ideas of power, authority, and prosperity. His immediate problem in *The Golden Bough* concerned the rule of succession of the priest of Diana's sacred grove at Nemi in southern Italy. Why did Diana's priest have to slay his predecessor and in turn be slain himself? In answer to this question, Frazer proposed an evolutionary scheme in which the institution of divine kingship developed from the figure of the magician, who belonged to the godless Age of Magic, to the magician man-god who arose in the subsequent Age of Religion. For Frazer, the central feature of primitive and ancient kingship all over the world was the magical power of the kingly man-god to control the fertility of the land and the people. When this power failed, the king had to be killed. Ritual regicide, the act of killing an ailing or aged king in order to save the divinity within, became the focus of the whole theory. What fascinated Frazer was the killing of persons to sustain life, a philosophy that equated human life with nature in an attempt to control the latter. Distantly behind it all was the figure of the suffering and crucified Christ, the dying-rising god-king, as well as Frazer's own deep ambivalence about the value of religion in the course of human history. Frazer was continually drawn to ritual violence as an expression of institutionalized power that compelled "people to kill in order to prosper," as Feeley-Harnick has aptly put it (1985: 273). Frazer's theory of regicide is best presented in his own florid prose:

> Now primitive peoples . . . sometimes believe that their safety and even that of the world is bound up with the life of these god-men or human incarnations of the divinity. Naturally, therefore, they take the utmost care of his life, out of regard for their own. But no amount of care and precaution will prevent the man-god from growing old and feeble and at last dying. His worshippers have to lay their account with this sad necessity and to meet it as best they can. The danger is a formidable one; for if the course of nature is dependent on the man-god's life, what catastrophes may not be expected from the gradual enfeeblement of his powers and their final extinction in death? There is only one way of averting these dangers. The man-god must be killed as soon as he shews symptoms that his powers are beginning to fail, and his soul must be transferred to a vigorous successor before it has been seriously impaired by threatened decay. (1911–1915 IV: 9)

Taking regicide as his central fact and the kingship of the Shilluk of the southern Sudan as his primary example, Frazer argued that all forms of ritual symbolism associated with kingship in Africa and elsewhere (for example, mock-kings, human scapegoats, blood sacrifice, cults of royal ancestors, ritual combats, dying-rising gods) were modifications of the ancient practice of regicide. Based on the Shilluk example, Frazer's divine king, especially in Africa, exhibited four major characteristics (cf. Seligman 1934: 5-6; Smith 1969: 347-49):

1. He was an incarnate god.
2. His life and vitality were bound up with the life and welfare of human beings and nature (his vitality sometimes being "invigorated" by human sacrifice).
3. He had to be killed when he grew old or ill.
4. His divine soul thereby could be transferred to a vigorous successor.

Contrary, perhaps, to Frazer's expectations, Buganda did not possess a divine kingship. The Kabakas were not regarded as incarnate deities; their life was not bound up with the vitality of the cosmos; and they were not killed (actually or symbolically) when they became old or ill.[17]

Nevertheless, Roscoe deliberately construed certain aspects of the Kabakaship in a Frazerian manner. He claimed, although not always in his ethnographic work *The Baganda*, that ritual regicide was practiced during the early period of the kingship, that the Kabakas were deified when they died, that they were the high priests of the kingdom, that their lives were strengthened and prolonged by human sacrifice, and that the person of the Kabaka was regarded as sacred. Putting these points together, Roscoe's portrait of the Kabaka was an attenuated version of Frazer's divine king. Frazer, for his part, picked up most of these points and fitted them into the theory of *The Golden Bough*. It will therefore be important to examine briefly both Frazer and Roscoe on each of these matters, for they concern important features of the kingship that will be discussed in more detail later on.

"There can be little doubt," Roscoe wrote,

that in the early reigns of the kings [of Buganda] the sovereign was expected to reign only so long as he enjoyed all his faculties, and when his powers began to fail, he was expected to put an end to his life or to have it taken from him either by one of his brothers or by one of his wives. There is one instance recorded when a king who was ill is said to have been smothered by his wives. (1921: 87-88)

In referring to regicide among the "early" kings, Roscoe had in mind the stories about the disappearance of the founder of the kingship, Kintu, and his son Chwa Nabakka I. However, these stories do not say that

Kintu and Chwa were killed. They say that Kintu, after reigning for many years, disappeared into a forest out of shame after inadvertently killing his Katikkiro and that Chwa disappeared some years later while searching for his father. Roscoe, influenced by Frazer, simply chose to interpret these stories as evidence of regicide. Roscoe's claim about regicide among the early kings appeared only in *Twenty-Five Years in East Africa*, a popular work that was free of Frazer's strictures against mixing theory with ethnography. Roscoe may have been persuaded to adopt this view on the basis of Frazer's already published statement in *The Golden Bough* that the disappearance of Kintu and Chwa "may well point to a . . . custom of putting them [the Kabakas] to death for the purpose of preserving their life" (1911–1915 IV: 28).

The stories about the disappearance of Kintu and Chwa stand in marked contrast to the accounts about the later kings, many of whom are said to have been murdered by rebellious princes or killed by supernatural powers. In these instances, it is clear that regicide was a matter of political intrigue or of supernatural retribution, not of royal infirmity. As for a king being smothered by his wives, Roscoe himself reported that this happened to one king accidentally and was said to be the reason why the king's wives were kept away from him when he was dying (1911: 103).[18] Even if such an event actually occurred, a single case of accidental regicide hardly counts as evidence of ritual regicide, and Roscoe undoubtedly knew it.

Roscoe also supposed that the Kabakas became gods after death: "The ghosts of the kings were placed on an equality with the gods, and received the same honour and worship" (1911: 283).[19] Later, he stated that the ghosts attached to the preserved jawbone and the royal Twin symbol together constituted a "perfect deity" (1921: 152). Both statements imply that the Kabakas possessed divine souls and achieved the status of gods when they died.

In one sense, Roscoe was correct; that is, the gods and the royal ancestors were metaphysically and symbolically the same. Both the gods (*lubaale*) and the royal spirits were spirits of deceased human beings, and both possessed the same ritual symbols: the preserved jawbone and Twin symbol. Like the gods, the royal spirits took possession of human beings who served as their mediums and prophesied about the welfare of the kingdom.

But sociologically, the gods and the royal ancestors were very different. The cult of the royal ancestors was a limited one that was restricted to the kingship; it formed part of the state religion, but played a minor role. None of the royal spirits could match the power and authority of the national war gods, Kibuuka and Nnende, or the lake god, Mukasa. Nor did the royal spirits perform acts of personal healing, which was one of the main functions of the lubaale. The ceremonies at the royal shrines were primarily acts of homage and divination, and attendance at them was limited to members of the royal family and to shrine officials. Although the major gods served the state, they were fundamentally rooted in the clans; the priests were appointed by the clans and sometimes challenged the kings, even killing them when they disobeyed.

The ritual terminology for the gods and the royal ancestors is also fundamentally different. Possession by a lubaale is called *kulagula* or *kusamira*, whereas possession by a royal spirit is referred to as *kukongoj-ja*, "to bear" or "to carry" the spirit of the king. Ceremonies at the lubaale temples are referred to as "divination" (*kulagala*), while those at the royal shrines are referred to as "paying court" (*kukiika mbuga*) to the king. The royal medium is never called a "priest" (*kabona*, *mmandwa*, or *mulaguzi*) but always a "bearer" (*mukongozzi*) of the king's spirit. While some Ganda writers in the past referred to the royal ancestors as lubaale, this was inaccurate and may have resulted from missionary influence (Taylor 1958: 217). The royal ancestors are never called lubaale but "honored kings" (*Bassekabaka*; singular, *Ssekabaka*), and their shrines are never referred to as "temples" (*ssabo*) but as "royal shrines" (*masiro*). To suggest, as Roscoe did, that the dead kings were deified and worshiped was to classify them as Frazerian deities to which the living kings succeeded on the throne, which was incorrect. The kings succeeded to the kingdom (*obuganda*), or rather they "ate the kingdom" (*kulya obuganda*). They did not attain the status of a divine being.

This, however, was precisely how Frazer fitted the spirits of Buganda's dead kings into his divine kingship pattern. In *The Golden Bough*, he placed Roscoe's material about the royal ancestors into his argument about the transmission of the king's divine soul to his successor (1911–1915 IV: 200–201). Although Frazer had to admit that the Shilluk kingship provided the only direct evidence of soul transference from the dead king to the living, he argued that "analogy seems to render it probable that a similar succession [by regicide] to the soul of the slain god has been supposed to take place in other instances, though direct evidence of it is wanting" (1911–1915 IV: 198). In Buganda, the spirit of the dead king did not pass into the body of his successor but into that of a priestly medium, the "bearer" (*mukongozzi*), who communicated messages to the living Kabaka. Frazer, ignoring the fact that his theory called for the soul of the dead king to pass directly into his successor, cited the Ganda example of the royal spirit medium in support of his view that "at death the spirit of the divine king or priest is believed to pass into his successor" (1911–1915 IV: 204). In this way, the Kabakaship was rather crudely forced into Frazer's god-man theory.[20]

In keeping with the Frazerian pattern, Roscoe also suggested that the Kabaka was the high priest of the kingdom. He wrote in *The Baganda*:

> The worship of the national gods was under the immediate control of the King; their first and principal duty was the protection of the King and the State. Although the King consulted them, sent presents to propitiate them, and followed their instructions, he would, if one of them vexed him, send and loot his temple and estate. He alone in the country dared to commit such an act of sacrilege, any other person violating the gods' property would have met with certain death at the hands of the guardian of the temples. The national gods had temples appointed for them by the King. (1911: 273)

Later, in *Twenty-Five Years*, Roscoe wrote that the monthly new moon ceremonies featured rituals whereby "the king showed himself to be the head of the whole religious worship" (1921: 186).[21]

Both these statements are incorrect. They were, perhaps, based on a misinterpretation. The Kabaka led the nation in supporting the gods and supplied them lavishly with gifts of tribute, but he did not control them or their cult, as some kings painfully learned. The Kabaka's obligatory gifts to the gods indicate a relation of asymmetrical exchange (cf. Kenny 1988: 604). Upon accession, the Kabaka rebuilt the lubaale temples and presented the gods with large endowments of women, slaves, cattle, goats, and cowrie shells in multiples of the sacred number nine. The gods, in turn, exhorted the new king to "always love the gods" and gave him their blessing (Kaggwa [1907] 1934: 21). Every year, the Kabaka made new presentations to the gods to secure those blessings. He also gave a large number of human victims to the war god Kibuuka whenever Kibuuka's temple was rebuilt. While responsible for the upkeep of the country's major shrines, the Kabakas never oversaw the worship of the lubaale or governed the priests. On the contrary, when the Kabakas refused to take priestly advice and proceeded to kill the priests and loot their temples, the chronicles say that the lubaale were quick to take revenge. They set illnesses and other afflictions upon the Kabakas in order to put them in their place. In the nineteenth century, the priests of Mukasa regarded Mutesa I as their "son-in-law" (Roscoe 1911: 298), even their "slave" (Ashe 1895: 102n.), a relationship that indicated his subordinate status. The chronicles also report that Mukasa's priests generally succeeded in forcing Mutesa I to do their will. To be sure, Mutesa's father, Ssuuna II, is said to have boasted that he was the lubaale on earth because he could with impunity plunder the temples of the lubaale of the sky (Roscoe and Kaggwa 1906: 50; Burton [1860] 1961 II: 191). But even the powerful Ssuuna was unable to force the gods to do his bidding. The dynastic accounts say that Ssuuna was struck by lightning sent by lubaale Kiwanuka because he mistreated one of Kiwanuka's priests (Kaggwa [1901] 1971: 119). Ssuuna is also said to have died of smallpox because he disobeyed the warnings of the priest of the war god Nnende (Nsimbi 1956b: 134). When Mutesa was ill in 1879, the priest of Mukasa attributed the malady to Mutesa's political ambition, which offended Mukasa. Mutesa was thus forced to return the powerful chieftainship of the Mugema to its rightful possessors, the Vervet Monkey clan (Rowe 1967: 154–56; Kaggwa [1901] 1971: 176). As Roscoe himself noted, the temple priesthoods were appointed by the clan heads (*Bataka*), and although it was necessary for the king to ratify priestly appointments, the priesthoods tended to support clan interests (Wright 1971: 4). Even though the king might summon the priest of the war god Kibuuka to the capital, the god could refuse to let him go and the priest would stay at home (Kaggwa [1907] 1934: 222). Kaggwa also notes that Kibuuka was treated like a Kabaka, and his seat was called Nnamulondo, which was the name of the king's enthronement stool. It was pointed out to me that ever since Tebandeke, the eighteenth Kabaka, who became a priest of Mukasa while on the throne, there was an institutional incompatibility between the Kabakaship and the priests, and the two could never be combined (cf. Kaggwa [1901] 1971: 56–59).

Thinking solely in Frazerian terms, Roscoe considered only the gods' service to the state, not the kings' service to the gods, on which the system was predicated.[22] As almost every Kabaka learned, the national gods were independent forces, allied to the clans, who acted both in support of the kingship and against tyrannical kings, thus checking their power. All the evidence shows that Mutesa, powerful as he was, had to walk a fine line, balancing his own ambitions against the power of the clans and their priestly supporters (cf. Wright 1971: 2–4; Kenny 1988). As for the new moon ceremonies to which Roscoe drew attention, these were celebrated both at the palace and at the temples of the gods, and only at the palace was the king in charge of them. Elsewhere they were supervised by the lubaale priests.

Another feature of Frazer's divine kingship pattern was the practice of "strengthening" the monarch's vitality by means of human sacrifice. Roscoe described several ritual killings, which he said were supposed to "invigorate" the Kabaka at his installation (1911: 209–10), although he did not explain how the Baganda thought this was done. Undaunted by lack of evidence, Frazer interpreted these killings as instances of soul transference: "[I]n all cases it would seem to be thought that the life of the murdered man was in some mysterious fashion transferred to the king, so that the monarch received thereby a fresh accession of vital energy" (1911–1915 VI: 223). Here Frazer was stretching his own theory. According to Roscoe, these killings occurred only two or three months after the installation ceremonies when, in terms of Frazer's theory, the new king should still be full of youthful vigor.

Another killing described by Roscoe took place at the estate of Nankere, one of the indigenous clan heads who confirmed (*kukula*) the king's accession to the throne. After administering an oath to the king, Nankere presented him with one of his sons. According to Kaggwa's account, Nankere said, "this child whom I have here will die for the Kabaka so that he will have long life (*aliwangaala*)" (Kaggwa [1907] 1934: 23; cf. Kakoma, Ntate, and Serukaga 1959: 11). The king then struck the boy with his fists, and he was taken away and killed; sinews from his back were made into anklets for the king. Roscoe, who did not realize that the kula rites were part of the installation process, thought that they occurred two or three years afterward for the purpose of prolonging the king's life.[23] Hence, Roscoe called them "prolongation of life ceremonies" (1911: 216), whereas they were actually called the "ceremony of confirmation" (*kukula*). These were the last of the accession rituals, and earned the king the right to be called Kabaka (cf. Kiwanuka 1971b: 36, n. 1). Roscoe also says that Nankere's son was a "substitute" for the king, and he was thus "fed and clothed and treated in all respects like a prince" (1911: 210, 151). Frazer had already published an account of this ceremony, based on Roscoe's field notes, in *Totemism and Exogamy* (1910: 485–86), and in it he referred to Nankere's son as a "substitute" sacrifice for the king. It is clear that Roscoe knew of this interpretation because at Frazer's request he checked through the page proofs of *Totemism and Exogamy* that contained material from his field notes (Frazer, 1 January 1910). Thus it would appear that Roscoe's designation of Nankere's son as a sacrificial "substitute" in *The Baganda* was a direct carry-over from Frazer's interpretation of the rite.

Unfortunately, Kaggwa's account does not say how Nankere's son was dressed, although Kakoma's more recent description says that he was dressed as a bride (*mugole*) (1959: 16). Kaggwa explains that the ceremony originated during the reign of one of the early kings, Kabaka Ttembo. Ttembo fell ill and became violently insane (*eddalu*). This type of illness is not uncommon in Buganda today, and it is greatly feared because of its intensity. Eddalu is one of several "strong" maladies that are said to be sent by human beings (through witchcraft) or by spirits; it is thought to be treatable only by Ganda medicines and is rarely cured (Orley 1970: 4ff). The dynastic accounts say that Ttembo tried several remedies before going to his uncle Nankere, who consulted a doctor. The doctor told Nankere to "put his medicine [*edagala*; literally, 'leaves'] into the back tendons of a human being, which were made into anklets and put on the legs" (Kaggwa [1901] 1971: 19). Kakoma's account says that the medicine was in fact sewn into the tendons (1959: 11). Henceforth, the anklets became part of the installation regalia of Ttembo's successors. As Audrey Richards has pointed out, the ceremony at Nankere's was one of doctoring the king and endowing him with strength (1966: 35), specifically fortifying him against the dreaded eddalu, so that the Kabaka "will have a long life (*aliwangaala*)" (Kakoma, Ntate, and Serukaga 1959: 11).

Frazer's idea of soul transference was an all-purpose theory by which he explained most royal ritual and symbolism. Roscoe ended his account of the rite at Nankere's estate with the description of a royal whip that was made from strips of skin taken from the corpse of Nankere's son. The whip was carried by an official and used when the king attended feasts at his council of chiefs. Anyone who was struck by the whip was believed to be made impotent, and he had to pay a fine of cowrie shells to the official in order for the curse to be removed. Frazer, attempting to explain the belief in the whip's power to cause impotency, proposed the following interpretation: "[W]e may conjecture that the life or virility of every man struck with the whip was supposed to be transmitted in some way to the king, who thus recruited his vital, and especially reproductive, energies at this solemn feast" (1911–1915 VI: 225). In *Empisa*, Kaggwa explained that the purpose of the whip was to make everyone who was standing up in the king's presence sit down, as custom required, and thus to maintain order in the king's council ([1907] 1934: 137). Kaggwa, too, referred to the whip's power to cause impotency, but neither he nor Roscoe said anything about its effect on the virility of the king.

Roscoe was, of course, well acquainted with Frazer's soul-transference theory, and in one instance he explicitly attributed it to the Baganda. In describing a drum called Kaula, he wrote that when a new skin was put on it a man was killed and his blood allowed to run into the drum "so that, when the drum was beaten, it was supposed to add fresh life and vigor to the King from the life of the slain man" (1911: 27–28). In this instance, Roscoe may have been misinformed. "Kaula" was not the name of a drum but of the king's chief drummer, and there is no evidence that any drum was refurbished in this fashion (Lush 1937: 15).

In keeping with Frazer's kingship theory, Roscoe affirmed in *Twenty-Five Years* that "the person of the king has ever been regarded as most sacred." He gave as evidence the fact that the king

> was never allowed to walk outside his own enclosure, but was carried . . .
> on the shoulders of chosen men, and even these men were each supplied
> with a piece of bark-cloth to place over their heads and shoulders for the
> royal seat, lest their flesh should come in contact with that of the king.
> (1921: 89)

On this point Roscoe was right, although the Kabaka's person was sacred not by virtue of his divinity but by virtue of his office. The office of the Kabaka was indeed the most powerful in the nation and required a high degree of symbolic behavior from both the king and those who came near him. Numerous proverbs and praise names attested to the Kabaka's power over life and death. He was likened to the queen termite that (the Baganda believed) devoured the termites of her colony, to the blacksmith's forge that melts iron in order to mold it, and to a hammer that crushes what it hits. Chiefs prostrated themselves before the king and writhed in the dust when thanking him for favors. In 1863, John Hanning Speke wrote about Mutesa: "[E]very man courts the favour of a word with the king, and adores him as a deity, and he, in turn, makes himself as distant as he can to give greater effect to his exalted position" (1863: 293). At the king's command, human life was frequently taken, not only as punishment but also as a display of royal power, and even as royal amusement. The CMS missionary Robert Pickering Ashe, who attended Mutesa's court in the 1880s, observed that Mutesa "was an object of deepest reverence, and even superstitious dread, to his people" (1895: 63). In the late 1950s, Audrey Richards was told that a father's authority over his family was modeled on that of the Kabaka, and "like the Kabaka— whatever he [the father] does is right. I suppose you would say he was just like God" (1964: 266).

As this last statement implies, the Luganda term for "god" or "divinity" (*lubaale*) is as much a status concept as a metaphysical one. When the CMS missionary Alexander Mackay demonstrated to the Baganda the operation of a mechanical water pump by shooting a stream of water twenty feet into the air, they called him a lubaale, believing he had unseen mystical powers (1890: 228). But *lubaale* was also a status term for supreme authority. Thus Mutesa once boasted to his chiefs that he was more powerful than lubaale Mukasa—that is, Mukasa's priest—because he could command greater honor and recognition (*kitibwa*) from the people (Mukasa 1938: 59). Because of the Kabaka's superior status and power, both Mutesa and his father, Ssuuna, were called "lubaale on earth" (*lubaale mu ensi*), for they sometimes punished the "lubaale of the air" by plundering their women, cattle, and goats (Roscoe and Kaggwa 1906: 50). To say, therefore, that the Kabaka was regarded as a lubaale or god was to attribute a very visible sort of power (*buyinza*) to him that had nothing to do with divine or mystical qualities.

Martin Southwold has suggested that it was the Kabaka's supreme authority over human life and death that both set him apart and evoked attitudes of sacredness about his person (1967: 21–22). Shils, too, notes that great power is the central, order-related event and as such "arouses the charismatic propensity" (1975: 263–64). But it was not simply the Kabaka's power to kill that raised him to the symbolic level; it was the fact that he was the embodiment of the nation, its order-creating principle. Hence, as Michael Kenny notes, the Kabaka "iconistically represents the total society" over which he rules (1988: 596). Evans-Pritchard thought of this aspect of sovereignty in terms of the throne's powers of unifying politically sectional interests. He noted in connection with the Shilluk kingship that the king "must be in society and yet stand outside it and this is only possible if his office is raised to the mystical plane" ([1948] 1962: 210). Clifford Geertz, thinking in more cultural terms, has referred to the "inherent sacredness of sovereign power" (1983a). The Kabaka was the center of the order of symbols, of the values and beliefs that governed Buganda. Hence, both he and his office partook of the nature of the sacred.

The king was set apart from both commoners and other royalty: he never walked on the ground, he could never be looked upon in a royal procession, and he had to take his meals in seclusion. Yet the person of the Kabaka was not holy or divine. The fact that the Kabakas were frequently murdered by rebellious princes, that they were believed to have been killed by vengeful gods, and that the lubaale priests regarded themselves as superior ritual authorities clearly indicates the very human dimensions of the king's person. The Kabaka was praised as "the Greatest of Men" (*Ssaabasajja*) and glorified as the "Father of Twins" (*Ssaabalongo*), but he was not regarded as a Frazerian man-god.

In using the expression the "inherent sacredness of sovereignty," Geertz does not have in mind Frazerian notions of divinity but the "symbolic aspects of power" and the "charisma of central authority" (1983a). This is because kings, no matter how secular they might otherwise be, define a "society's center and affirm its connection with transcendent things" (1983a). As agents of ultimate power and as symbols of the state, the Kabakas were extraordinary persons, set apart from society and given the highest respect and reverence, superior even to that accord-ed to the priests of the gods. In this sense, they were sacred personages or, as the Baganda put it somewhat paradoxically, "gods (*lubaale*) on earth."

The Golden Bough: Broken and Restored

Although Frazer did not derive any new theories from Roscoe's ethnography, he did pick up important evidence. In 1907, Roscoe obtained for the museum at Cambridge the relics of lubaale Kibuuka, the chief war god of Buganda. The relics turned out to include a human jawbone, an umbilical cord, and parts of what Roscoe described as human genitalia (1907a).[24] According to legend, Kibuuka was a heroic warrior who was slain in a battle with Bunyoro and became a god after he died. A temple was built in his honor, and he became the protector of Buganda's western frontier with Bunyoro. For Frazer, Kibuuka's remains were convincing evidence of euhemerism, the theory propounded by the ancient Greek writer Euhemerus that the ancient gods were human beings who were deified at death. In the third edition of *The Golden Bough*, Frazer pointed to Kibuuka's remains to support his theory that the Egyptian god Osiris was originally a human king who was deified after death (1911–1915 VI: 197). Partly on the strength of Roscoe's unique evidence from Buganda, Frazer held to the plausibility of euhemerism throughout *The Golden Bough* (cf. Ackerman 1987: 253–54). Euhemerism was, of course, a crucial part of Frazer's theory, which held that divine kingship originated in the idea of a deified human being.

However, at the end of *The Golden Bough* Frazer claimed that he had come to hold his theories very "lightly." In the final book, he dramatically confessed that the study of divine kingship had not been the real purpose of his work. Here, he abandoned his interpretation of the slaying of the priest-king of Diana at Nemi, the classical example on which he had founded his great project. In the preface, he declared the priest-king of Diana to be only a "puppet," the "make-believe" subject of the twelve-volume work, and he announced that "it is time to unmask him before laying him up in his box" (1911–1915 X: vi). The true subject, Frazer admitted, was not divine kingship per se but "the gradual evolution of human thought from savagery to civilization." He went even further and undercut the scientific standing of his theories by confessing that he had used them "chiefly as convenient pegs on which to hang my collections of facts" (1911–1915 XII: xi).

In what, then, lay the value of *The Golden Bough* if not in its theories about the origins of social and religious institutions? Was the theory of divine kingship merely a "peg" on which to hang the facts laboriously gathered by Roscoe and other ethnographers? Was *The Golden Bough* now to be regarded as merely an ethnographic encyclopedia?

It turned out that Frazer could not maintain this view very long. By 1922, when he issued the one-volume abridged edition of *The Golden Bough*, he had done an about-face. Without bothering to remind his readers of his earlier recantation, Frazer embraced his cast-off puppet, the priest-king of Diana, and reaffirmed his original project. "The primary aim of this book," he wrote, "is to explain the remarkable rule which regulated the succession to the priesthood of Diana" and to explore "kindred topics" (1922a: v). Although the historian of religions Jonathan Z. Smith believes that Frazer omitted his earlier retraction from the abridged edition so that its readers would not be "in on the joke" (1973: 370, n. 96), it seems clear that Frazer actually had changed his mind. Frazer's theory of kingship survived untouched from the completion of *The Golden Bough* in 1915. He would not, or could not, abandon or seriously call into question the work's original purpose or foundational theories. Thus he assured readers of the abridged edition that "the new evidence which has come to my knowledge in the meantime has on the whole served either to confirm my former conclusions or to furnish fresh illustrations" (1922a: v).

What was this "new evidence"? Frazer pointed out that most of it came from Africa, and he drew special attention to Roscoe's description of the annual ceremony of killing a mock-king in Bunyoro (1922a: vi).[25] Although Frazer did not say it, other evidence obtained by Roscoe on the Mackie Expedition, mainly from the kingdoms of Bunyoro and Ankole (Nkore), provided important illustrations of almost every aspect of the divine-kingship hypothesis: the sympathetic connection between the king and the fertility of the land and the cattle (Bunyoro, Nkore), the killing of the aged or ailing king (Bunyoro, Nkore), the invigoration of the king by human sacrifice (Bunyoro), the sacredness of the king's person (Bunyoro, Nkore), the cult of dead kings (Bunyoro, Nkore), and the sacred emblems of kingship (Bunyoro, Nkore). Such evidence, which Frazer gleaned from Roscoe's field notes and reported to the world, seems to have restored Frazer's faith in his divine-kingship theory. With these African parallels to the priest at Nemi freshly before him, Frazer even allowed himself to speculate about the early influence of Africa on ancient Italy and the possibility of African immigrants in southern Europe.

From this point onward, Frazer never again expressed any doubts. In 1936, when he published *Aftermath*, the supplementary volume to *The Golden Bough*, he was finally able to incorporate into the great work all of Roscoe's material on East African kingship. In the preface Frazer asserted, in response to criticisms about his method, that he based his conclusions "by strict induction on a broad and solid foundation of well-authenticated facts" and that he saw no reason to change "the superstructure of theory" that formed the framework of his life's project (1936: v). When he added his standard qualification, "Now, as always, I hold my theories very lightly, and am ever ready to modify or abandon them in light of new evidence," he was not to be taken seriously. He was eighty-two years old, blind, and unable to read or write, and he was not in a position to reexamine his views. In telling the reader that his theories would eventually give way to new ones, he was in fact laying claim to a permanent place in the progress of scientific knowledge. Moreover, in asserting that the facts of *The Golden Bough* would remain as a "picture or moving panorama of the vanished life of primitive man all over the world . . . groping and stumbling through the mists of ignorance and superstition," he was implicitly reasserting his theories of magic, primitive mentality, and divine kingship, for these formed the very structure of his "moving panorama."

By this time, however, Frazer's work had been dismissed by the anthropological establishment. It had long since proved to be an embarrassment because, apart from the African ethnography, most of Frazer's evidence came from classical literary sources, folklore, traveler's reports, and amateur ethnography. Regicide, it turned out, was very difficult to verify in colonial Africa. It was also recognized that there was a great variety of kings, whose power seemed to be composite and unstable, rather than absolute in Frazer's sense. From the 1930s through the early 1960s, studies of African kingship therefore shifted attention from the king and his royal prerogatives to governmental structure and political theories of state formation. As Feeley-Harnik perceptively notes, these studies coincided with the European task of transforming local African polities into colonial states (1985). In Buganda, anthropologists Lucy Mair, Lloyd Fallers, and Audrey Richards did not describe the power and legitimacy of the kings by examining royal mythology and ritual, but by scrutinizing the king's administrative functions and his rights over his subjects. Finding it impossible to classify the Kabakas of Buganda as divine kings, Mair and Richards touched on the royal rituals only briefly before moving on to lengthier discussions of economic, juridical, and military matters (Mair 1934: 178; Richards 1964: 279).

This, however, left some of the most striking features of the kingship unexplained. For example, Mair confessed that "the question precisely how the cruelties [mass killings] which are known to have been perpetrated by the last independent kings were reconciled with the conception of the 'good king' as expressed at the accession is one which cannot be answered" (1934: 182). Richards saw the king as a kind of father figure writ large, despite the evidence of her own investigations which showed that paternal authority in Buganda was conceived in terms of the power of the king, not vice versa.

By contrast, Frazer's theory of kingship, insofar as it was based on local myths and rituals, focused attention on indigenous ideas of power, especially the kings' prerogative for violence. Frazer, to be sure, forced indigenous ideas into his own scheme and badly distorted them. But he rightly conceived the study of kingship to be rooted in symbolic forms. Hence, it is now recognized that "investigations into the symbolics of power and into its nature are very similar endeavors" (Geertz 1983a: 152). The Kabaka of Buganda was not only a bureaucratic and political instrument in the evolution of centralized polities, as the British anthropologists saw him in the early 1960s, but also an ideological creation, the embodiment of a symbol, expressed most significantly in the royal myths and rituals recorded by Kaggwa and Roscoe.

Surprisingly, just when the colonial officials in Buganda thought they had transformed the Kabaka into an administrative figure of the colonial state, he rebelled against them, quickening the old images of the king as a heroic conqueror and as a personage of supreme power. At the center of these images was the figure of Kintu, the primordial progenitor of the Baganda and the founder of the kingship. As such, Kintu expressed the dual foundations of the state: the patrilineal clan system and the institution of kingship. The next two chapters examine the figure of Kintu in both aspects.

2

The Story of Kintu:
Myth, Death, and Ontology

Kintu is both the primal ancestor of the Baganda and the founder of the kingship. In keeping with these two roles, the oral traditions about Kintu fall into two narrative genres: story or legend (*lugero*) and history (*byafaayo*). As the primordial ancestor, Kintu is the subject of a story (*lugero*) that tells how he became the progenitor of the Baganda and the guarantor of their life on earth. As the founder of the monarchy, Kintu is the subject of historical narratives (*byafaayo*) that tell how he entered Buganda, established the kingship, and organized the clans. This chapter concentrates primarily on the tradition about Kintu-the-patriarch, although, as we shall see, this tradition overlaps with that of Kintu-the-royal-founder, and the two are finally inseparable.

The myth of Kintu's origin is called the "story of Kintu" (*olugero lwa Kintu*). Like other African creation myths, it explains the origins of the world in terms of polarities between sky and earth, divinity and humanity, life and death. In this way it expresses basic insights into the nature of the human condition and the structure of the universe.

The story of Kintu is also open to a number of interpretations. I shall discuss some of the meanings that the Baganda have ascribed to the story, including Christian interpretations and modifications that developed during the colonial period. In the end, I shall focus on the story's significance in relation to Ganda social structure and cosmology. I intend to show how the myth employs certain fundamental moral, social, ritual, and cosmological ideas that it projects onto the primordial past in order to explain the origins of the cosmos and the significance of life and death. An important consideration, of course, will be the sense in which the story may be properly called a "myth," and the possibilities for interpretation that this designation allows.

The Story and Its Christian Interpretations

Nowadays, the Baganda are acquainted with the story of Kintu in both oral and written form. The myth was first published in Luganda in 1882 by the Catholic White Fathers, who were among the first missionaries to reach Buganda (Le Veux [1882] 1914: 449–58). Since then, it has been available in printed vernacular versions, a recent one being an elementary-school textbook edition (Mulira [1951] 1959, 1965, 1970). The summary of the myth presented here is based on a Luganda version published by Kaggwa in *Engero za Baganda* ([1902] 1951). In the preface to the second edition, Kaggwa says that when he was collecting the stories for his book, he "tried very hard to ask older Baganda who knew the stories very well" ([1902] 1951: v). Although the oral accounts that I heard in 1972 basically agree with Kaggwa's, I have chosen to summarize his version because it is the most detailed. It also appears to have been the source of all subsequently published accounts in Luganda, and to have influenced contemporary oral tradition.

Kintu wandered alone into the uninhabited country of Buganda accompanied only by his cow. He was met by a woman called Nnambi, who came with her brothers from the sky. Nnambi took an immediate liking to Kintu, despite his unknown origins and barbaric ways (he ate only cow dung and drank only cow urine and did not know whence he came), and she told Kintu that she wished to marry him. After hearing of Nnambi's intentions, her father, Ggulu, ordered his sons to steal Kintu's cow and to take it to the sky. Then Nnambi invited Kintu to come to the sky to find his cow and to take her away. When Kintu arrived, Ggulu subjected him to a series of difficult tests to see if he really was Kintu. He was told to consume a houseful of food, to cut firewood from solid rock, to collect a potful of water from dew, and to find his cow in Ggulu's large herd of cattle. Through his own cleverness and with the help of circumstances, Kintu performed each of these difficult tasks, thus proving that he was truly the heroic Kintu. Ggulu then presented Kintu with his daughter, Nnambi, to be his wife and provided the couple with everything needed to establish their home on earth: cows, goats, sheep, chickens, plantain, and millet. Ggulu told Kintu and Nnambi to depart quickly before Nnambi's brother Walumbe (Death) returned, and he ordered them never to come back, even if they forgot something, otherwise Walumbe would want to go with them. Kintu and Nnambi immediately set forth on their journey. Along the way

Nnambi remembered that she had forgotten to bring the millet for her chickens. When she informed Kintu he reminded her of Ggulu's warning and told her not to go back. But Nnambi returned for the millet. When Ggulu saw her, he said: "Didn't I tell you not to come back for anything that you forgot and that if you met Walumbe he would not allow you to go with Kintu alone?" Then Walumbe arrived and said that Kintu had taken away his sister, and he told Nnambi that he wanted to go with her. "All right," said Ggulu, "you may go with your brother Walumbe," and they left to rejoin Kintu. When Kintu saw Walumbe, he said, "We are not going to be able to manage him because he is mad (insane) . . . [H]ow are we going to cope with Walumbe? All right, we shall finish the journey with him." After Nnambi had given birth to three children, Walumbe visited Kintu and asked him for one of his children to serve as a cook and a household servant. Kintu refused, saying that otherwise he would not have a child to give to Ggulu as his "share" (*ndobolo*) of Nnambi's children. Walumbe went away and remained silent. After Nnambi had given birth to more children, Walumbe again asked Kintu for a child, and again Kintu refused. Walumbe then told Kintu that he would kill his children, but Kintu was puzzled and asked how he would kill them (because no one had died before). When Kintu's children began to die, Kintu went to Ggulu and complained about Walumbe. Ggulu reminded Kintu of his warning and said if Nnambi had not returned, Kintu's children would not have died. Ggulu then told Kintu to take back Nnambi's other brother, Kayiikuuzi, who would try to catch Walumbe and bring him back to the sky. Kayiikuuzi's first attempt failed, and Walumbe fled into the ground at a place called Ttanda. Then Kayiikuuzi devised a plan. He told Kintu to order everyone to stay indoors for two days and to take their provisions with them; no one was to go out even to fetch water or to herd goats, and no one was to raise the alarm if they saw Walumbe so that Kayiikuuzi could catch him. Everybody did as they were told, except two young children who went out to herd their goats. When they saw Walumbe they cried out, and Walumbe fled back into the ground and went down beyond Kayiikuuzi's reach at the place called Ttanda.[1] Kayiikuuzi was angry and told the children that they had done wrong. "All right," said Kintu, "if Walumbe wants to kill my children, let him. But he will not be able to finish all of them because I, Kintu, will always continue to beget more." When Ggulu heard this, he said, "So be it. Let them [Kintu and his children] stay below. You, Kayiikuuzi, will stay with us." (Kaggwa [1902] 1951: 1–8)

This myth belongs to the type of narrative that the Baganda call lugero (plural, *ngero*). In Luganda, the term *lugero* shares some but not all of the meanings of the word "myth," and these similarities and differences warrant consideration. Ngero tell about the adventures of people and animals. Some are trickster tales, some hero tales, and some etiological tales; most are combinations of these (Nabasuta 1974). Almost all are didactic and allegorical in some way and convey a moral lesson. Every lugero is therefore thought to have one or more "meanings" (*makulu*), which may vary according to the context in which the tale is related and the teller's point of view. Kaggwa, for example, attached a set of "meanings" to his collection of tales in *Engero za Baganda*. Some of these meanings clearly reflect Kaggwa's own opinions and the circumstances of his time. However, many stories seem to have more or less fixed meanings that are stated at the end in the form of proverbs (*ngero nsonge*). Unlike historical narratives (*byafaayo*), which are full of royal names, clan names, and place names but devoid of deeper meanings, ngero involve timeless contexts and generalized social circumstances. Compared with byafaayo, which concern the facts of the past — literally, "things that have taken place" — lugero is an imaginative, fictional genre. The purpose of lugero is to provide verbal entertainment, teach moral truths, explain the origins of things, and often invite thought about the significance of human behavior and social values.

In keeping with its lugero form, the story of Kintu therefore lacks any specific sociological and geographical references, and its events occur in the timeless period of the beginnings. It is both etiological and morally didactic, and it is open to a variety of interpretations. By contrast, the historical narratives about Kintu are part of royal and clan traditions and are subject to official royal interpretation. The "historical" Kintu is, from the outset, a dynamic leader who later founds the Ganda throne and organizes the clans, whereas the "mythic" Kintu first makes his appearance as an acculturated being who must become socialized through the procedures of courtship, marriage, and the fathering of children. In this way, the story of Kintu tells about the establishment of the rules of courtship, exogamous marriage, patrilineal descent, and affinal relations — the basic elements of Buganda's social structure.

The story exhibits the typical lugero dramatic form: adventure→ predicament→resolution; in this instance, marriage→death→life. Kintu and Nnambi marry, settle on earth, and introduce Death into the world; and despite all efforts, Death remains. In the end, Kintu proclaims partial victory over Death and promises that even though Death will continue to kill, the Baganda will not die out, thus ensuring the collective life of the society. Hence the proverb "The descendants of Kintu will never be finished," which expresses the significance of Kintu's concluding words.

It is appropriate to classify the story of Kintu as myth for several reasons. It is a widely known dramatic tale about events that took place in the timeless period of the beginnings; it tells about the fabulous deeds of the heroic Kintu and his supernatural antagonist, Walumbe; and it explains how the Baganda originated as a society of exogamous, patrilineal clans and how they became mortal beings. In other words, it is a story about primordial events, involving supernatural beings, that explains the origins of human life and death. Although the story is not directly tied to cultic acts or priestly rites, it is implicitly related to the Ganda marriage ceremony, for which it provides a kind of symbolic archetype. It is therefore appropriate to interpret it in terms of these aspects of the word "myth."

Most Baganda regard the story as a simple tale about how the Baganda originated and how death came into the world; it is usually told to children to explain just these matters, and children tell it to one another for the same reasons. But Ganda commentary also goes beyond this etiological dimension and emphasizes the story's particular lesson about disobedience (*obutawulira*). Like many ngero, the story of Kintu illustrates a moral lesson by a negative example; it makes clear the norm of obedience (*obuwulize*) by showing the disastrous results that followed from a breach of that norm. Sometimes the Baganda say that it was Nnambi's disobedience that "brought (or caused) death" (*yaleeta olumbe*), and this is said to be the story's primary meaning. The story clearly portrays Nnambi as the bringer of death, and it suggests that she was ultimately responsible for human mortality — as Ggulu admonishes Kintu, "If your wife had not returned, your children would not have died." Even though Kintu and his children were also significantly responsible for this outcome, Nnambi is usually regarded as the primary agent because she was the first to disobey. As one Muganda explained to me, the one who strikes the first blow is fined more heavily, according to Ganda law, than the one who strikes back. Hence, the meaning of the story is often said to be about Nnambi's disobedience (*obutawulira*) and rebellion (*obujeemu*) against authority. For example, Enoch E. K. Mulira's primary-school version of the story has Nnambi lament, "[Why] did I rebel [*njeema*] and refuse to obey [*okuwulira*]?" ([1951] 1970 II: 6). As Roscoe reported, Nnambi "is said to have been the cause of all evil, sickness, and death" (1911: 136).

In light of this interpretation, some Ganda writers have suggested that the story explains the inferior position of women in precolonial Buganda. Writing in 1907, Kaggwa indicated that "all the ritual taboos imposed upon women might have been the result of Nnambi who brought Walumbe who killed Kintu's children" ([1907] 1934: 306). In 1955, Mulira added the following conclusion to his retelling of the story: "Because of the suffering which she [Nnambi] brought, the female in Buganda was treated like a slave and regarded as a mere piece of property until the coming of Christianity, which brightened her honor" ([1951] 1965 II: 30).

It is possible that the story once contained this meaning, although the social position of women in Buganda does not seem to have been greatly inferior to that of women elsewhere in East Africa. It is more likely that Kaggwa and Mulira, as educated Christians who abhorred much of the pagan past (as did their missionary teachers), sought in the Kintu story an explanation for the inferior social position of women, which Christianity and colonialism tried to change. Kaggwa's and Mulira's interpretations may also have reflected Islamic influence that preceded Christianity in Buganda by some fifteen years. According to Swahili tradition, the inferior social position of women in East Africa is explained by reference to Eve's behavior in the Genesis story, which Islam shares with the Judeo-Christian tradition (Knappert 1970).

In this connection, it is also significant that the first recorded version of the story collected by the Catholic White Fathers (in 1882), which is otherwise very similar to Kaggwa's account, attributes the initial misdeed of returning for the millet to Kintu, not Nnambi (Le Veux [1882] 1914: 449–58). This version was recorded during the first years of missionary activity from purportedly authentic sources, most likely chiefs associated with the royal palace. A similar version was collected in 1902 from peasant informants, who were also said to have been untainted by Islamic and Christian teachings (Johnston 1902 II: 700–705). Today, at any rate, the version in which Nnambi disobeys and returns for the millet is the accepted form of the story, perhaps because of its resemblance to the biblical account of Adam and Eve.

In precolonial times, the story of Kintu seems to have existed in several versions. An interesting variant, which portrays Kintu as the one responsible for bringing death into the world, was collected by a British officer in the early 1890s. Here Kintu is said to have been a favorite of the king of heaven (Ggulu) and to have frequently feasted at his court, always returning to earth with a gift for his people. He was, however, forbidden to go back to the sky for anything that he had forgotten. One time Kintu drank too much at the feast and returned home without the corn that he had been given. When he went back to fetch it, the king of heaven asked him why he disobeyed, and Kintu could only explain that the corn would be of great benefit to his people. But the king of heaven would not allow Kintu's misconduct to go unpunished, so he sent one of his servants to accompany Kintu as a perpetual warning to mankind of the consequences of disobedience. That servant's name was Death (MacDonald [1897] 1973: 134–35).

It is sometimes mistakenly assumed that myths, especially creation myths, are as timeless and changeless as the events they portray. Perhaps this is because they are usually thought to be intrinsically sacred forms of narrative and hence resistant to change. The story of Kintu is not sacred in this sense, and it has undoubtedly been altered and reinterpreted over time. Even though it tells about the timeless period of beginnings, the story itself was subject to the influence of new ideas introduced during the colonial period. It will therefore be useful to consider a number of versions, all written after Kaggwa's, that include Christian motifs and interpretations, so that Kaggwa's text, obtained from informants who heard it in the late nineteenth century, can be put into perspective.

During the early colonial period, the biblical account of Adam and Eve dominated literate Ganda interpretations of the Kintu story. Both attributed the origins of death to a woman's act of disobedience against the commandment of a sky-dwelling father-god. Because of these parallels, Ganda Christians, who were eager to relate their own creation myth to their newly adopted religion, began to interpret the story in Christian terms. Other Baganda came to regard the parallels between the two stories as evidence of an original and independent revelation from God.

It was the Catholic White Fathers who led the way by suggesting (in 1882) that the story of Kintu might contain the vestiges of an original divine revelation. According to the White Fathers, the story resembled Christian doctrine in several respects:

> Ggulu would be the King of the skies, the source of all being, Kintu the first man, Nnambi the companion given by God to man; Walumbe would be death, the result of the disobedience of Kintu; Kayiikuuzi [would be] the Son of the Sky, who devoted himself to the abolition of death on earth. (Le Veux [1882] 1914: 449)

Encouraged perhaps by their missionary teachers, Ganda writers began to comment on these parallels. In 1902, Kaggwa wrote an interpretation under the heading of "meanings":

> This story is very similar to the works of the Holy Bible of God where we read about Adam and Eve. We see how Eve, the wife of Adam, brought death, and in the same way Nnambi, the wife of Kintu, brought death. As the words of Adam begin with the creation of earth, so the story of Kintu also begins with the creation of the country of Buganda. ([1902] 1951: 115)

In 1912, a contributor to the newly founded Catholic journal *Munno* (Your Friend) pointed out that the Kintu story "tells us that wrongdoing [*kusobya*] came first from woman," as in the Bible (1912: 50). The same writer also saw a resemblance between "the fruit which came from a tree and the millet which also came from a 'tree.'" Similarly, the Protestant historian James Miti pointed out that "both Nnambi Nantuluntulu and Eve yielded to temptation through the question of food and it was that that caused death to come into the world" (n.d.: 9).

For some Baganda, these parallels proved that the story of Kintu contained divine revelation and that the Baganda possessed a genuine knowledge of God before the advent of the missionaries. One writer in *Munno* asserted that "our religion [*dini*; that is, Christianity] did not teach us something new [about God] but reminded us of something we already knew" (1916: 177). Thus the new, foreign teachings about God were identified as something old and intrinsically Ganda. Another writer commented on a tradition that told about Kintu's killing a legendary figure named Bbemba the Snake, who was the ruler of the country:

> They said that in the past the Kabaka of this country was a snake who was called Bbemba, and Kintu got rid of him. Now these things are made known to us that Kintu came with religion [*dini*] and got rid of Satan who was the snake. . . . God [Katonda] has shown it to us. (*Munno* 1912: 50)

Thus interpreted as veiled revelations from God, the stories about Kintu became a means of explicitly assimilating Christian ideas, at least on the part of some literate Baganda.

For both Catholic and Protestant converts, the figure of Ggulu became identical with that of the biblical God, who the missionaries and the Ganda alike called Katonda, or Creator. According to the Protestant clergyman Bartolomayo Zimbe, "the meaning of the name Kintu is from the expression *Kintu kya Mukama*, that is, 'the thing of the Lord,' which means *Muntu wa Katonda*, 'man of God'" (1939: 6). By equating Ggulu with God, the Baganda could not only interpret the Kintu story in light of Genesis, but also adapt it more closely to the Genesis account in order to imbue the story with Christian meanings.

James Miti was one of the first to retell the Kintu story in this way. In his version, Ggulu is replaced by Katonda, and Walumbe is no longer portrayed as the brother of Nnambi but as an independent "enemy" of man, analogous to Satan. Miti's account focuses on Nnambi's act of disobedience in returning for the millet, and on Katonda's curse that expels Nnambi and Kintu from the sky. "Go away from my sight, you rebels who rebelled against my orders," says Katonda, "and now you are taking with you your enemy [Death], he is sure to go on killing you." In this version, mortality is inflicted on Kintu and Nnambi by a righteous God as the punishment for disobedience, whereas in the traditional account death is seen as an inevitable, although accidental, consequence. Thus, Miti concludes, it was "through [the] disobedience of Muntu Benne [Kintu] and Namuntu Banddi [Nnambi] to the voice of the Lord God that we are subjected to death" (n.d.: 3–11).

A similar version appears in Ernest Kalibala's doctoral dissertation, written in 1946. According to Kalibala, Kintu accused Nnambi of disobeying both him and God, and he asked God to punish her. God responded by expelling Kintu, Nnambi, and Walumbe from heaven. "All of you have disobeyed me," God said. "You shall go to earth and toil." On their journey, each person blamed the others. "Kintu blamed his wife for her disobedience; [Nnambi] Nantululu blamed the chicken because she could not let it die; Mr. Walumbe blamed them all for plotting to leave him all alone in Heaven" (1946: 9–14). Because of constant quarrels, Kintu asked Walumbe to leave, whereupon Walumbe, after threatening to harm Kintu and his children, left heaven to become lord of the underworld, or hell. In this version, human life on earth is regarded as a punishment from God, while death is seen as the result of Walumbe's quarrels with Kintu.

Mulira's schoolbook version introduced into the story the Christian idea of salvation. An illustration in the second edition (1955 II) depicts Ggulu as an enthroned father-god surrounded by rays of light and by winged angels. Kintu and Nnambi appear as diminutive figures kneeling at Ggulu's feet, their hands raised in supplication. Toward the end of the story, Nnambi and Kintu confess that they have "sinned" (*kwonoona*) before Ggulu and that their sins have driven them from him. The Christian promise of salvation is prefigured in the image of Kayiikuuzi, who is referred to as the "Savior" (*Mulokozi*), the same term by which the Luganda Bible refers to Christ. When Kayiikuuzi arrives, he informs Walumbe that he has been sent "in the place of the Father," and he pursues Walumbe into the underworld (*Magombe*), as Christ pursued Satan into hell. After Kayiikuuzi fails to catch Walumbe because of the "sins" of Nnambi, Kintu, and their children, Ggulu declares that both Good and Evil will reign over the earth and that people will have to choose between them. The story also draws a prophetic contrast between "the first Nnambi who brought Walumbe" and "another Nnambi who will bring the Savior [*Mulokozi*]." The story ends with Ggulu's promise that "the Word [*Kigambo*] will be born in Buganda, and it will kill Death. It will save the Baganda. The Word will build my house on a firm rock against which Hell [*Magombe*] will have no power" (Mulira 1955 II: 34).

Although I have never asked Baganda whether the story expresses something like the Christian ideas of original sin or the fall of mankind, the myth is clearly open to this kind of interpretation, as the versions of Miti, Kalibala, and Mulira demonstrate. However, these interpretations do not appear to be consistent with the precolonial form of the story. The story, as Kaggwa tells it, did not imply that Kintu and Nnambi lived in an original state of moral perfection and only later fell into a state of moral decay. Rather, it showed human nature as it is: flawed from the beginning. But in the hands of educated Christians, the story of Kintu became a powerful vehicle for Christian teachings about obedience to God, the fall, damnation, and salvation. According to Mulira, "Nnambi had the freedom [*eddembe*] of a woman [to return for millet, despite her father's warning] and Kintu had the humaneness [*obuntubulamu*] of a man [in permitting his wife to return]" (1965 II: 6), suggesting that the story expresses essentially Christian values.[2] It would appear that the adaptability of cosmogonic myths to new systems of ideas is a subject that historians of religions might well explore further.

The Theme of Obedience

While Christian interpretations are still accepted today, Baganda also recognize the traditional meaning of the story of Kintu. Baganda have emphasized to me that when the story is seen in its Ganda social context, the theme of disobedience clearly extends beyond Nnambi's initial act and includes the acts of Kintu and his children. Thus Baganda say that Kintu could be considered responsible for Nnambi's act of disobedience. According to Ganda marital ethics, it was the husband's duty to make his wife act obediently. Indeed, Ggulu's words of admonishment to Kintu — "If your wife had not returned, your children would not have died" — can be interpreted as a reproach directed at Kintu.

A shorter version of the story published by Kaggwa also emphasizes Kintu's culpability. Here, Katonda rebukes Kintu and dismisses his complaint against Walumbe, saying: "Did I not tell you to depart early in the morning? Be gone! Do not ask me anything. Go away!" (Kaggwa [1901] 1971: 1). As the story also points out, Kintu's children "did very wrong" in disobeying their father and thus spoiling Kayiikuuzi's plan.[3] In Kaggwa's full-length version, Kintu explicitly assumes responsibility for his children's behavior and admits that he "made a mistake." In the text collected by the White Fathers, the matter is put more strongly. Kayiikuuzi accuses Kintu of permitting his children to disobey, and he asks rhetorically, "Is Kintu mad?" Mulira's version attempts to distribute the blame more equally and has Kintu confess: "I did wrong, and all my people did wrong before Ggulu."

It is not surprising that the theme of disobedience involves each member of the primal family. For, among other things, the story tells about the origins of the fundamental marital, affinal, and parental relationships that define the traditional Ganda family. Each of these relationships was conceived in an authoritarian way and required the "inferior" party to demonstrate acts of obedience and respect toward the "superior" party: wives toward husbands, husbands toward brothers-in-law and fathers-in-law, and children toward fathers. So fundamental were these norms that failure to abide by them was not just a case of disobedience but ultimately of rebellion (*obujeemu*), for it implied the refusal to recognize authority and hence was a subversion of the social order.

As the story of Kintu shows, the most important norms of obedience and respect are those that govern the family. In the past, a wife was expected to be submissive and obedient to her husband, or she was beaten. When a woman married, she left home and pledged herself to a new master. Children, too, had to obey and respect their parents, especially their father, and they were physically punished if they did not. Children knelt on the ground when speaking and acted instantly when told to do something. One child wrote in answer to a questionnaire (in the 1950s) that "to disobey a father is the worst crime a child can commit" (Richards 1964: 249). In the same survey, children also reported that disobedience and failure to show respect were the two acts for which they were punished most frequently. Children were often given small tasks and sent on minor errands as a means of obedience training. For boys, who were frequently sent away from home at a young age to live with their father's relatives, this training was a key to success in the wider world. In Buganda's traditionally competitive society, dutiful and respectful behavior could lead to one of the many clan offices and to one of the coveted royal appointments. As Audrey Richards has noted, the attitude of child to father was characteristic of all subordinate relationships in Buganda, of peasant to lord and of subject to king. For this reason, perhaps, filial relationships assume central importance in the Kintu story, which begins and ends with acts of filial disobedience.

It might therefore be said that the story of Kintu served as a powerful charter in Malinowski's sense of upholding the patriarchal norms of the family. By "mythical charter" Malinowski meant the way in which myths legitimate social institutions and practices by reference to ancient precedent ([1925] 1954: 107ff). Thus the story of Kintu might be thought to legitimate the norms of family authority by showing the disaster that occurred when these norms were transgressed.

It is doubtful that the story was told for the purpose of legitimating filial norms, but even if it were, Malinowski is wrong in asserting that "what really matters about such a story is its social function" ([1925] 1954: 116). The point is that although the story may have validated important social norms, it can have been only one of several means of doing so. Corporeal punishment, as noted above, was undoubtedly a more efficient and effective method of upholding the norm of filial obedience. Moreover, as recent critics of Malinowski's functionalist theory of myth have shown, to say that a myth performs a social function in any meaningful way requires us to hold that the society in question can function well *only* if the myth is present (Penner 1971; Oden 1979). Otherwise, all that is being said is that the myth's existence in a society is evidence of its social function, which either is a vacuous claim or begs the question. Since no one would seriously endorse the claim that a particular society functions well only if a certain myth is present, Malinowski's theory fails because it naively assumes too much.

The Ritual Dimension

Although Baganda usually discuss the significance of the Kintu story in terms of its domestic and social context, its meanings extend beyond that setting. According to Kaggwa, a symbolic act performed during Ganda funeral rites suggests that not Nnambi but her chickens were the ultimate cause of death. After the burial of the corpse, the period of mourning or "death" (*olumbe*) was ended by a ceremony called "destroying death" (*okwaabya olumbe*). This ceremony, Kaggwa points out, involved the eating of a chicken by the male relatives who gathered in the house of the deceased. In this house, whose temporary "owner" was Walumbe, or Death, the men killed and ate a chicken that they had roasted over a fire made from the center post of the house. Hence, in Kaggwa's view, the chicken was regarded as "the sorcerer who brought [or caused] death" ([1907] 1934: 202; cf. Roscoe 1911: 121). It was for the sake of her chickens that Nnambi returned and fetched the millet that brought death. By killing and eating a chicken while celebrating the "killing of death" (*okutta olumbe*), Kaggwa suggests, the male relatives thereby killed and disposed of the ultimate agent of death. After the ceremony, the heir to the deceased's household was installed, and the normal processes of life

were restored. From Kaggwa's point of view, the story of Kintu character-
izes the funerary fowl as a kind of scapegoat of death. In this context, the
moral significance of the myth is superseded by a ritual interpretation
that shows the funerary fowl/scapegoat to be the ultimate culprit.

Indeed, from the myth-ritual point of view, it might be argued that the
myth developed as an explanation of the ritual of the funerary fowl. But
the myth includes many features other than that of the funerary-fowl rite.
For instance, Mulira has suggested that the myth explains the origins of
the traditional marital procedures. His second school edition, as noted
above, concludes with a speech by Kintu and alludes to the Christian
promise of salvation. In a later version, Kintu declares that henceforth
men shall give cows as a marriage dowry, as Kintu himself did; women
shall no longer eat chicken, as a sign of Nnambi's fateful indiscretion;
husbands must always respect their brothers-in-law by giving them a
cock, thus avoiding Kintu's fatal mistake of insulting Walumbe; and
women must always carry chickens on top of their heads to their husband's house during the final wedding ceremony in remembrance of
Nnambi's forgetfulness ([1951] 1970 II: 29–30).

Mulira does not explain why he changed his mind and abandoned the
Christian conclusion of his first two editions, but he clearly intends the
reader of the later version to understand the story as a kind of ritual
paradigm for the traditional Ganda marriage. According to Mulira, all
men and women enter into marriage in the way that Kintu and Nnambi
did, and the basic Ganda marital procedures derive from their example.

There are further correspondences between the myth and traditional
Ganda marriage practices. In the past, a young man not only had to give
cattle to his prospective father-in-law, as Kintu did, but also had to visit
his home and serve him for a time doing domestic chores, such as brewing
beer and cutting firewood, to show that he would make a dutiful son-in-
law (Kalibala 1946; 243ff; Kakooza 1967: 119). In the myth, Kintu is
made to perform similar, although more difficult, domestic tasks to show
that he really is the fabulous Kintu, and thus to prove his worthiness to
his prospective father-in-law, Ggulu. Traditionally, it was the bride's
brother who helped to arrange his sister's marriage, as Nnambi's brothers
did, and one of them performed the role of presenting the suitor to the
father-in-law. In the 1930s, Lucy Mair recorded a betrothal ceremony in
which the brother jokingly voiced the same complaint against his sister's
suitor that Walumbe spoke against Kintu: "The brother presented the
suitor with jesting statements that he was trying to steal the girl and that
his sister was rebelling against him and no longer wanted to cook for

him." Speaking on behalf of the bride, the girl's paternal aunt said: "I am grown up, my time has come to marry, I have found my master" (1934: 80). Whereupon the father spoke to his wife and said: "This child has rebelled against us [*atujeemyeko*]; she has found her master." As this dialogue implies, every marriage required the bride to cease serving her brothers and to leave the household authority of her father for a new master. When the bride departed from her father's home for the last time, her father provided her with provisions for the wedding feast — livestock (including a cow, goats, and sheep, if her father was a chief), plantains, and chickens — as Nnambi's father did. So, too, the bride's brother visited his sister's home soon after marriage to establish affinal ties, and later asked the husband for one of his children as his "share" (*ndobolo*), as Walumbe did.

From a Ganda point of view, Mulira's interpretation of the Kintu story as a marriage charter or symbolic archetype is entirely appropriate. Although Ganda marriage rites contain no reference to Kintu or Nnambi, Mulira's interpretation is consistent with the Ganda tendency to justify institutional procedures by references to historical and legendary precedent, especially the founding deeds of Kintu.

Mulira's exegesis also suggests that the Baganda may in fact see themselves to be repeating in marriage the primordial, archetypal acts of Kintu and Nnambi. But to interpret the story in this fashion, as the theories of Mircea Eliade might lead us to do (1963), would be going somewhat beyond the evidence. Ritual repetitions do in fact occur in Buganda — for example, in some of the royal installation ceremonies (Chapter 3). But in such instances, the repetition is made explicit in the rites themselves, whereas no mention of Kintu and Nnambi is made in the marriage ceremonies. Although the story incorporates elements of the Ganda marriage practice, it does not appear to have served as a sacred model or paradigm that was explicitly repeated in ritual.

Eliade's mythical archetypes, however, are not always to be repeated in ritual but may be existentially repeated in the human condition itself. Or, like Victor Turner's "root paradigms," such mythic themes may exist as cultural models that are not explicitly recognized until they become deliberately actuated on the stage of events (1974: 64). Mulira's suggestion that traditional marriage practices were rooted in the story of Kintu was written during the turbulent period after Uganda gained its independence from Great Britain. This was a time of cultural crisis and renewal when many African writers encouraged their countrymen to reject Western values and return to their own heritage for principles of meaning and value. In Buganda, Kintu was, and still is, such a principle, a mythical archetype or root paradigm of "Ganda-ness" valid for all his "descendants."

It also seems evident that parts of the myth itself derive from the conventional marriage procedures. Ganda folktales (*ngero*) typically draw on well-known aspects of Ganda life and incorporate them in story form. This brings to mind Lévi-Strauss's *bricoleur*, who fashions myths from cultural materials that are already at hand (1966: 16ff). Although this view cannot be generalized to endorse the theory that myth always derives from ritual, it does pose an important question about the possible ritual sources of myths in specific cases. If a myth is framed in terms of elements drawn from local ritual and social structure, as most African myths are, then it is necessary to investigate these elements thoroughly in order to comprehend the myth. The question is not a chronological one: Which came first, the myth or the ritual? It is a hermeneutical one: How do a society's rituals illuminate its myths (and vice versa)? To answer this question, we must shift from a ritualist to a semiotic perspective.

Immortality, Mortality, and the Mother's Brother

Although the story of Kintu implicitly refers to certain features of the marriage process, its basic purpose is to explain the origins of death and ultimately to suggest a way of understanding the place of death in the Ganda scheme of things. The story does this by utilizing certain social and ritual elements associated with marriage. A central element is the figure of the mother's brother (*kojja*), who is made to represent death, and the story concludes with Kintu's declaration that death will not destroy Ganda society.

If we look at the story in this way, we can see that it attempts to explain the origins of death in terms of a series of oppositional relationships that are finally resolved. To look at it this way is of course to suggest the appropriateness of a structuralist interpretation, in this case one that is closely fitted to the story's narrative plot. As already noted, the story's narrative or diachronic sequence follows the form: marriage→death→ life. More specifically, the story moves from a condition of human immortality, to a condition of threatened extinction, to a final condition of normal human mortality — and it does so in terms of several oppositional relationships.

The first opposition appears in the unconventional behavior of Nnambi's father, Ggulu. Here it seems appropriate to assume that the myth reflects conventional Ganda marriage practices. Although such practices did not exist within the primordial time frame of the myth, the myth is obviously told against the background of these practices. Given the important role of brothers in arranging their sisters' marriages and in serving as their legal guardians, it is surprising that Ggulu should have deliberately given Nnambi in marriage to Kintu without her brother Walumbe's knowledge and tried to prevent Walumbe from joining his sister on earth. In doing so, Ggulu was implicitly avoiding one of the fundamental requirements of marriage — the establishment of affinal relations. If, however, Ggulu already knew that Walumbe would kill Kintu's children, as some versions of the story suggest, then his actions are understandable. Ggulu was attempting to save Kintu's children from the threat of mortality represented by Walumbe. In effect, Ggulu avoided acting according to standard Ganda marital practice in order to keep Kintu's children, the Baganda, immortal. Ggulu's action thus expresses an implicit opposition between immortality and marriage as the Baganda know it — including the bearing of children, which is the mark of the human condition.

The same conflict is apparent in the episode of Nnambi's return for the millet. Although millet appears to be an insignificant item, in one version of the story Kintu points out that without the millet the chickens will die. This is in fact implicitly assumed in all the versions, even though millet is not generally used to feed chickens in Buganda. While Nnambi's return for the millet to keep the chickens alive would seem to incur the disproportionate loss of human immortality, the loss of chickens would be disastrous for the conventional Ganda marriage. It would deprive Kintu and Nnambi of the chief symbols of paternal authority and affinal relations, without which the traditional Ganda marriage cannot exist. In the past, when a bride departed from her father's home for the last time, she took with her the provisions for the marriage feast, including a cock that was tied to a ring she wore on the top of her head. Upon arriving at her new home, the bride knelt on the ground in recognition of her husband's authority as the head of the household. The husband lifted off the cock, which the wife then killed, cooked, and served to her new mate. The gift of the cock meant that the woman was truly married (Roscoe 1911: 91; Kaggwa [1907] 1934: 175; Haydon 1960: chap. 6). (Women also gave a cock to their husbands as a sign of reconciliation after a quarrel.) The day after the marriage feast, the new husband was required to visit his brother-in-law and give him a cock in recognition of their new affinal relationship. He had to place the bird alive in his hands, and the brother-in-law returned it saying: "Go and kill it." Henceforth, whenever a male in-law came to visit, the husband provided him with a cock to eat.

Roscoe lists other occasions when fowls were needed:

> When a husband returned from war, his wife cooked a fowl for him. Every time that any of the husband's male relatives visited him, his wife cooked a fowl for them. When a woman's son returned from his first war, she cooked a fowl for him. When twins were born, a fowl was killed and eaten, to celebrate the event. When mourning was ended, a fowl was killed and eaten by male relatives. When a chief returned from war, his retainers paid him congratulatory visits and presented him with a goat and a fowl. When blood-brotherhood was made, a fowl was killed and eaten at the sacred meal which followed the ceremony. When clans which had been enemies were reconciled to each other, a fowl was eaten at the sacred meal held to ratify the event. When a son-in-law accidentally touched his mother-in-law, he gave her a present of a fowl. (1911: 424)

As the traditional signs and symbols of the marital state and of affinal relations, chickens were an essential possession for the married couple, and still are in Buganda.[4] If Nnambi had not returned for the millet, the death of her chickens would have deprived her of these essential domestic symbols. Nnambi's return for the millet thus poses again the opposition between immortality and conventional Ganda marriage. By returning for the millet, Nnambi secured the necessary symbols for her marriage, but did so at the risk of her children's immortality.

In contrast to the figure of Ggulu, who stands for the celestial principles of immortality and divinity, Walumbe represents the earthly principles of marriage and affinity that belong to the human situation. As we have seen, Walumbe's insistence on accompanying Nnambi to her new home is entirely justified by Ganda marital procedures. Indeed, a brother must pay a visit to his sister's home soon after her marriage in order to establish the affinal relationship. In tacit recognition of Walumbe's rights in this matter, Ggulu readily granted Walumbe's request and allowed him to accompany Nnambi, even though he seems to have known that the consequences would be fatal. As the bride's brother (*kojja*), whom Martin Southwold has appropriately defined as an "affine-parent" of his sister's children, Walumbe represents the institution of marriage and the affinal interests of the wife's clan (1973). Thus Walumbe's actions show that marriage, bearing children, and death go together in defining the human condition.

As for Kintu, his refusal to grant Walumbe's request for a child was, in effect, a refusal to recognize what came to be the traditional right of the mother's brother to the temporary possession of one (or more) of his sister's children. Such a child was called *ndobolo*, or "share," and represented the mother's clan's token share in her children.[5] After the birth of the third child, the kojja (specifically, the brother who had arranged the marriage) had the right to ask the husband for one of his sister's children to serve in his household. After a few years, the father could redeem this child by paying a token fee of two goats, and the child was returned to his father's home (Le Veux 1917: 546; Roscoe 1921: 165; Mair 1934: 61–63; Haydon 1960: 122). Kintu's refusal to recognize Walumbe's claim was thus an implicit avoidance of affinal relationships. Kintu rejected Walumbe's request by saying that he had already promised a "share" of his children to his father-in-law, Ggulu, and could not spare any for Walumbe. In saying this, Kintu was partly right, for his children could live at the house of his wife's parents as well as at his brother-in-law's. But Kintu was also partly wrong in light of Ganda practice; indeed, he was caught in a dilemma. By promising his children to Ggulu without Walumbe's consent, he was implicitly denying the rights of the kojja. In this respect, Kintu, like Ggulu (to whom he wished to give his children), aligned himself with the interests of immortality and patriarchy as opposed (initially, at any rate) to the affinal conventions of marriage.

Yet it was Kintu who finally resolved the "problem" of the myth and became the hero of the story. Although he was unable to prevent Walumbe from causing individual deaths, he promised that the people as a whole would survive. Instead of individual immortality, Kintu promised collective perpetuity: "If Walumbe wants to kill my children, let him. But he will not be able to finish all of them because I, Kintu, will always continue to beget more." Hence the proverb "The descendants of Kintu will never be finished."

At the sociological level, the story of Kintu may be seen as an exegesis of this well-known proverb. In Mulira's second school edition, the proverb is uttered defiantly by Kintu at the end of the story. The phrase "the descendants of Kintu" (*abazzukulu ba Kintu*) was, and still is, used by the Baganda as an expression of national pride. Traditionally, it meant that the Baganda were the members of a powerful kingdom founded by Kintu, which made them superior to their neighbors, and it implied that the Baganda were the bearers of a special inheritance associated with Kintu's name. The story shows this inheritance to be a vital, sociobiological one: the survival of the people despite the ravages of death. Kintu's promise was a "redemptive" prophecy, a promise of collective immortality. Kintu therefore stands as the source of Ganda vitality and existence through time.

The meaning of Kintu's prophetic declaration lies in the central metaphor of the myth, the portrayal of death as the mother's brother. As the mother's brother, Walumbe represents the interests of the wife's clan in the marital situation, while Kintu represents the interests of the husband's clan and of patrilineality. According to the rules of marriage and descent, members of patrilineal clans must give away their daughters in marriage to men of other patrilineal clans, and they must give up their claims to their daughters' children, reserving the right to retain only a temporary share, or "tax" (*ndobolo*). In return, the clans gain new members through the marriage of their sons and thus perpetuate themselves. As the symbol of the patrilineal-clan principle, Kintu ensures that the Baganda, as a society of exogamous patrilineal clans, will always gain new members. Thus the Baganda will collectively survive despite the fact of death, which will always claim a "share" of the living clan members. In this sense, the story of Kintu reflects the collective social life of the Baganda. Women marry men from other clans, who keep their children in order to perpetuate themselves; their clan brothers take back only a token share of the children as symbolic compensation. Within this circuit of exchange of women and children, originally portrayed in the Kintu myth, lies the collective life of the people and their guarantee of survival.

This interpretation of the myth turns on the central metaphor of death being "like" the mother's brother: Life is to Death as Children are to the Mother's Brother. It should be clear that these metaphorical relationships are explicit in the myth and have not been teased out of the narrative, as in so many structuralist analyses. The myth states as explicitly as possible, while still remaining a myth, that as the mother's brother takes only a token share of the father's children, so death (*olumbe*/Walumbe) will take only a small share of Kintu's living children—the Baganda. The hero of the myth and guarantor of its outcome is Kintu, who, as the principle of patrilineal-clan procreation, ensures that all the clans will gain children and thus that life will continue. The underlying hero of the myth is, of course, the exogamous patrilineal-clan principle itself, which Kintu represents. Without it, the clans would not gain children and therefore would become extinct.

The myth, then, presents a cognitive solution to a fundamental human question: survival in the face of death. The myth tells how the Baganda understand the advent of death and how they, as a society organized in terms of patrilineal clans, will always overcome its constant threat, thanks to the promise of Kintu.

Cosmology and Ontology

Another important feature of the story of Kintu is its cosmogonic dimension. The story explains why the Baganda live in a universe consisting of three realms: sky, earth, and underworld. Each of these realms signifies a different mode of being. As the realm of divinity, the sky (*ggulu*) is known as *olubaale*, or "abode of the gods." The earth (*ensi*) is the realm in which the Baganda live, and it is synonymous with "land" and "country." It is the realm of the "descendants of Kintu," who dwell in the kingdom that Kintu founded. The underworld (*magombe*) is the realm of the dead, whose spirits (*mizimu*; singular, *muzimu*) present themselves to Walumbe before returning to earth, where they hover around their graves. As the Kintu myth explains, these three realms are interrelated. The sky is the domain of Ggulu, the father god, and it was the original domain of Nnambi, the primordial mother; the earth is the realm of Kintu, the primordial father; and the underworld is the domain of Walumbe, the primordial mother's brother. The structure of the cosmos thus expresses the origin and destiny of the Baganda in this world. Through Nnambi, the Baganda are descended from the immortal realm of the sky; through Kintu, the Baganda came to live on earth and to seek their destiny; though Walumbe, the Baganda became mortal beings.

Sky	Immortality	Ggulu	Father God
Earth	Human Life	Kintu and Nnambi	Father and Mother
Underworld	Death	Walumbe	Mother's Brother

The myth also links the origin and structure of the universe to the human life cycle. All children are born of women, who live out their lives on earth as members of their fathers' clans. They take marriage partners from other clans and give birth to children who will succeed them. Eventually, they join their ancestors in the world below. Thus the story of Kintu is the story of the origins and destiny of every person. It enables the Baganda to see themselves collectively as the sons and daughters of Kintu and hence to affirm with Kintu the triumph of life over death in the proverb "The descendants of Kintu will never be finished."

In this respect, the myth has an archetypal dimension similar to that which Eliade ascribes to all cosmogonic myths (1959). Myth exemplifies a reality that is existentially repeated in the human condition. In this case, the myth exemplifies the patrilineal-clan principle that transcends time and lies at the core of Ganda social life. This principle is not, however, a sacred reality. That is, it is not extraordinary, supernatural, or hidden from the profane. Rather, it is the ultimate principle of everyday social existence. To the extent that anyone (male or female) is governed by the patrilineal-clan principle, he or she transcends time and participates in the ground of being, which in the myth is part of the very structure of the cosmos.

3

Myth, Ritual, and History: The Origins of the Kingship

In this chapter, I shift my attention from Kintu-the-patriarch to Kintu-the-royal-founder, and so from story or myth (*lugero*) to history (*byafaayo*). Here my concern is with the traditions about the founding of the kingship, which occurred in the late thirteenth century.[1] As in Chapter 2, both ritual symbolism and historical context will be considered.

The ritual repetition of founding deeds, which took place in the royal installation ceremonies, is a familiar phenomenon to historians of religions. In Buganda, these rituals not only installed the king, but also "reproduced" the kingship; that is, they reestablished it according to the deeds of its ancient founders. When the king died, the kingship temporarily ceased to exist, and it had to be reinstituted through a series of rites in which the new king and his chiefs enacted the founding deeds of the early kings. As we shall see, Ganda accounts of the founding of the kingship are based almost entirely on the installation rites. It is also evident that the installation scenario changed through time and that each ritual phase is embedded in its own historical context and contains important historical features. The question is whether one can extract any history from origin traditions that are fundamentally rooted in ritual symbolism. The answer appears to be a qualified "yes." We are limited by the few historical clues that are given within the installation rites, but these appear to be highly suggestive.

At first, scholars were disposed to treat the origin traditions as basically historical accounts. Apart from a few readily identifiable "mythical" aspects, judged to be dispensable, historians and anthropologists thought they were dealing with historical traditions featuring human actors in a realistic geographical and chronological framework. The story of Kintu's founding of the kingdom by conquest was also consistent with the long-held but now abandoned theory that the kingdoms of East Africa were established by culturally superior "conquering Hamites."[2] Beginning with Roscoe, historians who wrote about the origins of Buganda and the other kingdoms of East Africa drew on these accounts (Gray 1935; Oliver 1955).

The culmination of the historical approach was reached in the work of the British-trained historian Semakula Kiwanuka. According to Kiwanuka, "[W]hen dealing with traditional history, one must determine where mythology ends and where history begins. In the case of Buganda, history begins with the second version of the story of Kintu [his founding of the kingdom]" (Kaggwa [1901] 1971: 2). Nevertheless, in dealing with the various accounts about Kintu and the early history of Buganda, Kiwanuka admits that these narratives contain much that is "myth and legend" (1971a: 95). Obviously, if myth is somehow mixed in with history, some attention must be given to it and to how it relates to what actually happened.

Two scholars have rejected the historical approach to Buganda's origin traditions: Christopher Wrigley has proposed that these traditions are essentially folkloristic tales and fertility myths (1958, 1959), while Ronald R. Atkinson has argued that they consist of mythic statements about structural themes in the Ganda theory of kingship (1975). On entirely different grounds, Michael Twaddle has proposed that the story of Kintu's conquest was a fraudulent account perpetrated by Apolo Kaggwa for political reasons (1974). While each of these views contains important insights, none examines the imprint of ritual on the origin traditions and none recognizes the significant historical clues that lie within the installation rites themselves. The importance of the rites for historical analysis has clearly been overlooked.

The Ritual Paradigm

I will begin by describing the clan-based ritual succession pattern that was universal in Buganda, for this was the paradigm on which the royal rites were based.[3] Every adult who died was succeeded by an heir who took over the social role or clan office of the deceased. Succession was therefore linked to the funerary ritual, and it was both hereditary and elective. If the deceased were male, the successor had to be a son, nephew, brother, or grandson, and he was either designated by the incumbent in advance or chosen by the clan authorities at the time of the funeral. In either case, the ratification of the successor as the official heir (*musika*) took place at the incumbent's home immediately following his death. An important clan office, such as a clan or lineage chiefship, was always attached to a piece of land known as the *butaka*, or "estate of the office." This is where the incumbent lived and where the funerary and succession rites took place. Before the deceased was buried, the heir went to this estate to be confirmed. Then he and the other relatives entered into a period of mourning, during which their food, clothing, and cultivation were restricted for up to six months, depending on the social importance of the deceased. Afterward, the heir went again to the estate of the chiefship to attend the burial of the deceased and to take part in the end-of-mourning rites, which formally installed him in office.

A male was installed together with a woman of the clan called the clan sister (*lubuga*). Both the heir and the lubuga stood on a barkcloth mat in front of the house of the deceased. The clan representative robed the heir with barkcloth and presented him with the spears and shield of his office and gave the lubaga a knife and a basket in recognition of her role as the food provider and housekeeper of the estate. The clan representative also administered an oath of office to the successor, telling him to perform properly the duties of the office. If the office were that of a clan or lineage headship, the successor took the name of the founder of the clan or lineage, for that name was the title of the office.

The new officeholder and the lubaga received gifts from members of the clan in acknowledgment of their succession. In the evening, the new chief and the lubaga went into the inner room of the house and performed the *kukuza* rite, in which the chief stepped over the legs of the lubuga, signifying sexual intercourse. The lubuga also lived in the house for a period of time. According to Nsimbi, "The idea of the *lubuga* is to show people that the heir will welcome people to his house since he has a wife that will never leave him (the *lubuga* being of the same clan as the heir)" (1956a: 33). The new chief then toured his estate, and everyone paid their respects by offering gifts to him.

The succession process may therefore be divided into three phases: (1) death of the incumbent, formal ratification of the heir, burial of the deceased; (2) mourning (liminal) period; and (3) installation of the successor and the lubuga at the estate of the chiefship. The last rite contains important historical implications because the title of the office and the butaka on which it was conferred belonged to the clan and derived from the clan ancestor. By performing the succession rites on the clan estate, the territorial, social, and historical foundations of the office were clearly expressed and perpetuated through time. In the case of the royal installation ceremonies, the several clan estates on which the Kabakaship was conferred, the clan heads who conferred it, and the investiture symbolism involved present important clues to the possible origins of the office.

In the late nineteenth century, the royal installation ceremonies followed a three-part sequence.[4]

1. When the king died, the royal fire was extinguished as a sign of his death, and the prime minister (*Katikkiro*) and other senior chiefs formally chose the successor in front of the palace. Afterward, the king-elect went to Buddo Hill, the estate (*butaka*) of the Kabakaship, where he reenacted Kintu's conquest and was installed as the Kabaka together with his Lubaga (Queen Sister), a half-sister, by the officials at Buddo. These rites are said to have been instituted by Kabaka Namugala in the mid-eighteenth century.

2. The Kabaka-elect went into mourning and lived in seclusion for a five-month period until the body of the deceased king was embalmed and entombed.

3. The king-elect ended mourning by engaging in a ritual hunt that reenacted Kimera's return to Buganda, and he was invested with Kimera's regalia as Ssaabataka, or Head of the Clan Heads. These rites are said to have originated with Kimera (the third Kabaka) in approximately the fourteenth century, and they marked the end of the installation ceremonies.

Afterward, the Kabaka received gifts and wives from representatives of the clans, sent gifts to the major gods and rebuilt their temples, entered his new palace, built his new capital, and took leave of his mother, the Nnamasole (Queen Mother). Five months later, the chiefs presented the Kabaka with the skull of his predecessor so that the jawbone could be removed and installed in a shrine.

For our purposes, it will also be important to consider a fourth and final set of ceremonies that was discontinued by Ssuuna II at the time of his accession in approximately 1826. It consisted of a set of rituals called *kukula kwa Kabaka*, the "confirmation (or maturation) of the Kabaka." They took place after the three phases described above and were held at the estates of the four most important indigenous clan heads (*Bataka*). The first of these ceremonies is said to have been established by Kabaka Ttembo, the successor to Kimera, who was Kintu's great-grandson; the second is associated with Chwa Nabakka I, Kintu's son and successor; and the third is associated with Kimera and Kintu. The last two rites, associated with Kintu and Chwa, the first two kings, were therefore the oldest according to the dynastic chronology. Although they were terminated in the early nineteenth century, Kaggwa and others provide detailed descriptions of them, and they contain significant implications for the origins of the Kabakaship.

Kintu's Conquest at Buddo

It is appropriate to begin investigating the story of the origins of the kingship by examining the installation ceremonies at Buddo Hill, which are said to commemorate Kintu's founding of the kingship. Roscoe's and Kaggwa's informants provided an important historical clue when they indicated that these rites were instituted by Kabaka Namugala in the mid-eighteenth century. Prior to this time, Kaggwa explains, "the first Kaba-kas of Buganda, from Kimera to Namugala, did not go to Buddo; they went to Nankere's [estate] to be confirmed (*kula*). And the Kabaka was not called 'Kabaka' until he went to Nankere's" ([1907] 1934: 7; cf. Nsimbi 1956b: 259). After Namugala established the rites at Buddo Hill, they took precedence over the "confirmation" rites at Nankere's and the other clan estates, and the Buddo rites were performed first (Roscoe 1911: 191–92; Kaggwa [1907] 1934: 7–8; Kakoma, Ntate, and Serukaga 1959: 15).

The question therefore arises whether the story of Kintu's conquest at Buddo Hill originated in Namugala's reign as a justification for the new ceremonies that he established there. Kaggwa's account strongly suggests that this was the case. According to Kaggwa (and Roscoe), Buddo Hill was chosen as the new ritual center of the kingship because it was the place where a new charm (*jjembe*) was put in the ground for the protection of the king. During the reign of Kabaka Mawanda in the early eighteenth century, the king's four nephews banded together to overthrow him. Before they acted, a diviner named Buddo, who came from the Ssese Islands in Lake Victoria, made a jjembe and told the brothers that if "any of you becomes king and steps on the jjembe, he will never be overthrown. But whoever fails to step on it will never become Kabaka of Buganda" (Kaggwa [1901] 1971: 75). He also told them that "after you have defeated Mawanda, the successor must choose some people to take care of it [the jjembe]" ([1901] 1971: 75). The brothers buried the jjembe in a mound on Naggalabi Hill, later named Buddo Hill after the diviner who made the charm. Then the brothers killed Mawanda, and one of them, named Mwanga, acceded to the throne.

The chronicles do not say whether Mwanga, who was killed soon after his accession by his maternal uncle, went to Buddo Hill and stepped on the charm, but they do say that his brother Namugala did. Namugala also appointed Semanobe of the Lungfish clan to guard the hill together with Makamba and Nalungu of the Pangolin clan. Henceforth, these officials were in charge of the installation ceremonies at Buddo. Then, according to Kaggwa's account, "Buddo explained to Namugala that 'It was on this very hill, called Naggalabi, that your ancestor Kintu conquered Bbemba the Snake [Bbemba Musota] who was Kabaka of Buganda, and after Kintu killed him, he became Kabaka of Buganda'" ([1907] 1934: 8).

The priest named Buddo may therefore have been the first to attribute the origins of the kingship to an act of conquest by Kintu at Buddo (Naggalabi) Hill. It is possible that the priest drew on a story about Kintu's defeat of a local chief named Bbemba. But it seems unlikely that such a story originally functioned as an account of the origins of the kingship; otherwise, the installation ceremonies would certainly have been held at Buddo Hill, the butaka of the Kabakaship (as Buddo was later called), not at the estates of the indigenous clan heads, which were not royal lands. Significantly, the traditions say that Kimera, Kintu's alleged great-grandson, who is said to have returned to Buganda and restored the Kabakaship, did not go to Buddo Hill to be installed but went instead to an estate of a woman called Nakku, who belonged to the indigenous Civet Cat clan.

Analysis of the Kintu conquest story shows that it follows the pattern of the succession process. The following summary is based on several published versions.

> After Kintu and his followers, who belonged to several different clans, arrived in Buganda (some accounts say that Kintu came from the sky), he was asked by Mukiibi, the head of the Pangolin clan, to help rid the country of a tyrannical ruler named Bbemba the Snake. Bbemba is said to have been either an actual snake (*musota*), specifically a python (*ttimba*), or a half-snake, half-human creature. Bbemba ruled at Buddo Hill, which was then called Naggalabi, and he was notorious for raiding and plundering his subjects. He even killed the son of Mukiibi, who was Bbemba's prime minister (*Katikkiro*). When Kintu heard Mukiibi's request, he lent his men to the cause. Mukiibi's companion in this enterprise was a tortoise (*nfudu*), or someone called "Tortoise," who succeeded in tricking Bbemba into cutting off his own head. Then Mukiibi and Tortoise attacked and defeated Bbemba's men. After they extinguished the fire at Bbemba's hearth and buried his body on the hill, they presented Kintu with Bbemba's head and asked him to succeed to the Kabakaship. Kintu went to Naggalabi for the succession, and he spent the night in Bbemba's house, which was called the House of Buganda. Later he built his capital at Magonga and established many of the clans of Buganda by assigning totemic animals to them.[5]

Both the structure and the content of this story reflect the royal succession pattern, including the ceremonies that were established at Buddo by Namugala: (1) death of the king, extinguishing of the royal fire, selection of the new king by the Katikkiro and his men; (2) journey of the king-elect to Buddo Hill for the mock combat and succession; (3) nocturnal stay by the new king (and the Lubuga) in the House of Buganda; (4) departure from Buddo, installation as Head of the Clan Heads, recognition by the clans; (5) building of the new capital; and (6) presentation of the skull of the dead king to his successor.[6]

In keeping with this succession pattern, the story's plot and message are primarily ideological: every succession to the throne is both an election and a conquest, and every tyrannical king may be justly killed. From the beginning, succession depended not only on royal status, but also on selection by the Katikkiro and the ability of the king-elect to subdue any opposition from rival princes. The story also legitimated the relatively new practice of replacing kings by regicide, which occurred quite frequently in the eighteenth century.

Following the structuralist methods of Edmund Leach and Claude Lévi-Strauss, Ronald Atkinson has interpreted this story in the context of the other traditions about the early kings. He argues that, taken together, these traditions constitute "a myth comprised of an interrelated set of variants on a few basic structural themes": legitimacy/illegitimacy, king/antiking, royal/nonroyal, autochthony/nonautochthony (1975: 44). Curiously, Atkinson does not say why the Baganda should be preoccupied with these themes, or how they relate to the actual institution of kingship. He concludes that although these particular structures derive from Ganda history, "the synchrony of structure dominates the diachronic concerns of history" (1975: 44). To be sure, any narrative, historical or otherwise, requires a framework or structure, but to posit such a structure requires showing how it is related to the institution with which the narrative is concerned.

Atkinson fails to see that the structure of the Kintu story derives from the ideology, symbolism, and sequence of the succession pattern. Thinking in structuralist terms, he argues that the story expresses a general conceptual problem, which he calls a "paradox of legitimacy." Kintu is portrayed as the legitimate ruler because he is the dynastic founder, even though he is a usurping foreigner; Bbemba is portrayed as the illegitimate ruler because he is opposed to Kintu, even though he is the legitimate indigenous ruler. To express this opposition between two types of legitimacy (nonautochthonous versus autochthonous), and the superiority of the one over the other, Kintu is represented as a royal, nonautochthonous, superhuman being; Bbemba is represented as a nonroyal, autochthonous, snakelike creature. Thus "the paradox of ultimate legitimacy in Buganda appears unreal and easily resolved because Kintu has everything in his favor and Bbemba nothing in his" (Atkinson 1975: 22).

However, by concentrating on only the general import of the symbolism (so that it will fit Lévi-Strauss's analysis of similar symbolism), Atkinson misses its specifically Ganda meaning.[7] Kintu's nonautochthony is a matter of both historical tradition, which we shall examine later, and the clanless nature of the kingship. In Buganda, there was no royal totemic clan. Although the throne descended in the male line, all princes (and princesses) took their mother's totems. The result was that the kings were chosen from different totemic clans, and the kingship circulated among them; the emblems of the kingship lay in the hands of various clan officials. By representing Kintu as a foreigner, especially as a sky-born being, the royal traditions portray him as an outsider without any totemic clan affiliation, thus placing the kingship above the clans. Kintu's foreignness, as Kenny points out, was a structural requirement of royal tradition, emphasizing the transcendent nature of the Kabakaship (1988: 609). For the same reason, Bbemba is represented as clanless so that the Kabakaship will not appear to have derived from an indigenous Ganda clan. Kintu's nonautochthonous status is therefore a function of the clanlessness of the kingship, not his "royal" status or his "superiority" over Bbemba. To be sure, there are clan traditions that claim that Kintu was both an indigenous Muganda and a member of a particular totemic clan, but, as we shall see, the royalist response to this assertion was to maintain that Kintu was a clanless foreigner.

Succession to the Ganda throne could take place only upon the death of the king; hence in the story or origins, Kintu could succeed only upon the death of a previous Kabaka. Regicide was justified only in the case of a tyrannical king. Bbemba therefore had to die as a tyrant to justify the rebellion of his chiefs and the succession of Kintu. In this connection, Bbemba's snakelike character not only expresses his autochthony, as Atkinson notes, but also undermines his legitimacy. In Buganda, almost all snakes are feared as dangerous predators, hence the proverb "King Bbemba [the snake] cannot make a friendly visit, he only raids" (Kaggwa [1907] 1934: 5). Bbemba's unsuitability is not a matter of his autochthonous status, as Atkinson believes, but of his tyrannical nature.

Snakes also appear in Ganda folklore as stupid creatures that are easily tricked.[8] In the story of Kintu's conquest, the trickster is a tortoise. Atkinson, thinking in generalized structuralist terms, argues that the tortoise is the central mediating figure: "[H]e is autochthonous and less than human (like Bemba), but because he has legs and can walk he is *more* human than Bemba, and he is on the side of Kintu who is more than human, non-autochthonous, and the first of Buganda's royal line" (1975: 23). But this rather forced interpretation misses the point. The tortoise's role is that of a trickster, and his purpose is to decapitate Bbemba. It is the tortoise's ability to draw his head into his shell, thus appearing headless, which tricks the gullible Bbemba into cutting off his own head, believing that he will never die. The chiefs then present Bbemba's head to Kintu. The presentation of the predecessor's head is a primary feature of the succession process so that the deceased Kabaka's jawbone can be removed and enshrined. In another version of the story recorded by Kaggwa, the tortoise assists Bbemba's Katikkiro, Mukiibi, who plays the central mediating role. Politically, the Katikkiro was the pivotal figure because he represented the chiefs to the king and the king to the chiefs, and he officially announced the king's successor. By turning against Bbemba, Mukiibi led the rest of the chiefs in revolt, and by asking Kintu to succeed, he legitimated Kintu's succession. Without Mukiibi's support, Bbemba could not have been overthrown or Kintu installed. Kintu did not succeed simply because he was royal or superhuman or nonautochthonous, but because he was the properly chosen king. Nor did he succeed simply by might of conquest, as Southwold supposes (1967: 22). Indeed, one of the main points of the story is to show that Kintu's conquest and succession were arranged by the king-making chiefs, led by the Katikkiro.

Another point is to show that Kintu's succession, like that of all the kings who followed him, was a conquest over rival forces. Once the Katikkiro announced the king-elect at the capital in front of the assembled princes and county chiefs, the chosen prince had to face the prospect of rebellion by rival princes backed by one or more chiefs. On this tension-filled occasion, the Katikkiro was obliged to hand out spears to any chief who wished to prepare for war (Roscoe 1911: 190). If the king-elect met with no resistance or if he and his backers were able to subdue any resistance that arose, then the prince and his party went to Buddo Hill to begin the installation rites. As Kabaka Mwanga was told at the time of his installation in 1884: "Fight your enemies and conquer Buganda." According to Bartolomayo Zimbe, this statement meant that "a kingdom is always conquered, not succeeded to" (1939: 89). Zimbe's interpretation expresses the Ganda ideology of royal succession by conquest, for succession to the Kabakaship was both ascriptive and achieved. Like Kintu, every king-elect who went to be installed at Buddo Hill was a chosen prince who had "conquered" his enemies and emerged victorious. The story of Kintu's conquest therefore expressed both the succession process and the ideology behind it. There is no structuralist "paradox" involved here, for the story represents the paradigm of royal succession in Buganda.

Christopher Wrigley has looked at the same story from a folkloristic perspective. Noting that it brings together the figures of tortoise-trickster and snake, Wrigley argues that the story is "an ordinary fable, one of the many which celebrate the cunning of the tortoise, and in part an ancient myth of rejuvenation, of which the snake, with its ability to renew its skin, is a widely used symbol" (1958: 13). But this interpretation hardly seems appropriate, since in the story the snake is killed, not rejuvenated, and there is no theme of renewal. Although the tortoise and the snake are obviously folkloristic elements, the story's purpose is to attribute the origins of the kingship to Kintu and to support the legitimacy of his conquest over Bbemba.

If the story of Kintu's conquest at Buddo is indeed rooted in the installation ceremonies created by Namugala, it is necessary to understand why Namugala created the new ceremonies and why the story of Kintu's conquest suited his purpose.

The period immediately preceding the Kabakaship of Namugala was marked by expansion of territory and development of royal power. The ambitious Mawanda, whom Namugala and his brothers overthrew, succeeded in greatly increasing Buganda's territory in the west and east. At the same time, he augmented the monarchy's power by creating new chiefships to govern these territories and by appointing his own men to several of the existing chiefships that had been held by the clans. This was the beginning of a new type of chief, the military (*mutongole*), the so-called king's man, whom Mawanda and his successors used to expand the monarchy at the expense of the hereditary clan aristocracy (Southwold 1961). Even so, the overthrow of Mawanda and the numerous king-killings that preceded his reign in the eighteenth century indicate that the monarchy was falling victim to competition among the clans, each benefiting by putting its man on the throne. The traditions say that Mawanda tried desperately to secure a blessing for a long reign from Kintu at his shrine at Magonga (Kaggwa [1901] 1971: 71–73), possibly because he wanted to appropriate Kintu's shrine as a ritual center to support himself in the face of his rivals. But he failed to obtain Kintu's blessing. Mawanda's nephews, however, succeeded in securing a magical charm that would strengthen the security of the king, and they placed it at Buddo Hill, which they designated as the site of Kintu's founding of the kingship. As the new butaka of the kingship, Buddo therefore became the locus of the installation ceremonies.

When Namugala inaugurated the ceremonies at Buddo, he performed the necessary rituals before going into seclusion for the mourning period. Henceforth, it was possible for the king-elect to obtain the Kabakaship

almost immediately after his election without waiting for the end of the
five-month mourning period, when the succession wars flared up. Even
though the king still had to go into seclusion, he now did so in full
possession of the title of Kabaka. Symbolically, the effect was to nullify
the five-month interregnum associated with the mourning period. This
was in keeping with the stated purpose of the Buddo rites, which was to
strengthen the king's hold on the throne and to prevent rebellion.

Equally important, the Buddo rites gave the Kabakaship its own territorial foundation. If the Kabakaship, which had now grown more powerful than the indigenous clan heads who conferred the office, were symbolically to express its new autonomy, it had to possess its own butaka,
one that was both indigenous and associated with the founder Kintu.
Before Kabaka Namugala, the kings were installed at the end of mourning as the successors to Kimera and as Ssaabataka. Then they went to the
estates of the four most important indigenous clan heads to be "confirmed" and receive the title of Kabaka. These rites were necessary because the traditions say that the Kabakaship was originally founded on
these indigenous estates. With the advent of the Buddo rites, the king
acceded to the Kabakaship on his own territory, thus demonstrating the
autonomy of the Kabakaship in relation to the indigenous clans.

The Buddo Rites

At Buddo, the kings enacted the two central deeds of the Kintu story: the
succession combat and the overnight stay in the House of Buganda.[9]
The mock combat, or "battle of reeds" (ebirembirembi), took place
when the Kabaka-elect and his party arrived at Buddo Hill. They were
met at the entrance gate by the Semanobe, the guardian of the hill, who
challenged the king-elect and barred his way. Then the king's men and the
Semanobe's men picked up elephant-grass reeds and fought. The combat
ended when the Semanobe and his men fell back before the king's party
and the king advanced and touched a barkcloth tree at the entrance gate.
This signified the king-elect's right to advance up the hill, for barkcloth
trees were symbols of land tenure. The tree stood near the shrine called
Serutega, which guarded the hill and contained the Twin symbol of lubaale Kibuuka, the chief war god of the kingdom.

According to Nsimbi, the battle "commemorates [kutujjukiza] the battle that Kintu fought with Bbemba and defeated him" (1956b: 154).
Although the story says that it was Mukiibi and Tortoise, not Kintu, who
defeated Bbemba, Nsimbi and others attribute the victory to Kintu when
explaining the ritual, perhaps so that the king-elect could be said to be

repeating an act performed by Kintu himself. Nsimbi also says that the rite shows that "the Semanobe guarded the hill well and did not accept any man as the descendant of Kintu to eat the drum of Buganda" (1956b: 154). Symbolically, the ceremony demonstrated that the king-elect was the rightful heir to the "estate [*butaka*] of the Kabaka," as Buddo Hill was called, and hence to the Kabakaship itself.

The second of Kintu's deeds "repeated" by the new king was the over-night stay in the House of Buganda. This act followed the standard clan succession pattern in which a successor to office was required to spend the night in the house of his predecessor, together with his clan sister, the lubuga. It showed that the successor and his clan sister had taken full possession of the office on behalf of the clan to which the office and estate belonged. At Buddo, the Semanobe took the king-elect's right hand, the Makamba took his left, and together they led the king into the House of Buganda and seated him on a barkcloth. The king feasted with his officials and spent one or two nights in the house with his Queen Sister (*Lubuga*). According to Nsimbi, the House of Buganda originally belonged to Bbemba and his predecessors, and it was the place where Kintu slept at the time of his accession (1956b: 154). While this interpretation lends support to the historicity of the Kintu conquest tradition at Buddo, Kaggwa says that the House of Buganda was built by Kabaka Namugala when he instituted the ceremonies at Buddo Hill ([1907] 1934: 6). Kaggwa's view, which seems to be the correct interpretation, is consistent with the fact that the House of Buganda contained no royal insignia belonging to either Kintu or Bbemba. The absence of such insignia is understandable if Buddo Hill were established *de novo* by Namugala as the new butaka of the kingship.

All the regalia at Buddo Hill belonged to Buddo, and two of the four shrines also belonged to him. The Shrine of Lumansi held Buddo's Twin symbol (*mulongo*), called Lumansi; and the Shrine of Buddo contained his jawbone and spirit. The Semanobe, the guardian of the hill, served as the medium for Buddo's spirit in divination séances. Prior to the king's investiture, the Semanobe took the king to the Shrine of Buddo and told him: "This [jawbone] is Buddo which I have given you to hold and this is his 'twin.' He is the one who gave your grandfathers the kingdom. You will live longer than your ancestors. May no one speak evil against you" (Kaggwa [1907] 1934: 6). Thus in addition to the repetition of Kintu's deeds, it was the spirit and jawbone of Buddo that legitimated the king's succession at Buddo Hill and "gave" him the kingship.

The ceremonies at Buddo ended with the king's investiture at the mound of Nakibuuka, the site of Bbemba's defeat. The remaining cere-monies took place at nearby Kisozi Hill, where the Makamba told the king about his obligations to conquer other nations, defend his people, and ensure that there be food and peace in the kingdom. The king also played a mock game of *mweso* in which he "defeated" the Katikkiro and the Kasujju, his two chief ministers of state, to demonstrate his superiority over them. Finally, the king went to Sumba Hill, where a local priest said a prayer for the king's life and for his reign.

There seems to be convincing evidence, then, that the story about Kintu's conquest at Buddo was created in the reign of Kabaka Namugala for the purpose of providing the Kabakaship with its own territorial estate (*butaka*). Thus we can propose that, like so much ritual symbolism, the story was an "invented tradition" (Hobsbawm and Ranger 1983).

Kimera's "Return" to Buganda

The next episode in the royal history tells of the restoration of the kingship by Kintu's alleged great-grandson, Kimera. Here Kimera is portrayed as a "lost prince" who returned from the neighboring kingdom of Bunyoro to reclaim the vacant throne of Buganda, after the disappearance of Chwa Nabakka I and the death of Kimera's father, Kalemeera. The story is a common one in interlacustrine history, and it accounts for the origins of new dynasties. The Ganda story goes as follows:

> Kintu's son, Chwa Nabakka I, succeeded to the throne after Kintu disappeared from Buganda. Chwa later grew to resent his own son, Kalemeera, because he kept constant surveillance over him. Kalemeera was afraid that his father might disappear like Kintu and leave him alone. So Chwa devised a plan to get rid of Kalemeera. He told his Katikkiro, Walusimbi, whose daughter, Nakku, he had married, to accuse Kalemeera of committing adultery with his wife. Kalemeera was accused and subsequently judged guilty by the king's council. He was sent to the court of his uncle, Mukama Winyi, the king of Bunyoro, in order to raise funds by obtaining hoes (which were made in Bunyoro) to sell in Buganda to pay his fine.
>
> Kalemeera was warmly received by his uncle and allowed to sleep in the same house with Wannyana, Winyi's chief wife, who was a Muhima woman of the Grasshopper clan. That night Kalemeera seduced Wannyana and made her pregnant. Later, he confided his indiscretion to Mulegeya, a potter, who belonged to the Vervet Monkey clan. Mulegeya interceded with Winyi on Kalemeera's behalf. He told the king a prophecy and persuaded him not to punish Wannyana. He said that as soon as Wannyana gave birth, the child should be thrown into a clay pit; then the king would live a long life. Convinced by Mulegeya's prophecy, Winyi permitted Kalemeera to leave Bunyoro. On his way to Buganda, Kalemeera fell ill and died. His

companions cut off his head as proof of his death, brought it back to Buganda, and put it in a shrine in Busiro county. After Wannyana gave birth to her child, Kimera, he was cast into a clay pit. Mulegeya rescued him and brought him home and raised him with his own infant son, Katumba. Wannyana gave Mulegeya some cows to provide milk for Kimera, and she also gave Kimera a beaded bracelet for his right hand to distinguish him from Mulegeya's other children, who wore anklets. Kimera grew up without knowing his true mother, and he became a skillful hunter.

Meanwhile, in Buganda, Chwa had disappeared from the throne. He had been told that Kintu had returned, and he was afraid of meeting him (or, alternatively, he became lost while looking for him). The chiefs then appointed Walusimbi, the Katikkiro (also head of the Civet Cat clan), to rule over them. Later, they deposed him and appointed Ssebwana of the Pangolin clan to serve as Katikkiro. When the chiefs learned that Kalemeera had left a son named Kimera in Bunyoro, they asked him to return to Buganda and to succeed to the vacant throne. Kimera agreed and brought his mother, Wannyana, as well as a number of followers from several different clans. He hunted buffalo as he entered Buganda, and was immediately recognized as a prince by Chief Natiigo, head of the indigenous Pangolin clan. Kimera also left large footprints on rocks in the countryside.

When Kimera arrived in Buganda, he was welcomed to the palace at Gganda by Nakku, Walusimbi's daughter and Chwa's former wife. She tricked Ssebwana into leaving the palace, and when he heard the drums welcoming Kimera as the new Kabaka, he fled to the Ssesse Islands. Wearing his calfskin hunting garb, Kimera succeeded to the kingship by stepping on the royal carpet (*kiwu*) in the presence of Nakku at Gganda. Then he married Nakku and appointed Mulegeya's son Katumba, head of the Vervet Monkey clan, to the newly created office of the Mugema in honor of the deceased Mulegeya, who had protected him in Bunyoro, and Katumba was given the county of Busiro to govern. He also created the offices of the royal executioner (*Ssebatta*) and of the Mukwenda. Then he built a palace for his mother at Lusaka.[10]

As others have noted, Kimera's heroic biography resembles that of Ndahura, the legendary founder of the Chwezi dynasty of Bunyoro. Ndahura was born illegitimately in a foreign land, cast away as an infant, rescued by a potter, raised as a cowherd, welcomed into his grandfather's kingdom by a female guardian of the throne, and restored to the kingship (Nyakatura 1973: 18–21). Like Ndahura, Kimera left giant "footprints" on rock surfaces around the countryside. The Kimera story may have been modeled on the Ndahura legend, or it may have derived from a common source. In either case, the resemblance suggests that the story is a dynastic-founder tale and that its origins lie among interlacustrine societies with traditions of kingship.

Kimera's biography also fits the basic pattern of the Ganda succession process, including the ritual acts that repeat Kimera's deeds: (1) death of the previous king, election of the successor by the chiefs; (2) seclusion and interregnum; and (3) ritual hunt, succession and investiture (with a female figure), entrance into the palace and taking of wives (including a woman called Nakku), separation of the Kabaka from the Queen Mother (*Nnamasole*). These parallels suggest that the Kimera story was shaped according to the succession pattern, so that every new king could be seen to repeat the example established by Kimera and properly assume his title.

Leaving aside for the moment the story's historical implications, it is clearly a tale about the legitimacy of the Kintu–Kimera line of descent. As Atkinson points out, the structural theme of political relations surfaces toward the end of the tale and centers on the Kimera/Ssebwana, king/antiking episode. To Atkinson, the story represents "a temporary and anomalous resurgence of the priority of autochthones . . . [and] the (re)establishment of the 'legitimate' (but non-autochthonous) royal line in a variant replay of the coming of Kintu" (1975: 30). Thus he sees the opposition between Kimera (nonautochthonous king) and Ssebwana (autochthonous antiking) to be a variant of the opposition between Kintu (nonautochthonous king) and Bbemba (autochthonous antiking).

However, the story's emphasis does not fall on the question of autochthony, but on the question of Kimera's legitimacy. First, it shows that the heir to the Kabakaship must be a descendent of the Kintu line. Kimera was immediately recognized as the proper heir to the throne because of his royal descent, unlike Ssebwana, who, although he was properly chosen, was not of royal descent and had to give up the throne as soon as Kimera arrived. Second, the story implies that the heir to the throne must be installed as "Kimera" and invested with his regalia. For this reason, every king-elect ended the mourning period by hunting game, thereby reenacting Kimera's triumphant, "royal" return. The Mugema then pronounced him to "be" Kimera and invested him with Kimera's regalia. Before Namugala's institution of the Buddo rites, this was the procedure that made the king the heir to the throne and Ssaabataka, or Head of the Clan Heads. After the establishment of the Buddo rites, the Kimera installation ceremony still retained its importance as the procedure by which the clan heads made the Kabaka the Ssaabataka and installed him in his palace at the end of the mourning period.

Wrigley has interpreted the Kimera story as a tale about a Frazerian divine king. He notes that Kimera's name derives from the verb *kumera*, "to sprout" or "to grow up" (as plants do), and he refers to a story about the young Kimera, who wanders unwittingly with his cows into his mother's millet field, where he is discovered by servant girls who raise the alarm. On this basis, Wrigley argues that "we are in the presence of the oldest of agricultural rites, the dance of women who greet, or more properly summon, the young green shoots." Concerning Kimera's mother, Wannyana, whose name means "calf" or "heifer," Wrigley suggests that she is "kinswoman of Hathor and of 'cow-faced holy Hera,' goddess of fertility in plant, beast and man" (1959: 39). Wrigley concludes by indicating that the story of Kimera's succession refers to a Frazerian ritual drama: "Kimera has come to manhood, and the time has come for Ssebwana to yield his place. . . . Kimera has come to his people; the fear of famine is over for another season; the days of feasting and dancing can begin" (1959: 40).

Despite its ingenuity, this interpretation is farfetched. Nsimbi explains that the Banyoro conceive of Kimera historically as a Nyoro prince who broke away from Bunyoro and "rooted" himself in Buganda and founded the Ganda throne. Here, *kumera* refers to the establishment of a new dynasty in Buganda as the sprouting of a young shoot or transplanted tree. As for Wannyana, the Baganda believe that she was a member of the cattle-herding Bahima people of the western grasslands where millet grows. Her name ("heifer") does not denote a "goddess of fertility" but is an ordinary female name in the Grasshopper clan (Kaggwa [1912] 1949: 14). Although there is no doubt that the stories about Kimera portray him as a mythical persona, Wrigley himself admits that the notion of corn rites and corn-kings is singularly inappropriate to Buganda, where corn is not grown.

Investiture as Kimera and Ssaabataka

At the end of the mourning period, the Kabaka left the seclusion of his mourning enclosure (*kakomera*), where he was surrounded by chiefs who were loyal to him. Before the hunt, Kalibala of the Grasshopper clan freed a gazelle for the Kabaka to kill. The hunting party was evidently a well-organized affair. In October 1884, after Mwanga ended mourning for his father, Mutesa I, he was told: "Let us go hunting, for your grandfather Kabaka Kimera came hunting from Bunyoro before he became Kabaka, and he sat well on the throne of Buganda" (Zimbe 1939: 75). Mwanga then set out with his hunting dogs, named Semagimbi and Senkungo after those of Kimera, and killed four antelope.

In the story, the hunting motif legitimates Kimera's royal status, for hunting large game, especially buffalo, was the sport of kings and princes, and only royalty could roam freely about the land and trespass on clan estates. According to Kaggwa's account, when Kimera and his followers entered Buganda to hunt game, the local clan head, Natiigo, exclaimed: "Who are these coming through the back of my land as if they were princes?" ([1901] 1971: 13). In the ritual context, the ceremonial hunt also brought the Kabaka out of his secluded state of mourning and symbolically "returned" him to his kingdom to enter his palace like the heroic Kimera and to receive new wives and the homage of the clans.

The dynastic account also says that the office of the Mugema, who invested the king, was created by Kimera. The Mugema was called the "Father of the Kabaka" in honor of Mulegeya, who rescued Kimera from the clay pit, and Kimera is said to have given the office to Katumba, as head of the Vervet Monkey clan. On the day after the ceremonial hunt, the Mugema sat the king on the stool of the kingship, called the Nnamulondo. The stool rested on a royal carpet made of lion and leopard skins. This carpet (kiwu) is said to have been made by Kintu. The Mugema also invested the king with four robes of office. The first was a barkcloth that he tied over the king's right shoulder, signifying that the king was "the man who owns the country." The second was a calfskin that was also tied over the right shoulder. The calfskin is said to recall the tradition that Kimera succeeded to the kingship while wearing the calfskin garb of a hunter. Then the Mugema declared to the Kabaka: "You are Kimera, indeed! You must always rule over your people well. You have succeeded Kimera" (Kaggwa [1907] 1934: 93; Nsimbi 1956b: 43–44). The Mugema also declared: "You are Ssaabataka [Head of the Clan Heads], treat your bataka with honour" (Mair 1934: 181). After tying a barkcloth over the king's left shoulder to indicate that the king was to be honored as the Head of the Fathers of Twins (Ssaabalongo), the Mugema knotted a leopard skin over the king's left shoulder to signify that he was "a leopard and his subjects were [merely] squirrels" (Kaggwa [1907] 1934: 93). Finally, the Mugema wrapped a barkcloth around both of the king's shoulders to show that the king had succeeded properly to the throne of Buganda.

The Mukwenda, another official appointed by Kimera, presented the king with the two spears and shield of the kingship. According to several sources, including Mutesa I, the spears and shield originally belonged to Kimera (Bellefonds 1876–1877: 63; Stanley 1893: 151). Next, Kajubi of the Grasshopper clan placed a bracelet of beads on the king's left wrist and announced: "You are Kimera" (Kaggwa [1907] 1934: 12). Segulu of the Pangolin clan then placed a bracelet of copper and brass on the king's right wrist and said, "This is the prince who succeeded to the kingship because it [the bracelet] cannot be put on all the princes, only the one who succeeds" (Kaggwa [1907] 1934: 12). Kasujju then handed the king a drum called Kyebabona, which belonged to Kintu, and the king beat upon it (Kaggwa [1907] 1934: 12). Next the king was taken over to the royal Mujaguzo drums and told to beat on the chief drum, called Ttimba ("python"). The sounding of this drum, which is said to have been brought by Kimera (Lush 1937: 9; Nsimbi 1956b: 44), signaled the completion of the ceremonies. The new king, after being put on the shoulders of his bearer and shown to the people, wounded with a spear a Munyoro who was taken away and killed in Bunyoro. The following day, the king entered the Twekobe, the house of the kingship, and received new wives and the homage of the clan officials who were responsible for providing services to the royal palace.

Thus ended the fourth phase of the installation sequence. The fact that these rites occurred at the end of the mourning period, when succession to office normally took place, suggests that the historical Kimera (whoever he was) was fitted into the installation process as the heir to the Kabakaship founded by Kintu. The fact that Kimera is credited with so much regalia and with the naming of several new officials, the most important being the Mugema, implies that Kimera introduced some major innovations in the Kabakaship.

The "Confirmation" Ceremonies

Before the advent of the Buddo rites, the new king was installed as Kimera and Ssaabataka, but could not become Kabaka until the completion of the kula rites, which "confirmed" him in office. These ceremonies required the king-elect to travel to the estates of the four most important indigenous clan heads to be invested by them on their land. This requirement clearly reflects the segmentary nature of the early Ganda state, in which the king was *primus inter pares* among autonomous clan heads (*Bataka*) who retained significant authority (Southwold 1961; Richards 1966: 35). As these ceremonies indicate, the indigenous Bataka regarded the king-elect as an outsider, a trespasser on their ancient clan lands. They therefore had to "confirm" (*kukula*) his accession on their own territory and hand over some of their regalia to him, thus making him superior to them. Institutionally, the Kabakaship rested in their hands because, as these rites indicate, it was originally conferred on their lands.

First, the king went to the estate of Nankere, the head of the indigenous Frog section of the Lungfish clan, who was in charge of the "confirmation" ceremonies. On the way, the king passed by the rear of the house of Kalonda, the head of the Mushroom clan. This was regarded as an act of trespass, and the king was reprimanded and fined. Kalonda then took him to see Nankere, who was dressed in ceremonial barkcloths, wore a beaded crown, and carried his spears and shield of office. Nankere greeted the king and led him into a house called Namirongo, where they dined with the Queen Mother. Later, Nankere administered an oath of office to the king:

> You have come to Kyanjove [Bukerekere] to see how your grandfathers were confirmed [*kula*]. May you live longer than your ancestor Kungubu. You should rule Buganda in peace; no one should oppose you. All people should kneel down because you are Master [*mpanga*, Cock]. To anyone who is insolent [i.e., refuses to obey] you should shout the proverb: "The queen termite eats her drones." (Kakoma, Ntate, and Serukaga 1959: 16–17)

When Nankere finished, the king struck with his fists one of Nankere's sons who was dressed as a bride. The boy was taken away and killed, and his back sinews were removed and made into a pair of anklets for the king to wear in order to have "long life" (*kuwangaala*). According to the traditions, Nankere originally made such anklets for Kabaka Ttembo, Kimera's grandson and successor, to cure him from madness (*eddalu*), and he performed this service for his successors. Here Nankere's ceremonial role expresses the common African theme of the subdued autochthonous leader who possesses ritual potency that he gives to the politically superior "outsider" chief or king at the time of his installation (cf. Turner 1969: 98–99). Nankere then invested the king with the double barkcloths of Bukerekere. He also removed some beads from his own crown, placed them on the king's head, and gave him his own two spears of office. The ceremony ended when Nankere officially dismissed the king from the presence of the Queen Mother, telling him that he could no longer see his "companion Kabaka."

The king proceeded to the clan estate of Kasujja, the head of the indigenous Colobus Monkey clan. Kasujja set the king on a rock, called Nanfuka, and said, "I am your ancestor. My sister Nnambi Nantuttulu gave birth to Chwa Nabakka I. That is why I am showing you this land" (Kaggwa [1907] 1934: 23). This rite installed the king as the heir to Chwa Nabakka I, who is regarded as Kintu's son and successor.

Lady Nakku then presented the king to Gunju of the indigenous Mushroom clan, who in turn took him to the estate of Walusimbi, the head of the indigenous Civet Cat clan. The king was again made to commit an act of trespass for which he was admonished, and he paid Walusimbi a fine of nine cows, goats, barkcloths, women, and slaves. Walusimbi, standing on a carpet made of lion and leopard skins to signify his royal status, administered an oath to the king (who presumably stood on another lion-and-leopard-skin carpet).

> You have been brought here that I should instruct you in the administration of the kingdom. Now I solemnly charge you: Rule all the people well. I shall keep a close watch over you and over this land as I did when your ancestor Chwa I was no longer here. I give you this wisdom: Judge cases wisely, rule the people with mercy, and punish those who rebel against you. You are the Kabaka [*Gwe Kabaka*], you are now grown up [*okuze*]; you cannot see your mother who gave birth to you. (Kaggwa [1907] 1934: 24)

As this statement implies, Walusimbi acted as the ultimate authority over the title of the Kabakaship, which he held in the absence of a Kabaka on the throne. He was the last to invest the king, and thereafter the king was called "Kabaka." At Walusimbi's, the Kabaka ordered a number of people to be killed for acts of disobedience (Roscoe 1911: 211–12; Kaggwa [1907] 1934: 25). These killings, which we shall examine later, demonstrated that the Kabaka had now acceded fully to the authority of the throne. The "confirmation" ceremonies ended after the new king spent the night with Lady Nakku on here estate at Kavumba. By spending the night at Lady Nakku's ceremonial hut (called *Lukuwadde*), the new king succeeded to the kingship on her estate, as had Kimera when he "returned" to Buganda. Lady Nakku then joined the Kabaka at his palace and became one of his principal wives.

In the early nineteenth century, when the monarchy reached the peak of its power with the accession of Ssuuna II (ca. 1826), the king no longer needed to be confirmed by the indigenous Bataka on their estates, and these ceremonies were discontinued (Kaggwa [1907] 1934: 24; Kakoma, Ntate, and Serukaga 1959: 15). By this time, the indigenous Bataka refused to see the king after his installation because they resented his political gains at their expense (Kaggwa [1907] 1934: 151).

Historical Clues in Ritual Symbols

From a historical point of view, the most striking fact about the installation ceremonies is the modest amount of regalia that is attributed to Kintu compared with the abundance attributed to Kimera, Buddo, and the indigenous clan heads. Kintu's meager legacy is a drum, which was beaten at the end of the Ssaabataka investiture ceremonies, and the royal carpet, made of lion and leopard skins, on which the king sat on his enthronement stool. Both are symbols of succession, and both firmly link Kintu to the office of the Kabakaship. The carpet also links Kintu to the Lion clan, whose secondary totem was the leopard. According to Kaggwa, Kintu killed the lion that became the totem of the Lion clan, and he established the lion-and-leopard-skin carpet as the royal emblem ([1912] 1949: 2). This suggests that Kintu was himself a member of the Lion clan or, perhaps, that he was a Lion clan deity or ancestor. Indeed, Mutesa I is said to have thought that the Kabaka must be a member of the Lion clan, since one of his titles is "Lion" (Kaggwa [1912] 1949: 2; cf. Roscoe 1911: 41). But given the lack of other symbolism of political hierarchy and centralization (of the sort introduced by Kimera), the drum and carpet do not themselves imply the existence of kingship.

The ceremonies at Walusimbi's estate also present important historical clues. The significant ceremonial role played by Walusimbi is in accordance with the tradition that Walusimbi—who was also known by the title "Buganda"—governed the indigenous clan heads at Bakka before Kintu came to Buganda (Nsimbi 1956b: 194). Roscoe goes further and says that Kintu deposed Walusimbi (also known as Ntege), but allowed him to retain the title of Kabaka (1911: 145). Roscoe also points out that Walusimbi possessed a carpet made of lion and leopard skins. Nsimbi, too, notes that after Kintu's son Chwa I disappeared and the Kabakaship was vacant, "Walusimbi ruled like a Kabaka" (1956b: 195). Moreover, the traditions say that Walusimbi's daughter Nakku was Chwa I's wife, and that Nakku expelled Ssebwana and welcomed Kimera to Buganda and installed him on the throne. The fact that the Civet Cat clan always provided a woman, whose title was Nakku, to the new Kabaka suggests that Nakku's role may originally have been that of the Lubuga of the Kabakaship. All these ritual clues reinforce the traditions that say that Walusimbi was the leading autochthonous chief before Kintu's arrival (cf. Southwold 1968: 143; Nyakatura 1973: 25), and that Walusimbi's estate was the original butaka at which the office of Kabaka was established.

The fact that the Kabakaship was conferred on the estate of the Civet Cat clan, while the symbols of the office belonged to Kintu's Lion clan, suggests that the Kabakaship was the joint creation of the two clans. Succession to the office on Walusimbi's estate tied it to the most important of the indigenous clans. Additional evidence is the fact that members of both the Civet Cat and Lion clans were barred from the throne (Kaggwa [1912] 1949: 2; Southwold 1968: 143). The result was that the Kabakaship was shared by the rest of the clans. This unusual principle—the absence of a chiefly clan—seems to have been firmly established by the time of Kimera's arrival, for both Kimera and his successors came to the throne as members of their mothers' clans.

It is also significant that the practice of preserving the chiefly jawbone is not said to have begun with Kintu but with Kalemeera, the traditional father of Kimera. Kalemeera allegedly died on his return from Bunyoro, where the custom of preserving royal jawbones was practiced. The remains of neither Kintu nor Chwa I were treated in this fashion, and no one knows where the grave of either Kabaka is located, which is perhaps why they are said to have "disappeared" from Buganda. Lacking a jawbone, Kintu's shrine at Magonga is empty except for a small grass hut that contains coffee beans and monetary offerings. Unlike the shrines of Kimera and his successors, Kintu's shrine has no royal throne-platform, screen of spears and shields, or inner "forest." Instead, Kintu's spirit is said to dwell in the forest grove outside the shrine. According to Kaggwa's clan history, it was Kimera who first built a shrine for Kintu at Magonga, where he is said to have disappeared, thus incorporating him into the dynastic shrine tradition ([1912] 1949: 10). As Roland Oliver has noted, there is good reason to believe that the practice of preserving the jaws and skulls of chiefs came from Bunyoro (1959), although the practice itself does not seem to have been a Bito custom (Kiwanuka 1971a: 59). The fact that in Buganda the origin of this custom is linked to the death of Prince Kalemeera, who went to Bunyoro, suggests that it may be one of the few Nyoro customs that was adopted in Buganda upon the accession of Kimera.

It is significant, too, that Kintu's shrine contains no royal Twin symbol (*mulongo*). Like the jawbone, this royal emblem was put in the shrine after the king's demise. According to dynastic history, Kimera (whom the Banyoro regard as a twin) was the first Kabaka to possess a mulongo, and he may have started the practice. The absence of any such dynastic emblem associated with Kintu suggests that until the accession of Kimera, the Kabakaship may not have been a dynastic office but one that circulated among the leaders of the Kintu–Walusimbi clan confederacy. This, together with the building of Kintu's royal shrine by Kimera, points strongly toward Kimera as the one who transformed the office of the Kabakaship into a royal, dynastic institution.

Historical Reconstruction

The suggestion that Kintu was the leader of a Lion and Leopard clan complex who entered Buganda and founded the Kabakaship together with the indigenous clans is consistent with his role in the oral traditions of southern Busoga (Cohen 1972: 86-94). In this area, numerous Kintu shrines and traditions depict him as a clan leader associated with the Lion and Leopard clans who traveled westward across southern Busoga. He is not depicted as a royal figure or as the founder of any royal centers or dynasties. What he, or the clan leaders who acted in his name, may have created in Buganda was a clan confederacy of the sort that Kintu is said to have established in Busoga. Such a confederacy was not a "kingdom," with all the political centralization and hierarchy that that term implies. In Busoga, Kintu's clan groups and their most important chiefs formed the basis of the more centralized polities that developed later. The Kabakaship founded by Kintu and Walusimbi thus might be regarded as the period of proto-kingship in Buganda.

There is reason to suspect that during this period a political relationship developed between Buganda and the western Chwezi kingdom of Kitara, and that Chwa Nabakka I may have formed an alliance with the Chwezi kingdom (Kiwanuka 1971a: 35). About the time when the Chwezi throne fell to the Luo Bito from the north, the Grasshopper clan, to which Kimera belonged, came into Buganda from the western grasslands of the Chwezi region, together with other cattle-herding clans. The Kabakaship was then held by Ssebwana of the Pangolin clan, whom Ganda traditions say Kimera ousted from office. When the Bito (Bushbuck) clan took over the Chwezi throne of Kitara, Buganda may have briefly fallen under Bito control, as the Nyoro traditions claim, and later been liberated by Kimera.

According to the Nyoro account, Kimera was the younger twin brother of Isingoma Mpuga Rukidi, the Luo founder of the Bito kingship of Bunyoro. When Rukidi acceded to the throne, Kimera was given Buganda to rule. Kimera supposedly took a number of clans from Kitara (later Bunyoro) to Buganda and founded an independent kingdom (K. W. 1936: 75; Nyakatura 1973: 64-65). Since Ganda tradition says that Kimera was a prince who came from Bunyoro, most scholars initially supposed that the Ganda version of the Kimera story concealed the fact that Kimera conquered Buganda and established a Bito subdynasty on the throne (Gray 1935; Oliver 1955; Southwold 1968; Cohen 1970).

However, the Ganda historian Semakula Kiwanuka has argued convincingly that Kimera was not a Bito prince but a leader of migrating clans from the western lands of the Chwezi kingdom. Somewhat before the time of the Bito takeover of the Chwezi throne, Kimera arrived in Buganda and established a new dynasty (Kiwanuka 1971a: 36-63; cf. Oliver 1977: 639). The ritual evidence also supports this view. Kimera did not introduce any Bito ritual symbols into Buganda, an astonishing fact if he is supposed to have conquered Buganda and established a Bito subdynasty. Instead, most of Buganda's royal symbolism and most of the offices of the kingship originated *de novo* with Kimera. While the practice of building royal jawbone shrines, introduced by Kimera, was also followed by the Bito kings in Bunyoro, it does not appear to have been a Luo custom, but a Bantu practice that Kimera brought from the western Chwezi region (Kiwanuka 1971a: 59). Moreover, Kimera did not impose the Bito royal clan on the Kabakaship: he adopted the prevailing policy that no royal clan existed. Indeed, the Kabakas were prohibited from marrying into the Ganda Bushbuck clan, a practice that is entirely foreign to Nyoro custom.

Nevertheless, Kiwanuka's theory of the origins of Kimera leaves Kimera's associations with the Nyoro court unexplained. Although Kiwanuka suggests that in the Ganda tradition "Bunyoro" simply stood for Kimera's western origins in the region of the Chwezi kingdom of Kitara, he does not explain why the Ganda tradition makes the king of Bunyoro the "brother" of Chwa I, or why Prince Kalemeera is portrayed as a visitor to his "uncle's" court. If Kiwanuka's version is correct, Ganda tradition should simply have cast Kimera in the role of a "lost prince" from the west who returned to "reclaim" the Ganda throne.

The answer is evidently twofold:

1. Kimera's accession to the Kabakaship had to be legitimated according to the Chwezi paradigm of the royal founder as a "lost prince" in a foreign kingdom, a paradigm familiar to the western clans that put Kimera in the Kabakaship.
2. The Kabakaship may have been briefly subject to Chwezi control, requiring successors to the office to go to the Chwezi court for approval, episodes that were later remembered as a Ganda prince going to the court of Bunyoro.

In the nineteenth century, such a relationship existed between Bunyoro and the chiefdoms of northwestern Busoga. At this time, the local Soga princes, who belonged to the Bushbuck clan (called the Baisengobi), regarded themselves as descendants of the royal Babito of Bunyoro, and the princes were sent to the court of Bunyoro to be trained as pages. Upon the death of the Soga chief, the Mukama of Bunyoro appointed a Soga prince to succeed him, and the prince returned to Busoga to take over the throne (Roscoe 1915: 200–201; Nyakatura 1973: 130). The Mukama also confirmed the prince's accession by sending iron hoes from Bunyoro, where they were made, to the capital in Busoga (Roscoe 1924a: 132).

The Ganda tradition about Kimera's return from Bunyoro may have been based on the memory of a similar arrangement with the Chwezi rulers. Sons of the Kintu–Walusimbi line, of which Kalemeera may have been one, may have been sent to the Chwezi kingdom to be trained at the court of their "uncle" and then returned to Buganda to succeed to the title of the Ganda confederacy. Alternatively, they may have gone to the Chwezi court to obtain hoes, as Kalemeera was required to do, as a sign of their "uncle's" approval. In either case, the accession to the Kabakaship, when the Chwezi rulers were in control, might appropriately have been portrayed in ritual terms as the "return" of a Ganda heir from a foreign kingdom. When Kimera's Grasshopper clan, which possessed its own chiefly line and symbols of office associated with the petty kingdom of Bwere, arrived in Buganda, it may have joined with the local Kintu–Walusimbi clan confederacy and established Buganda as an independent kingdom, thereby freeing Buganda from Chwezi overlordship and ousting their appointed ruler, Ssebwana. Kimera may thus have been the first to establish Buganda as a kingdom in its own right, which is essentially what the Nyoro account says. The overwhelming amount of royal symbolism attributed to Kimera at the time of his accession, and the number of important royal offices established by him at this time, point strongly to this conclusion.

If it is true, as Kaggwa's informants from the Otter clan stated, that Kimera built a royal shrine for Kintu at Magonga ([1912] 1949: 10), the "enshrinement" of Kintu had the effect of grafting him onto Kimera's newly founded royal line. It also gave the kingship of Buganda its own ancient origin tradition, separate from that of the Chwezi of Kitara and from the Bito kings of Bunyoro, a tradition that was firmly rooted in the local clan confederation founded by Kintu. Later, when the Ganda monarchy wished to assert its superiority over the indigenous Ganda clan heads, Buddo Hill was established as the ritual center of the kingship and the Kintu conquest story was developed.

In this connection, it is significant that the early European travelers were told that both Kintu and Kimera were the founders of the kingdom. In 1862, several informants, including a chief named Natiigo, whose ancestor welcomed Kimera to Buganda, told Speke that Kimera was the first Kabaka (1863: 246; cf. Kaggwa [1901] 1971: 13). In 1875, Mutesa told Stanley that the first king was Kintu. At the same time, he told Linant de Bellefonds, whose visit overlapped with Stanley's, that the first king was Kimera, whom Mutesa described as a breakaway prince from Bunyoro-Kitara. Although Mutesa clearly recognized Kintu as the original founder of the Kabakaship, he also regarded Kimera as the founder of the dynastic line to which he was heir and which he associated with Bunyoro-Kitara. Indeed, he boasted to Bellefonds that he was the "true heir of the ancient kingdom of Kitara" (1876–1877: 63). As we have seen, this tradition of dual founders was embedded in Ganda traditional history and ritual. The Kintu/clan-patriarch tradition, associated with the Kintu clans, was tied together with the Kimera/royal-dynastic-heir tradition, associated with the Kimera clans, to form a single dynastic history. Hence, in the royal installation ceremonies, the deeds of Kintu were performed at the initial "founder" stage, and those of Kimera at the subsequent "heir" stage.

We shall never know, of course, whether this theory is correct. It does, however, make sense of the history and symbolism of the installation ceremonies and the historical traditions that are reflected in them. It is also consistent with Nyoro accounts and with evidence from Busoga.

The Kintu Controversy

I have left until last the controversy about the historical origins of Kintu. This debate, which began in Buganda in 1915 in response to Kaggwa's dynastic history and still continues, is best understood against the background of the competing interests of the kingship and the clans. The point at issue is whether Kintu was a foreigner or an indigenous Muganda. An authoritative answer to this question, couched in Western historical terms, is important to both the kingship and the clans.

In Buganda, oral history was kept both by the clans and by the kingship. Each retained its own traditions, and these overlapped at certain points—for example, when a clan member became Kabaka or was appointed to an important royal office. When literacy was introduced at the end of the nineteenth century and Kaggwa published the history of the kingship, clan heads began to write down their histories. For the most part, there were no major differences between these accounts and Kaggwa's record of dynastic traditions, except on the question of the origin and identity of Kintu. As Twaddle has pointed out, the shift from oral to written communication did not significantly change Ganda modes of thought (1974). Nor did the introduction of foreign ideas about history; although certain details were altered, history remained a matter of institutional concerns, and no structural changes were made.

The royalist point of view held that Kintu was a stranger to Buganda; he was even said to be a semimythical being who came from the sky. According to one of Roscoe's informants, Tefiro Mulumba Kulungi, who was Mutesa I's personal steward, the "old idea was that Kintu came from Heaven [*ggulu*, or 'sky']. We knew that he was a human being, but we thought he had been dropped by the creator [Katonda]. His father is not known, but he was said to be the son of Ggulu or the 'Heavens'" (Roscoe and Kaggwa 1906: 51; cf. Nsimbi 1956b: 151). The missionary writer Julien Gorju was also told that "whence Kintu came, we know nothing, we know no more than his name. . . . [When he came] he said 'I am the thing [*kintu*] from the sky, sent by the God of the sky to arrange the country'" (1920: 100).

With the arrival of the Arabs at Mutesa's court in the 1870s, the matter of Kintu's origins took a historical turn, at least in royalist circles. Gorju says that the Zanzibari traders told the first Catholic missionaries who arrived in Buganda in 1879 that Kintu was Ham, the father of the black race in Africa (1920: 99). As in the Bible, Muslim tradition holds that Ham was the founder of the African peoples, and the Zanzibaris appear to have supposed that Ham was the figure whom the Baganda called Kintu, the stranger who entered the country and became the progenitor of the people and founder of the nation.

This view, or some version of it, was accepted by Mutesa I, who learned Arabic and encouraged his people to follow Islam. According to Tefiro, Mutesa's steward, "After Mutesa had 'read' [that is, adopted Islam] he formed the opinion that Kintu was a descendant of Ham, the son of Noah" (Roscoe and Kaggwa 1906: 50–51). In 1875, the explorer Stanley found that Mutesa believed that Kintu was Ham himself (1878 I: 345). Mutesa also told one of the first CMS missionaries that Kintu was descended from Ham and that Ham's tomb was in Buganda, presumably at the site of Kintu's shrine at Magonga (*CMS Intelligencer* April 1878: 213; cf. Felkin 1885–1886: 739). Whatever Mutesa's precise belief, it seems clear that the Muslim traders introduced the figure of Ham as an interpretation of Kintu's identity and that the historicization of Kintu in royal tradition began with Mutesa's acceptance of this view. In this way, Kintu became part of the wider historical tradition of the Islamic and Christian world with which Mutesa sought greater contact. As Mutesa was well aware, by identifying Kintu with Ham he enhanced his own status as the direct descendant of a figure recognized by the outside world as the ancient patriarch of black Africa.

By association with Ham, the figure of Kintu also acquired more definite geographical origins. Stanley, who obtained his information from Mutesa's court, wrote that Kintu was believed to have come into Buganda "from the north" (1878 I: 345). Later, the CMS missionary Robert W.

Felkin reported that Kintu was said to have crossed the Victoria Nile at the village of Foweira in Bunyoro before turning south toward Buganda (1885–1886: 764). In the opinion of Mutesa's steward, the northern direction was also linked to scriptural teaching: "We don't know where he [Kintu] came from, we think he came from Egypt through Ganyi country [Bukedi]. . . . Egypt is about the place where Noah's ark settled and all scriptures tell us that Ham was the father of all black men" (Roscoe and Kaggwa 1906: 50–51). In the second edition of *The Kings of Buganda*, Kaggwa added that Kintu came through Podi in Bunyoro and then into Buganda (cf. Twaddle 1974: 87). Although it is uncertain whether Kaggwa obtained this information from his informants or whether it was his own idea, it is clear that by the time Kaggwa published his history, Kintu's historical nature and "northern" origins were well established in royal circles. On this matter, Kaggwa was clearly neither an innovator nor party to a "fraud" to deceive Europeans, as Michael Twaddle has argued (1974: 94). He was following a relatively new version of the tradition that stemmed from Arab contact and was believed by Mutesa himself.

In recording the traditions about the early kings, Kaggwa wrote down what he learned from members of the royal family and the guardians of the royal shrines. These were the custodians of dynastic history whom Kaggwa listed as his sources. From the indigenous Bataka, he received different accounts of the origins of the kingship, which he rejected and did not record. This is confirmed by Semu K. L. Kakoma, a member of the indigenous Frog lineage of the Lungfish clan, who told the anthropologist Martin Southwold that he was present when Kaggwa was compiling *The Customs of the Baganda*. Kakoma said that he, together with another man, wrote down what the old Bataka said, and they told Kaggwa that there were seven Kabakas before Kintu and that Kintu did not come from another country but was a native Muganda. According to Kakoma, Kaggwa dismissed these accounts as mere "fables" (*engero*) (Southwold field note 1955: Fallers Collection).

Not long after Kaggwa published *The Kings of Buganda*, the newly founded CMS newsletter *Ebifa mu Buganda* (Events in Buganda) published an article that listed five pre-Kintu Kabakas whom Kaggwa had ignored (Rowe 1969: 218; Kiwanuka 1971a: 18–19), spurring the long controversy about whether Kintu was a native Muganda and was the original founder of the kingship. As clan spokesmen, the Bataka challenged Kaggwa and his royalist version of Kintu's origins. Theirs was clearly a political view, for they had lost much of their power in the settlement in 1900, which was jointly drawn up and administered by

Kaggwa and the British. Their insistence on Kintu's indigenous status, and on an indigenous pre-Kintu line of rulers, indicated that the kingship was originally a clan-based institution in which the Bataka possessed important rights.

In 1916, Eriya M. Buligwanga published a lengthy history of the Lungfish (Mmamba) clan in which he claimed that Kintu was a native Muganda and a member of the Mmamba, and that Nnambi was his Lubuga from the Mmamba clan (1916: 19–20). In the 1920s, the Bataka of the Heart and Lungfish clans also claimed in separate publications that Kintu was not only an indigenous Muganda, but also a member of their own respective clans. The head of the Heart clan went so far as to argue that the men of his clan should all be regarded as princes! He submitted his claim first to the Lukiiko, the Buganda parliament, and then to the Head of the Princes (*Ssaabalangira*), Ggomotoka. Ggomotoka, of course, refused to recognize the Heart clan's claim to royalty, and he later rejected a similar claim by a member of the Bushbuck clan.

This was not the first time that certain clans had tried to make Kintu one of their own. During the reign of Kabaka Kateregga in the early seventeenth century, the Leopard clan made such a claim and was severely persecuted for it (Kiwanuka 1971b: 42). Some members of the Lion clan did the same and were forced to flee to Busoga.

In the 1920s, Ggomotoka wrote a series of essays in the Catholic newsletter *Munno* in which he endorsed the view that Kintu was a foreigner whose origins lay outside Buganda. Here he relied on a theory published earlier in the same newsletter by W. Kizito Tobi (*Munno* April–May 1914). Tobi took as his premise the fact that the kings of Buganda and Bunyoro were traditionally referred to as brothers, which Mutesa had emphasized in trying to persuade Mukuma Kabalega of Bunyoro to adopt Islam (Mukasa 1938: 17). Drawing on Nyoro informants and on traditions collected in Busoga, Tobi's version of the story identified Kintu as Rukidi's younger twin brother, Kato (whom Nyoro royal accounts identified as Kimera), and said that Kintu and Rukidi parted company before they reached Bunyoro. Kintu then traveled south through southern Busoga, meeting several clan leaders who joined him on his journey to Buganda, where he eventually became the first Kabaka.

The important point about this new history is that it utilized traditions from outside Buganda to uphold the royal tradition about Kintu's foreign origins, thereby lending "objectivity" to Ganda dynastic tradition. In endorsing this account, Ggomotoka recognized that it made Kintu a member of the royal Bito (Bushbuck) clan of Bunyoro, and that the Ganda princes were therefore members of the Bito dynasty. Ggomotoka explained, however, that although according to this account the Ganda princes were once members of the Bito clan, they had changed their clan affiliation in Buganda by taking the totems of their mothers' clans. At the same time, Ggomotoka denied the implication that this account entitled members of the Ganda Bushbuck clan to be regarded as princes, as one clan member had assumed (*Munno* December 1922).

As far as Ggomotoka was concerned, the new version showed that Kintu did not belong to any Ganda totemic clan, and that his Bataka opponents were therefore wrong in thinking that he was an indigenous Muganda. In defending the new version, Ggomotoka accused the Bataka-backed nativist school of trying to "mislead the people" (an expression that implies political disloyalty and subversion) and of ignoring the authority of royal tradition, which, he pointed out, was best known by Kintu's descendants. Like Kaggwa, Ggomotoka dismissed the stories about the pre-Kintu rulers as "mere legends" (*lufumo bufumo*), and he cited clan traditions, recorded by Kaggwa, which stated that some of the clans met Kintu when he came into the country and that others had come with him (*Munno* December 1920). Ggomotoka therefore upheld Kaggwa's version of the Kintu tradition as the legitimate tradition of the royal establishment, because it protected the monarchy from clan ambitions. To call Ggomotoka's version of the Kintu story a fraud directed at Europeans, as Twaddle proposes (1974), is clearly to miss the point.

Ggomotoka did take note of one of his Ganda critics who pointed out that if Kintu came from outside Buganda, then Europeans might feel free to displace the Baganda from their country on the grounds that they were not the original inhabitants. To this Ggomotoka responded that the Europeans themselves had migrated into Europe, implying that Europeans had no greater claim to their lands than the Baganda to theirs. As for Kintu's heavenly origins, Ggomotoka drew on his missionary education and dismissed this view by saying that Jesus Christ was the only person known to have come to earth from heaven.

The originality of Ggomotoka's new version lay in its conflation of the Nyoro tradition about Kimera with the Soga tradition about Kintu. This, however, did not change the essentials of the Ganda royal tradition. Kintu was still a foreigner; Buganda was founded independently of Bunyoro, and its dynastic continuity reached all the way back to Kintu.

4

The King's Four Bodies: Ritual Change, 1856–1971

In Chapter 3, we saw that elaborate ceremonies marked the death and succession of the Kabakas of Buganda. These rites were perhaps the most effective expression of royal ideology. During the colonial period, when the kingship was virtually powerless, the ceremonies were greatly modified but still performed under colonial authority as an expression of the ancient legitimacy of the throne. In 1971, the rites were held for the last time at the reinterment of Buganda's last Kabaka, Sir Edward Mutesa II, who had died in exile in London two years before. This time they marked the end of the kingship, and inadvertently helped to legitimate General Idi Amin's military regime.

In this chapter I do not intend to examine the entire ritual program, which traditionally lasted for more than five months. Instead, I shall concentrate on a single theme: the theory of kingship as expressed in royal body symbolism. The installation rites were not merely ceremonial trappings, as previous accounts suggest, but primary components in what Clifford Geertz has called the "symbolics of power."[1] Ritual symbolism expressed the nature of the kingship by defining the royal person, for the person of the king symbolized the office he held. This is why Frazer devoted so much attention to the rites surrounding the king's body. As Mary Douglas has pointed out, "The [human] body is a complete structure. The functions of its different parts and their relation afford a source of symbols for other complex structures" (1966: 115). My concern is not with matters of ritual purity and pollution, the subject of Douglas's study, but with the theory of kingship that the royal rites and body symbolism expressed. Here I follow the lead of Ernst Kantorowicz's masterly study, *The King's Two Bodies*. This work, which Kantorowicz calls a

study of "medieval political theology," argues that European royal ceremonies, especially funerary ritual, articulated a theory of state. I shall
also be concerned with the changes that occurred in the royal body symbolism before, during, and after the colonial period, roughly from the
accession of Mutesa I in 1856 to the reinterment of his great-grandson,
Mutesa II, in Buganda in 1971. Here it is evident that royal ritual was a
means not only of expressing political change, but of transacting it.

The Person of the King

In Chapter 1, I noted that Roscoe recognized correctly that the person of
the Kabaka was regarded as "most sacred." Although the Kabaka was not
considered to be holy or divine, he was treated as an exalted and extraordinary personage because he was the political and symbolic center of the
state. Hence he possessed what Geertz has called the "charisma of central
authority," and may be called "sacred" in this particular sense. The king
derived all his powers from the installation ceremonies that marked his
accession to the throne. In the late nineteenth century, these ceremonies
followed a three-phase "passage" structure. In the first phase, the new
king was elected at the capital and installed as Kabaka at Buddo Hill; in
the second, he was kept secluded during the long period of mourning
until the burial of his predecessor; and in the third, he was invested as the
Ssaabataka, or Head of the Clan Heads, and installed in his palace by the
clan officials.

The state was constructed anew by the succession ceremonies, and the
king was invested with ritual images of royal power and prosperity. This
was the underlying logic of Frazer's theory of regicide. Although the
Kabakas did not kill their predecessors in order to obtain their divinity,
they did reenact the deeds of the founding kings, Kintu and Kimera, in
order to acquire dynastic legitimacy and reestablish the kingship. Each
king fought a mock combat at Buddo Hill that recalled Kintu's founding
of the kingship through conquest, and each took part in a ritual hunt that
commemorated Kimera's triumphant return to restore the throne. In this
way, every new king was identified with the founding ancestors and took
his place within the dynastic line. Henceforth, he personified both the
institution of the kingship and its history — he embodied the kingship in
his person.

The royal rites did not, of course, make the Kabaka divine, but they did
make him a symbol, the kingdom's leader and source, at once the continuation and personification of the dynastic line. As such, the king was no

longer an ordinary person but the embodiment of an idea: *obwakabaka*, or "kingship." Etymologically, the term *obwakabaka* means "the power (*buyinza*) of the Kabaka," and it refers to both the kingship and the kingdom (Le Veux 1917: 273; cf. Southwold 1973: 56). In fact, the Baganda did not distinguish between these two; they regarded both the kingship and the kingdom as the manifestations of the king's actions. Thus Southwold says that, for the Baganda, "a kingdom is produced, maintained, sustained, only by operation of kingship, that is, kingly power; equally, kingly power is realized only in operation, and it operates only within a field of a specific king, namely kingdom" (1973: 56). Enoch Mulira also points out that the welfare of the kingdom was bound up with the king's activity on the throne: "If he were an active *Kabaka*, then the whole kingdom was on the move, but on the other hand, if he were inactive, things went wrong" (1945: 48).

The Kabaka's extraordinary role as the pivotal figure of the kingdom placed him outside of the general community; he was made socially invisible and the object of the greatest fear and respect (*kitiibwa*), a kind of sacred personage whose exalted status was maintained by the ceremonial treatment accorded him at court and by his arbitrary power of life and death over his subjects. Richards calls such symbolic measures "keeping the king divine": "All rulers without standing armies or other institutionalized means of control have to balance on the knife edge of their people's belief, but in cases of divine kingship the pose is surely a precarious one, between god and man, between *rex* and *dux* for instance" (1969: 24).

It is a common ritual principle that whatever is sacred or exalted is ordinarily kept hidden from view, and whenever it is brought into view, it is elevated above the masses. Such was the case with the Kabaka. He was rarely seen outside his large palace enclosure, but when he did appear he was carried on the shoulders of his bearers, and no one was permitted to look directly at him. Most of the time, the king stayed in his palace, located within the capital at the juncture of the kingdom's system of roads. The royal palace was both the center of communication within the kingdom and the source of its wealth. Along the roads ran the king's messengers, who carried information by word of mouth directly to and from the monarch. The roads also conveyed the royal taxes in the form of livestock and produce, and, most important, they conveyed the king's armies, which were raised during wartime to plunder Buganda's neighbors of slaves and livestock.

Within the palace, the king held council (*kukiiko*) with his chiefs. They sat on the ground in a semicircle before the king's audience hall while he sat on a throne above them. In 1862, Speke's companion, James A. Grant, sketched a picture of this scene (Plate 5). On this occasion, Speke and Grant were given the extraordinary privilege of sitting on chairs that were level with the king's platform throne. In Grant's rendering, the king's spears and shield of office stand against the rear wall to Mutesa's right, and at his left sit several of his wives. The king was dressed in the royal manner, as he always was on such occasions. His hair was cut in the style of a cock's comb, signifying that he was the "Cock" (*Sseggwanga*; that is, the superior power) of the kingdom. He also wore beaded anklets that indicated his exalted rank above the territorial clan heads. When he walked before his council of chiefs, he affected the waddling gait of a lion to show himself as the "lion" of his kingdom. In keeping with the image of a powerful predator, he held court with a hunting dog at his side, one of a pair of such dogs that were named after those of the heroic hunting king Kimera. Speke, who was familiar with the story of Kimera's return to the throne, recognized that the "dog, spear, shield, and woman" were emblematic of the kingship of Buganda (Speke 1863: 284).

A strict code of etiquette governed the behavior of those who sat in the king's presence. Coughing, sneezing, or exposing the legs from under the robe (while sitting on the ground) were forbidden on pain of death. To enforce these rules, the king's executioners sat on the front porch of the audience hall ready to seize any offender and take him or her away. Chiefs who received royal appointments came forward and knelt before the king to express their gratitude, then threw themselves on the ground and twisted from side to side, uttering repeated thanks. Chiefs who were appointed to lead the king's armies pranced before him in front of the palace gates, vigorously thrusting their spears at him in a display of military prowess and loyalty.

Such ceremonial behavior does not, however, fully explain how the Kabaka maintained his subjects' reverence and respect, since most people did not live in the capital. In nineteenth-century Buganda, the most important means of maintaining the king's charisma was his arbitrary power to kill his subjects, a complex subject that I take up in a later chapter. Here it is sufficient to note that, while capital punishment and human sacrifice were common, Buganda was not simply a despotic state, nor was the Kabaka a brigand king. On the contrary, the Kabaka was the source of justice and order, and his state was a highly bureaucratized polity.

Nevertheless, a fundamental paradox lay at the heart of the kingship: the Kabaka was at once the chief executor of the law and a law unto himself. Capital punishment, which was a common means of maintaining order under the nineteenth-century kings, could also be employed by the king for purely personal reasons. Anyone who aroused the king's displeasure could legitimately be put to death, no matter how insignificant the offense. The king and the law were one. To quote Mulira, "They [the Baganda] put him in such a position of power that he could kill as many of them as he liked, without anyone objecting" (1945: 48). The person of the king signified ultimate authority in its most deadly form. Not being divine and lacking mystical powers, the Kabaka relied on his arbitrary power to kill to express his supremacy and inspire his subjects' fear and respect.

During the colonial period, when the Kabaka was reduced to an administrator and figurehead, he was still accorded great respect as the symbol of the nation. Later, when the British exiled Mutesa II in 1953, he became a more potent political figure, Buganda's "symbol of ultimate concern," as Welbourn aptly put it (1965: 45), a status he held until his death in 1969.

The Royal Corpse

It was Frazer who saw the regeneration of the kingship in the ritual killing of kings, and thereby made the connection between the king's body and the course of time (Feeley-Harnick 1985: 300). In Buganda, the royal corpse received special treatment that was crucial to the whole installation process. Without it, the rites could not begin, a new king could not be installed, and the royal spirit could not be placed in a shrine for posterity. The proper treatment of the corpse was therefore central to the continuity of the kingship and dynastic history.

The Kabaka's death was kept secret until the royal electors had agreed on a successor and secured the capital against impending anarchy. The period between the reigns, when all the king's chiefs left office, was literally a period without kingship and without political order. After all preparations had been made, the monarch's death was signaled at the capital by the beating of the death rhythm on the royal Mujaguzo drums. Officials announced the Kabaka's death with the euphemisms "the fire has gone out," "the Lion has released his hold on the shield," or "Buganda is quiet." No one said that the Kabaka had died. Instead, people referred to the king as having "gone away" or "disappeared," both common Ganda euphemisms for death. In reference to the Kabaka, these expressions also recalled the disappearance of Kintu, the founder of the kingdom, who was not said to have died but to have vanished into a forest at his capital at Magonga.

The succession rites were linked to the funerary rituals. After the announcement of the king's death, the royal corpse was displayed in the palace enclosure. This confirmed the king's death and symbolized the temporary suspension of the kingship. The body was laid in state in the house of the king's principal wife, the Kaddulubaale. In ordinary funerals, the middle partition of the deceased's house was pulled down and made into a bier. The body was placed in the bier, which rested on dried plantain stalks; dried plantain leaves lay over the floor to signify death. The center pole (*eggwagi*) of the house was pulled down and burned to show that the owner had died and that his house was broken up (Roscoe 1901: 128; Kaggwa [1907] 1934: 202; Gorju 1920: 361–62). In the case of the king, who was called the Owner of Buganda, the removal of the center post of his tomb house effectively signaled that his reign had come to an end. "Buganda is dead," cried the king's chief pallbearer, "we have brought him for burial" (Roscoe 1911: 106). As this statement implies, the king's death meant that both the kingdom and the kingship temporarily ceased to exist.

Within the palace enclosure, the Kaddulubaale's house was the scene of wailing, and the royal drums sounded the funeral beat for several days and nights. The kingdom as a whole was plunged into mourning. Everyone wore a dried plantain fiber belt as a sign of death and decay, and all were forbidden to cut their hair, brew beer, or cultivate their fields. As in ordinary Ganda funerals, agriculture was curtailed to show respect for the dead. In the case of the king, the ban on cultivation lasted for five months and showed that the whole kingdom lay under the pall of the monarch's death. Nor was trade with the outside world permitted or wars undertaken beyond the borders of the kingdom. The nation's prosperity and activity, with which the living king was identified, came to an abrupt halt.

The king's death also brought to an end the peace of the realm. In Luganda, the word for "peace" (*mirembe*) also refers to a king's reign. When the king was alive and living in his palace, the royal fire that burned continuously outside the palace gates signified that the king was alive and that the kingdom was "at peace" (Nsimbi 1956b: 57). When the king died, the fire was put out and its keeper, the Musolooza, was strangled. The kingdom was no longer at peace with itself, and the forces of anarchy were let loose during the brief interregnum. All the dead king's chiefs were dismissed from office; people tried to rob one another; chiefs looted their subordinates; and all prepared to fight for or against the new king. The people remained in their compounds on guard against attack.

Having assembled a strong military force at the palace and decided on a successor, the royal electors lined up the princes in the open space (*mbuga*) in front of the palace gates. The Katikkiro, or prime minister, called for a new prince to reign. The Kasujju, the guardian of the princes, walked down the row of princes, selected the one who had been chosen, and handed him over to the Katikkiro with the words, "This is your king." The Katikkiro then told the people that the remaining princes were ineligible "squirrels," and he offered spears to any of the chiefs who wished to fight on behalf of another prince. The chiefs themselves came prepared with their own forces, and if a battle broke out, the victorious prince became king. Afterward, the rest of the princes were taken into custody, and most were killed to ensure the safety of the new king.

The next day, the king-elect and his party of electors went to Buddo Hill and performed the first part of the installation ceremonies, called "eating Buganda." The new king then went into mourning and seclusion. Although he was officially recognized as Kabaka, he was not allowed to receive public recognition, establish his palace, or build a new capital until the body of the previous king had been buried and the mourning period completed. Mourning lasted for five months. During this symbolic interregnum, the king-elect lived in a temporary enclosure (*kakomera*), which was sturdily built and surrounded by the compounds of his loyal chiefs. Here he was subject to the customary mourning restrictions. He wore old barkcloths and a belt of dried plantain fiber, ate "burnt" (uncooked) food, refrained from washing and from cutting his hair, and abstained from sexual activity. These prohibitions, which expressed the presence of death (*olumbe*), lasted until the end of the mourning period, at which time death was "destroyed" (*kwabya olumbe*) by rites of cleansing, celebration, and the enshrinement of the king's jawbone (Roscoe 1911: 103–11; Kaggwa [1907] 1934: 4–18). The mourning period was a time of political transition; old chiefs left office, new chiefs were appointed, and succession wars were fought and settled. During this time, the Mugema, the governor of Busiro, retained possession of the royal Mujaguzo drums so that no rebel prince might seize them and have himself proclaimed king.

Meanwhile, the body of the king, representing the defunct kingship, was taken to Busiro county under the supervision of the Mugema, the Kaggo (the king's ritual representative), the Ssaabaganzi (the king's maternal uncle), and the Ssebatta (the head of the royal executioners). The body was eviscerated, washed in beer, pressed, and dried over fires in order to preserve it during the five-month period. The new king or his representative then went to Busiro and placed a barkcloth over the corpse. This signaled the beginning of the final installation ceremonies. The corpse was taken to the royal cemetery at Merera and placed on a frame over a shallow grave inside a tomb house from which the center pole had been removed, and the front porch was collapsed over the entrance. Later, the skull was detached and the jawbone was removed, washed in milk and beer, and presented to the new king.

The rites of succession to hereditary office were part of the funerary procedures and linked to the corpse of the deceased, thereby establishing the continuity of the succession. In clan ceremonies, from which the royal rites derived, the heir was appointed by the clan authorities before the funeral. Upon the death of the incumbent, the heir was required to pass under a barkcloth held over the body or to cover the body with a barkcloth or, if he arrived late, to spread a barkcloth over the grave. In each case, the barkcloth rite (*kubiika akabugo*) showed that the individual who performed it was the designated heir to the office, land, and wives of the deceased. At the end of the mourning period, the heir was installed by clan officials at the estate of the deceased. He was also invested with a new barkcloth and with the spear and shield of office, and seated on a stool before the house of the deceased with his clan sister (*lubuga*) to receive his clan's acknowledgment of his succession.

The royal installation ceremonies followed the same pattern, except that they included two investitures instead of one. At Buddo Hill, where Kintu is said to have founded the kingship, the king was installed in the Kabakaship by the Semanobe and the Makamba, the guardians of Buddo. But the new king could not exercise the full power of the kingship until the end of mourning. At that time, the clan officials invested him with the robes of Kimera, making him the Ssaabataka, or Head of the Clan Heads. The king-elect's act of "covering with barkcloth" (*kubiika akabugo*) was therefore a necessary prelude to his final installation as king. It showed that the chosen prince was not only the new Kabaka, but also the heir to the headship of the clans. As such, he was qualified to receive the title of Ssaabataka, which would give him authority over all the Bataka and hence authority over the kingdom as a whole. He would then have the right to establish his capital and build his palace. The performance of the barkcloth rite was thus the first step in the second phase of the installation process, which began after the burial of the king and the end of mourning.

Before his death in 1884, Mutesa explicitly forbade the practices of embalming the royal corpse and removing the skull and jawbone. He also made his chiefs promise to bury him in his own palace instead of at the royal burial ground at Merera (Kaggwa [1907] 1934: 17).

Mutesa's funerary reforms apparently were motivated by both political and religious considerations. According to Kaggwa, Mutesa announced his burial instructions immediately after launching an attack on the office of the Mugema. The Mugema, who was the head of the Vervet Monkey clan, was the governor of Busiro county and the guardian of the royal shrines located in Busiro. As such, he was known as the "Katikkiro [prime minister] of the Dead" and played an important role in the royal funerary procedures. He was also the chief investor of the king, the one who made him "Kimera" and Ssaabataka; in this capacity, he was known as the "Father of the Kabaka" (*Nakazadde*). For centuries, the Mugema was the highest ranking clan head; his was the last of the county governorships to remain in clan hands, the rest having been usurped by the throne over the years. Sometime after Mutesa became king (Kaggwa does not say when), he accused the Mugema of shirking his duties by not accompanying the body of Mutesa's father, Ssuuna, to its burial place. Mutesa remarked sarcastically, "If he is called the 'Father of the Kabaka,' does he give birth only to the living [and not the dead king]?" (Kaggwa [1907] 1934: 16–17). Mutesa took the governorship of Busiro away from the Mugema and gave it to a member of the Grasshopper clan. In 1879, during another purge of senior chiefs, he gave the Mugemaship to a Muslim favorite from the Pangolin clan, but he was eventually forced to return the office to its rightful clan. Mutesa also abolished the Mugema's mortuary duties, together with those of the Ssebatta, Kasujju, and other clan officials, whom he accused of charging exorbitant fees and of "torturing" the royal corpse.

Mutesa's intention seems to have been to bring the royal mortuary practices under the sole supervision of the monarchy, and to preserve the integrity of the royal person even after death. The clans, which over the decades had lost much of their power over the king, now lost their ritual control over the disposition of his body.

Mutesa's reforms may also have been based on Islamic notions about the afterlife. In 1869, two years after Mutesa began to keep Ramadan (which he kept for ten years in succession), Kaggwa says that Mutesa consulted with his senior chiefs (some of whom had already converted to Islam) and his Arab friend Khamis ibn 'Abdullah about the reburial of his father's remains. Upon their advice, Mutesa ordered Ssuuna's body to be disinterred from the graveyard at Merera in Busiro and brought to Wamala, rejoined with its jawbone, and reburied in a tomb inside Ssuuna's shrine. Afterward, Mutesa disinterred and rejoined the bodies and jawbones of eight other kings in similar fashion (Kaggwa [1907] 1934: 80; [1901] 1971: 160). Mutesa's actions probably stemmed from his acceptance of the Muslim doctrine of bodily resurrection, a subject that he is known to have discussed with his Muslim teachers, and from the desire to see that his ancestors would be resurrected intact. His own instructions to be buried "with my head whole" were most likely given for the same reason. Mutesa also prohibited the customary looting that occurred after the death of the king (Zimbe 1939: 85–86), perhaps with the intent of abolishing the brief interregnum following the king's death, thereby smoothing the transition for his successor.

The effect of Mutesa's burial reforms was to shorten the succession ceremonies considerably, which enabled his son, Prince Mwanga, to gain a hold on the throne more quickly than usual. Mutesa died on October 9, 1884, and two or three days later Mwanga's first act of succession was to place a barkcloth over his father's body. The body lay in state for a day or two and then was buried beneath the floor of the palace, as Mutesa had requested. This occurred just five days after Mutesa's death (Zimbe 1939: 72) instead of the usual five months. After spending two days at the estate of one of his chiefs, where he was protected by 7,000 armed men, Mwanga went to Buddo and was installed in the Kabakaship. A few days later — less than two weeks after Mutesa's death — he declared the end of mourning and was installed as Ssaabataka with full authority over the kingdom.[2]

The relative swiftness of Mwanga's installation was almost certainly the doing of Mutesa's powerful Katikkiro, Mukasa. Mutesa had designated Mwanga as his heir, and Mukasa, who was devoted to Mutesa's wishes, wanted to secure the young prince's succession over the opposition of some of the senior chiefs. After Mutesa's death, Mukasa assembled 4,000 armed men at Mutesa's palace to protect Mwanga during the barkcloth ceremony. On this occasion, the eighteen-year-old Mwanga was so frightened that despite encouragement from Mukasa he dropped his corner of the barkcloth. A few days later, Mwanga declared the end of mourning, almost certainly on Mukasa's advice, and thus set the stage for the early completion of the installation (Zimbe 1939: 69–84). Undoubtedly, this helped to forestall resistance to Mwanga's appointment, for the traditional five-month mourning period had been the time when political adjustments occurred. Having been so quickly installed on the throne, the young and ambitious Mwanga was uneasily poised between the old and the new. Almost immediately he began to collide with the older chiefs, both pagan and Christian, and these conflicts eventually led to his downfall four years later.[3] Had the succession process not moved so rapidly, owing to Mutesa's ritual reforms, Mukasa and the older chiefs would have had greater opportunity to impose their will on the young Mwanga before he came to the throne and began to turn against them.

The Royal Corpse in Modern Times

The link between succession and the royal corpse made possession of the king's body all-important. Semakula Kiwanuka has pointed out that "the prince who had it [the corpse] would be the prince who performed the funeral rites and then went through the accession ceremonies" (1971b: 82). This meant, in effect, that a prince could not succeed to the throne while the Kabaka was still living and that the prince who had the dead king's body would succeed almost automatically after performing the barkcloth rite.

Exceptions to both rules occurred during the colonial period, however, when the reduction of the king's powers led to a corresponding loss of the political significance of the royal corpse. In 1910, the British protectorate government agreed to return to Buganda the body of Kabaka Mwanga, who had died in exile in the Seychelles in 1903. Without the body, Mwanga's successor, the young prince Daudi Chwa II, could not be properly installed. To be sure, in 1897 Katikkiro Apolo Kaggwa and his rebel chiefs attempted to install the infant Daudi Chwa in the Kabakaship after the defeated Mwanga fled the country. In a bogus rite, Kaggwa and his chiefs took the one-year-old Chwa to the palace gates at Mmengo, where the Mugema placed him on the Nnamulondo stool of succession and robed him in ceremonial barkcloths of the Ssaabataka. Two spears and a shield were held over him, and he was made to strike the Mujaguzo drums, after which it was declared that he had "eaten Baganda." An eight-year-old girl was also robed in barkcloth and installed as the Lubuga (*CMS Intelligencer* December 1897: 912; Mullins 1904: 98; Kaggwa [1901] 1971: 208). But this was a trumped-up ritual, and everyone knew it. Many Baganda therefore continued to regard the exiled Mwanga as their Kabaka until he died in 1903 (Tucker 1908: 347; *Uganda Journal* 1947: 118; Mutesa II 1967: 58). In the meantime, Kaggwa and the other regents, in collaboration with the British, attempted to promote Prince Chwa's legitimacy by holding annual celebrations of his "accession," as the British called it (*Uganda Journal* 1942: 145–46).

After Mwanga's death, Kaggwa and the regents sought the return of his body. With it, they could legalize Chwa as Mwanga's heir in the traditional manner and legitimate their own regency as well. In August

1910, the body was brought back to Buganda, and Mwanga, who had been dethroned in life, was accorded full royal honors at his burial in order to effect the succession. His body was taken to Mutesa's tomb and laid in state. The Kasujju took the fourteen-year-old Daudi Chwa to Mwanga's coffin and presented him to Katikkiro Apolo Kaggwa with the words: "Here is our Kabaka." The young king then placed a barkcloth over Mwanga's coffin, assisted by Kaggwa, the Ssaabaganzi, and the Kaggo (Kaggwa [1907] 1934: 91). Thus Chwa performed the first act of his succession over a decade after it had been declared by Kaggwa and his rebel chiefs. The next day, Chwa was invested as Ssaabataka by the Mugema and Kasujju on behalf of the clans and installed in his palace at Mmengo.[4]

However, despite this attempt to return to traditional procedures, the ceremonies reflected the two major political changes that had occurred in the colonial kingdom: the regency of chiefs led by Apolo Kaggwa and the imposition of British rule. The power of the regency was made evident by the fact that Chwa was not allowed to proceed to Buddo Hill to be installed in the Kabakaship after covering his father with barkcloth. Instead, he was taken to the palace and installed as the heir to Kimera and as Ssaabataka by the clan heads. The regents held the Kabakaship in their hands for four more years until Chwa reached his majority at age eighteen, as prescribed by "The Uganda Agreement of 1900."[5] Then he went to Buddo Hill and "ate" the Kabakaship. Never before had the Kabakaship remained so long in the hands of the king's men.

Kaggwa and his chiefs were also the servants of the protectorate government, to which they had sworn an oath of loyalty. During the installation ceremonies, the government was represented by Bishop Albert Tucker. When Mwanga's body arrived in Buganda, it was taken first to Namirembe Cathedral, where the bishop read the first part of the burial service. The next day, the body was taken to Mutesa's tomb, where Chwa covered it with barkcloth. Bishop Tucker and his assistants then completed the burial service and placed Mwanga's body inside the tomb (*Uganda Journal* 1949: 224–25). As the most prominent colonial official participating in the burial ceremonies, Bishop Tucker effectively communicated the fact that the royal corpse, on which succession ritually depended, belonged as much to the British as to the chiefs of Buganda.

In 1939, the burial of Daudi Chwa was handled in similar fashion. As in Mwanga's case, the royal corpse no longer symbolized the temporary suspension of the kingship, nor did it have much to do with the political realities of succession. According to the Uganda Agreement, the new Kabaka had to be a descendant of Kabaka Mutesa. He then had to be elected by the Lukiiko (the king's council), but his election could not be officially recognized until it was approved by the protectorate government.

Following Chwa's death, the Lukiiko met immediately and selected Edward Mutesa II from over a dozen of Chwa's sons. That evening, Mutesa, who had just turned fifteen years old, covered his father's body with barkcloth and reappointed the ministers and chiefs of the Lukiiko. The governor, Sir Philip Mitchell, found the Lukiiko's choice of successor "most satisfactory." He therefore anticipated that the next day Mutesa and the three ministers of state would come to Government House "to go through some ceremonies before me and the succession would be completed without fuss or difficulty" (*Diaries* 22 November 1939). When Mutesa and the ministers arrived, the governor conveyed the condolences of the British Crown to the young Mutesa and spoke of his confidence in the ministers. Then Mitchell "swore in the Ministers as regents and congratulated them on their loyal and faithful service" (*Diaries* 23 November 1939). This took place in the privacy of Government House, without any other Baganda in attendance. As far as the governor was concerned, the accession was complete. All that remained were the ceremonies to be performed by the Baganda, which the governor did not attend.

Chwa's body lay briefly in state in the royal palace before being taken in procession to Namirembe Cathedral, where the bishop of Uganda conducted the service. At the Kasubi, the Ganda chiefs again brought the king's body to the bishop; it was lowered into the ground, and the bishop read the last rites. By taking charge of the royal corpse, the colonial officials conveyed the fact that they were fundamentally in charge of the succession process.

When Mutesa II died in March 1971, his body, too, played an important political role, only this time the beneficiary was General Idi Amin. In order to win all-important Ganda support for his coup d'état of January 1971, Amin called for the return of Mutesa's body from London, where the exiled Kabaka had spent his last years. Ganda royalists in London wished to have Amin declare that the Ganda throne would be restored before permitting the Kabaka's body to be returned, but the Ganda authorities at home, who were in charge of the burial rites, were overjoyed at Amin's proposal and gave their consent (Kiwanuka 1979: 66–67). For five years, the Baganda had lived without their Kabaka, and he still remained, in Welbourn's phrase, their "symbol of ultimate concern" (1965: 65). In Ganda eyes, the return of Mutesa's body meant not only the return of their beloved leader, but also the possibility of the monarchy's restoration. At this time, K. S. Katongole, the Ssaabaganzi, said that the "return of the body of the late Sir Edward Mutesa and his burial . . . anticipate a bright future . . . " (*Uganda Argus* 6 April 1971).

Although Mutesa II's funeral was entirely a Ganda affair, General Amin made it a state occasion for the purpose of legitimating his recent coup, just as Kaggwa and the British had used Mwanga's body to legitimate the colonial regency. When Mutesa's body arrived at Entebbe airport, Amin received it on behalf of the nation and stood by it to receive the presidential gun salute. Then he took the body by helicopter to Kololo Hill in Kampala, the site of Uganda's independence ceremonies in 1962. By circumventing the twenty-mile road trip through Buganda (a maneuver that disappointed thousands of Baganda who had lined the road waiting to see the Kabaka's body pass by), Amin kept the body under his control and took it to a place of national rather than local Ganda significance. Standing before the body at Kololo, Amin delivered a speech in which he reminded the Baganda that although Mutesa had been Kabaka of Buganda, he had also been president of "all" Uganda. In this way, he tried to direct Ganda loyalty from the late Kabaka to himself as the new president. Then he had the body taken to the Parliament building, where he made another speech, again emphasizing the national significance of the Kabaka's return. The next day Amin attended services at Namirembe Cathedral, where Mutesa's body lay in state. Although Amin was a Muslim, he joined with Ganda leaders and with representatives of Britain and other European countries who paid their respects at the Anglican service for the Kabaka. The following day, the *Uganda Argus* printed a report containing some of the remarks addressed to Amin as he left the cathedral: "You have saved us, Dada"; "Dada, you have redeemed us"; "Long life Dada"; "We have nothing to give you except to give you our love and loyalty. We pledge to continue to be always obedient to your government" (3 April 1971).

For the Baganda, the return of Mutesa's body raised hopes for the restoration of the kingship. With Mutesa's body in their possession, they could install Mutesa's son, Prince Ronald Mutebi, as his royal heir and successor. At Kasubi, where Mutesa's body had been taken for burial, the Kasujju brought Prince Mutebi to his father's coffin and handed him over to the former Katikkiro, J. S. Mayanja. Then Mutebi, assisted by the Kaggo, placed a barkcloth over his father's casket on top of the Uganda flag in which the coffin had been draped. Afterward, the casket was placed in front of the entrance to the tomb, and Mutebi was taken around to the rear and kept out of sight for the remainder of the ceremonies. As prayers were being said, General Amin arrived and placed a wreath at the foot of the casket. He was followed by diplomatic representatives from the African and European nations that had recognized his regime. After the departure of Amin's soldiers, the Ganda chiefs took the casket inside the tomb and placed it in a grave next to the graves of Mutesa I, Mwanga II, and Chwa II.

Initially, Prince Mutebi's performance of the barkcloth rite gave rise to some confusion about his status. Foreign Minister Wanume Kibedi said that the government had been urged not to let Prince Mutebi perform the barkcloth rite because it "would signify his virtual enthronement." The next day, Kibedi reiterated the stand of his government against the restoration of the Kabakaship. "The government," he said, "is not worried about the placing of the barkcloth on the coffin, the act being only a rite" (*Uganda Argus* 6 April 1971). As far as Amin's government was concerned, the Kabakaship had been buried with Mutesa II. This, indeed, was an important point. Until the return of Mutesa's body, many Baganda refused to believe that the Kabaka was dead and that the Kabakaship had been abolished. By arranging for the return of Mutesa's body, Amin was able to win Ganda support and to demonstrate effectively the termination of the Kabakaship.

The Ganda authorities, for their part, complied with the prohibition against installing a new Kabaka. The barkcloth ceremony, they pointed out, did not make Prince Mutebi a Kabaka, but rather Mutesa's official heir. Later, at the royal estate at Bamunanika, Mutebi was invested by the Mugema and the Kasujju as the successor to Kimera and as Ssaabataka. The royal fire was rekindled and Mutebi was paraded around on the shoulders of his bearer and taken to Twekobe, the Kabaka's house (*Munno* 6 April 1971). He was not, however, allowed to strike the royal Mujaguzo drums, nor was he taken to Buddo Hill and installed in the Kabakaship (Ssaabalangira Lukongwa, personal communication, August 1972). Investiture as successor to Kimera and as Ssaabataka gave him the recognition of the Bataka, but not the authority to govern as Kabaka. It did, however, ensure the continuation of the royal line. The royal corpse thus fulfilled its ancient function of confirming the death of the Kabaka and of legitimating the heir to the throne. But in this case, the corpse also symbolized the demise of the kingship.

The Royal Jawbone

Before Mutesa I abolished the practice of removing the dead king's skull and jawbone, they were taken from the royal corpse five months after burial. At this time, the new king told the Kaggo and the Ssaabaganzi to "go to Merera and get the Kabaka." After the removal of the lower jaw, the skull was taken back to Merera, one of the royal cemeteries, and buried near the body. The jaw was cleansed and washed in milk and beer to make it white, and the chiefs of the late king, the Kaggo, the Ssaaba-ganzi, and the Kimbugwe, drank mouthfuls of the second washing. Afterward, the jaw was decorated and given to the king, who ordered a shrine to be built for it on a hill in Busiro county. The Mugema's son, the Ssentongo, saw to the shrine's construction.

The dynastic accounts say that the practice of removing the jawbone began with Prince Kalemeera, the alleged grandson of Kintu, who died on his way home from Bunyoro.[6] As proof of his death, the clan heads who accompanied him cut off his head and brought it to Buganda. The jawbone was removed and placed in a shrine, and a guardian was posted to watch over it. Kaggwa says that the jawbone was preserved because the king needed it in the afterlife, but he does not explain why it was selected over some other part of the body ([1907] 1934: 18–19). According to some Baganda, the jaw was removed and placed in a shrine because it was the "most important" and "strongest" bone of the body and showed that the Kabakas were strong and would not disappear from the country, as did Kintu and his son Chwa I. Roscoe says that the jawbone was preserved because the spirit (*muzimu*) of the deceased person was attached to it (1911: 113, 202). On this point, the Head of the Princes, Paul Lukongwa, told me that there was no connection between the Kabaka's spirit and the jawbone, the spirit being completely "free in the air," as he put it, and not attached to the jaw. This question is complicated by the fact that attendants at the shrines do not normally use the word *muzimu* in referring to the deceased Kabaka. Instead, they use the title Ssekabaka, the same term that is used for the jawbone relic. Thus in ordinary conversation, the Ssekabaka and his jawbone are identified. Both are referred to as "Kaba-ka," and both are located in the inner sanctuary of the shrine called the "forest." Without the jawbone, the Ssekabaka could not be enshrined. But there is also a difference between them. At the shrine of Kabaka Mulondo, the attendants said that the Ssekabaka kept close watch over his jawbone and that his vigilance had foiled attempts to steal it and once caused the stolen jaw to be returned.

The Kabaka's jawbone, bound in barkcloth and decorated with cowrie shells, was placed in a wooden bowl and set on a "bed" of cowries and beads. The cowries and beads were those that had been presented to the king by the clan heads (*bataka*, including the heads of major lineages) who had succeeded to office and been confirmed by the king during his reign. Known as the king's "wealth," the cowries and beads represented the Kabaka's authority over the clans and the clan heads' allegiance to the king as Ssaabataka. The more the king possessed, the greater his honor, and he was said to have "many chiefs with him." According to Roscoe, the jawbone and its bowl were wrapped in barkcloth, decorated all over with cowries, and made into a large conical container about two and one-half feet high and eighteen inches at the base. Roscoe has described this structure as an "effigy of the king" (1911: 109–10), although the photograph in his book does not look at all like a human figure. Earlier, however, Roscoe wrote that the cone containing the jawbone was wrapped in barkcloths "until it assumed the proportions of a man" (1902: 45; cf. 1901: 130), suggesting that perhaps the reliquary he photographed was only part of a full-size effigy figure.

In 1972, I saw a large, effigy-like figure at the shrine of Kabaka Mulondo, one of the kings whose jawbone Mutesa I did not reattach to the body. The jawbone container sat at the top of a tall, four-legged stand that was about five feet high and was referred to as a "chair" (*entebbe*). The stand was completely wrapped in barkcloth, which concealed the conical jawbone container at the top, and covered by a large piece of embroidered cloth. Although I did not ask whether this figure was intended to be an effigy—the attendants simply referred to it as the "Kabaka"—the whole assemblage looked something like a standing or seated human figure. Spears, a dagger, and a shield were attached to its sides at the position of the figure's "arms." Unlike the small jawbone reliquaries that Roscoe photographed and saw on the throne-platforms (*mwaliiro*) of the shrines, Mulondo's effigy stood behind the platform in the inner "forest" (*kibira*) and was visible only through an opening in the barkcloth curtain. Kimbugwe's shrine at Bugwangya also contained a tall, four-legged frame at the rear of the building, but it no longer held the jawbone container, which had been deposited elsewhere for safekeeping. Kimbugwe was another of the kings whose jawbone Mutesa had not reburied in 1869.

Unlike the funerary effigies of the European monarchs, the Kabaka's reliquary did not serve as a symbol of the undying nature of the kingship during the royal funeral. In Renaissance England and France, the funerary effigies were made immediately after the death of the king and were displayed during the funeral procession. They symbolized the "dignity" of the monarchy, which was vested in the body politic and "did not die" (*dignitas non moritur*), in contrast to the personal aspect of the monarchy, which died with the king (Kantorowicz 1957: 419–37; Giesey 1960: 79–92). From this practice, the English derived the Christologically inspired doctrine of the king's "two bodies," the one corporate and immortal, the other personal and temporal. The king's resplendent effigy, displayed on top of his casket, symbolized the triumph of the royal "dignity" over death and the unimpaired continuity of the kingship despite the death of kings.

In England, the sixteenth-century doctrine of the king's two bodies superseded the medieval view that the king's death created an interregnum when the peace of the realm was destroyed and robberies and public disturbances occurred. Once the Renaissance jurists developed the doctrine of the immortal kingship, the purpose of the effigy, which represented both the immortal character of the office and the immortal aspect of the king, was to fill the gap between the death of the king and the coronation of his successor. As we have seen, in precolonial Buganda emphasis was placed on the identity between the king and the kingship, and on the discontinuity of the kingship at the time of the king's death. There was a brief, chaotic political interregnum before the new prince was chosen, followed by a long symbolic interregnum when the new king lived in seclusion during the five-month mourning period. Then the dead king was buried and his successor's installation completed. This was the pattern that Mutesa I and his son Mwanga abolished. In Renaissance France, the new king was also kept in seclusion until the burial of his predecessor, during which time the dead king was treated as though he were still alive — in effigy form. The new king, who was legally empowered from the moment of his predecessor's death, could not appear in public lest there seem to be two kings of France, an impossible situation. In Buganda, the successor was kept hidden or secluded as long as the royal corpse, which symbolized the defunct kingship, remained unburied. Only after the corpse was interred and the mourning period ended could the new king be publicly installed by the clan officials as Ssaabataka and acceed fully to the throne.

As a polity, the kingdom of Buganda consisted of the unity between the kingship and the clans. It was the clans that kept the regalia of the kingship during the interregnum and mourning period, and they conferred these emblems on the new king when they installed him in office. They also built the king's palace, supplied him with servants, and sent women to be his wives. The same fundamental unity between the king and the clans was expressed in the composition of the jawbone reliquary, the jawbone resting on the bed of beads and cowries representing the king's superiority over the clan heads.

Because political unity did not exist apart from the reign of a king, both the kingship and the kingdom were dissolved at the king's death, and the kingship reverted to the various agencies and symbols that constituted it: the chiefs who chose the king, the guardians at Buddo Hill who installed him, and the clan officials who made him Ssaabataka and invested him with the symbols of the Kabakaship. Unlike the sixteenth-century European jurists, the Baganda did not think of the kingship as something that possessed a "real" existence apart from the living king, but as something that existed only during the reign of a king. On the death of the king, every chief, except the Katikkiro, left office so that the vacancies could be filled by the new sovereign.

The kingship therefore had to be created anew at every succession. In the late nineteenth century, the installation rites began with the ceremonial repetition of Kintu's founding of the kingship at Buddo and concluded with the repetition of Kimera's return and restoration of the monarchy. The jawbone reliquaries, referred to by the kings' names, represented the individual Kabakas, not the kingship itself, which had no existence apart from the living kings. Nevertheless, the idea of the historic continuity of the kingship clearly existed in the jawbone relics contained in the royal shrines in Busiro, which is one of the reasons why the Baganda continued to hold the shrines in such high regard.

Although the jawbone reliquary represented the king's person, it did not exhibit his personal likeness, as did its European counterpart, the funerary effigy. A year after the new king was installed in his palace, the jawbone was installed in its shrine. The shrine was also called a "palace" (*lubiri*), and it possessed its own retinue of officials, all of whom had served during the reign of the deceased king. The deceased king was thus installed in a palace in Busiro county where his royal ancestors dwelled, while his successor took up residence in a new capital. The jawbones were kept hidden in the shrines and never taken out to public view, perhaps because they belonged to the "hidden," spiritual world of the ancestors.

It might be said, then, that the Kabakas of Buganda possessed two "bodies" whose parts were united in the living king but separated after death: (1) the king's physical person, which at death represented the mortal aspect of the Kabaka and the demise of the kingship; and (2) the king's enshrined jawbone reliquary, which represented the Kabaka and his reign.

As in seventeenth-century France, the disappearance of the royal reliquary-effigy in Buganda coincided with the development of monarchical absolutism. Like the "Sun King," Louis XIV, who equated the state with himself ("L'état, c'est moi"),[7] Mutesa I and his son Mwanga II began to think of Buganda as consisting primarily of themselves. In accusing the clan authorities of "torturing" the royal corpse and in objecting to the fees they charged, Mutesa was objecting to ritual actions that signified, among other things, the once-powerful role of clans in the affairs of the kingship. By prohibiting their ritual manipulations of the royal corpse, Mutesa intended, perhaps, to abolish this expression of clan control over the person of the king.

Mutesa's thinking may have been the culmination of a process that originated when his father, Ssuuna II, began reattaching some of the royal jawbones to their skulls. In this way, Ssuuna, perhaps under the influence of Islam, may also have intended to restore the integrity of the royal person. By suppressing the political anarchy associated with the king's death, Mutesa's Katikkiro also suppressed any evidence of an interregnum, implying that a new reign (*mirembe*, or "peace") began immediately after Mutesa's death.

The Royal Medium

The person of the deceased Kabaka was also represented by a spirit medium through whom he maintained contact with the living king. The Ganda view was that a person's heart (*mutima*) became a spirit (*muzimu*) after death. The spirit could travel in the air and inflict illness on people. In the case of important chiefs, the spirit took possession of someone at the grave site and was periodically offered beer in order that its benevolence toward the living be secured. Possession lasted about a year, and then the spirit left the grave site and went to the underworld of the dead (*magombe*), whence it was reborn among the chief's descendants, the common fate of everyone about two years after death.

In the case of kings, spirit mediumship lasted indefinitely, through generations of mediums, and the royal spirit was never reborn. Soon after the jawbone had been installed in its shrine, a medium, called a "bearer" (*mukongozzi*), became possessed by the Ssekabaka. According to Roscoe, the mukongozzi was a person who had served the king. When the spirit came upon him, he spoke as the king used to speak and acted as the king had acted, imitating his gestures and mode of walk (1921: 151; cf. Kaggwa [1907] 1934: 16). The attendants at the shrine asked the medium questions about the Kabaka's personal life to which, presumably, only the Kabaka and his close associates knew the answers. If the medium's answers and ritual behavior while possessed proved convincing, he was formally "married" to the Ssekabaka and took up permanent residence as his "wife" at the shrine. The mediums I encountered in 1972 were both male and female, and I was told that they could belong to any clan; normally, there was only one medium to a shrine.

Sometime before his death, Mutesa I ordered that anyone who pro-
fessed to be a medium for his spirit be made to read the Koran, because
he himself was able to read it. Mutesa also ordered that the would-be
medium be given his rifle to shoot down birds in flight, as Mutesa himself
was able to do. These tests, Mutesa claimed, would prevent "liars" from
imitating him. It seems clear that Mutesa proposed these tests because he
did not believe in the mediumship rites and wanted them discontinued
(Kaggwa [1907] 1934: 17; Zimbe 1939: 77–78; cf. Mackay 1908: 161). One
of Mutesa's custodians told Roscoe that Mutesa put a stop to anyone
representing his father's spirit and did not want anyone impersonating
him either (Roscoe and Kaggwa 1906: 52).[8]

The purpose of the mediumship ceremonies was twofold: to display the
"living" spirit of the deceased kings, and to maintain the connection
between the royal ancestors and the living monarch. At regular ceremonies, held at the time of the new moon (or even daily, according to
Roscoe), the mediums became possessed by the royal spirits, danced in
the shrines, greeted royal visitors, and received offerings of beer and
requests for health and prosperity. The deceased king's court was arranged as though he were alive, and the assembled officials sat in front
of the royal throne-platform, where the king's spirit was supposed to
be present. The mediums also sent private messages to the king about
matters of state and warned him about the possibility of war and rebellion. Although the royal ancestors were specifically protectors of the
throne, they served as guardians of the nation as a whole, like the war
gods Kibuuka and Nnende. Ontologically, the gods (*lubaale*) and the
royal ancestors (*Bassekabaka*) were identical; that is, both were spirits
(*mizimu*) of former human beings. But the gods' independence of the
kingship and their foundation within the clan system gave them greater
powers and enabled them to oppose, even kill, the king for the sake of the
kingdom.

It is difficult to estimate the significance of the royal mediums in the
affairs of the precolonial kingship. During his early years on the throne,
Mutesa I is said to have paid special attention to the spirit of his father,
Ssuuna II. He had a small shrine (*ssabo*) built within the capital so that
he could pay his respects to Ssuuna's Twin symbol and receive messages
from his medium (Roscoe 1911: 113, 283–84; 1921: 151–52). Speke reported that when Mutesa received warnings from Ssuuna in dreams,
telling him to kill someone who was dangerous to him, the order was
carried out (1863: 424). Several times during his reign, Mutesa also held
mass executions at Ssuuna's shrine at Wamala, once at its inauguration
and again whenever it was rebuilt. The last of these occurred in 1879,
when an estimated 2,000 people were killed. Ssuuna's shrine was also

linked to Mutesa's capital by a road that ran some seven miles directly to the capital. Messages and offerings presumably traveled back and forth along this route. Newly appointed chiefs also went to Ssuuna's shrine to give thanks for their appointments after paying their respects to the three Kabakas at the capital: the king, the Queen Mother (*Nnamasole*), and the Queen Sister (*Lubuga*) (Ashe [1889] 1970: 109). Ssuuna's spirit therefore played an important role in the appointment and dismissal of chiefs. Ssuuna's shrine was governed by his Royal Sister, who had succeeded to the kingship with him, and it was administered by Ssuuna's former Katikkiro, together with the former Kimbugwe (keeper of Ssuuna's Twin), the Kaggo, and a large retinue of other former officials and wives belonging to Ssuuna's court.

Yet despite the apparent regularity of the mediumship rites, and apart from two notable instances when Kintu's spirit spoke to Kabaka Nakibinge and to Kabaka Mawanda (Kaggwa [1901] 1971: 26, 71–73), the chronicles give no information about the transactions between the Kabakas and their ancestors. This suggests that the ancestors' role was not of great significance in the politics of the nation. The mediums, it appears, were primarily ritual figures who kept alive the spiritual reality of the deceased kings by regularly "holding court" (*kukiika mbuga*) at their shrines. In contrast to the living kings, who heard legal cases and delivered political pronouncements, the mediums heard prayers for health and prosperity from the shrines' attendants and delivered ritual greetings. Although the royal mediums gave political advice to the king, this function must have been largely an extension of their ritual duties and of minimal political importance. Nevertheless, it is clear that during the early period of Mutesa's reign, the royal mediums played an important role in the politics of the kingdom. In abolishing this office, Mutesa was able to increase his power over the traditional authorities.

In 1972, no medium impersonated Mutesa I at Kasubi. His immediate descendents, Mwanga, Chwa, and Mutesa II, who were buried with him also lacked mediums. But Mutesa I's abolition of the office of royal medium did not extend to the other shrines, most of which did have mediums affiliated with them. Every shrine was the pride of the clan whose "son" became king; it was kept up by this clan and by the clans who supplied men and women to fill the posts held by the original officials at the king's court. For a shrine to function, it had to have a medium who became the "bearer" of the king's spirit and impersonated him during the ceremonies. Any clan might supply this figure, who then became the focus of the shrine's activity.

In colonial times, Mutesa II, who was educated at the University of Cambridge, gave funds to rebuild the shrines, but he had no use for the advice his ancestors communicated to him through the mediums. According to Audrey Richards, these messages contained only general pronouncements, rather like a daily horoscope, which Mutesa said he ignored (personal communication 1977; cf. Taylor 1958: 210). Nevertheless, the shrines remained active centers of royal ritual both for the clans and for members of the royal family, who often visited them.

The Royal Twin

A fourth symbolic representation of the deceased Kabaka was his *mulongo*, literally, "twin." Although the king himself was not regarded as a twin and was never referred to as such, he was said to have been born with a double. All royalty, not just kings, were said to have had a stillborn twin at birth. The stump of a prince's or princess's umbilical cord was preserved and placed in the cylindrical base of a tall, vaselike object. The base consisted of tightly wound barkcloth and was about five inches in diameter and eight inches high. A long loop handle, fashioned from a thick fiber cord bound with barkcloth, was fastened to the top (Plate 4). The base and handle were decorated with small red, yellow, and blue beads in a zigzag pattern. When standing upright, the Twin is about two and one-half to three feet high.

Formerly, the Twin symbols were egg-shaped, about six or eight inches in diameter, with a leather strap, which served as a loop handle, attached to one end (Plate 4). The egg-shaped container appears to have been made from a lump of barkcloth-covered clay, with cowhide sewn tightly around it. The outside was covered with cowrie shells and beads and decorated with a triangle made of yellow, blue, and red beads. Nowadays, the Baganda refer to this form of Twin as the "old" style (of which only a few examples remain), in contrast to the cylinder-and-handle style, which they say is of more recent construction.[9] However, the latter style has been in existence since at least 1862 when Speke and Grant described cylinder-and-handle containers at Mutesa's court. It may also be noted that the more recent style resembles the umbilical-cord containers made for the siblings of actual twins. These held the stump of the umbilical cord wrapped in barkcloth and attached to a loop of string. Stumps were worn around the neck during a special ceremony "to honor and please the twins" of the family and to protect the children from the twins' dangerous powers (Mair 1934: 48, plates 1 and 4).

As for the actual nature of the royal Twin, Roscoe initially thought it was made from the placenta (1901), since the placenta is sometimes spoken of as a twin (cf. Mair 1934: 42), but he later discovered that the Twin was thought to exist in the dried stump of the umbilical cord (Blackman 1916: 199). The placenta itself was regarded as a second child (literally, "the child who is behind"), and, according to Roscoe, its ghost became attached to the royal umbilical cord (1911: 235).

Kaggwa states that the twin was made from a long clot of blood (*ebbuba eggwanvu-wanvu*) that was "born" after the placenta ([1907] 1934: 194), a view that was held by Ssaabalangira Lukongwa as well. However, a member of the Leopard clan, the clan whose duty it was to decorate the royal Twins, told Kaggwa that the Twin was made from the stump of umbilical cord (*kalira*) taken from the navel of the child (Kaggwa [1912] 1949: 62).

The Twin symbols were cared for by the mothers of the princes and princesses, and they accompanied their human counterparts throughout their lives, because the health and welfare of the person was thought to be bound up with them. Princes, who became kings, gave them names that expressed attributes of royal power and authority. The Twin was clearly personified and endowed with mystical powers. Kaggwa says that in Busiro the Twins were cared for as though they were "the living kings themselves" ([1907] 1934: 129). Today, attendants at the royal shrines refer to the Twin as the "Kabaka." They also refer to the base (containing the umbilical-cord stump) as the Twin's "stomach" and to the loop handle as its "arms." When the Twin is wrapped in barkcloth, they say that it is "dressed." Like a human twin, the royal Twin is also wrapped in bbombo vine on ceremonial occasions; and like the living king, the royal Twin is carried on the right shoulder of its bearer (Plates 7 and 8).

Surprisingly, the Baganda appear to possess no myth or legend that explains why every king was born with a double. The first reference to a royal Twin in the dynastic accounts is to the Twin of Kabaka Kimera, the alleged great-grandson of Kintu, who came from Bunyoro to claim the vacant throne. Kimera, whom the Banyoro regard as the twin brother of the founder of the Bito dynasty, is said to have buried his Twin symbol after the death of his mother, Wannyana, who used to care for it. Five generations later, it was found by Kabaka Tebandeke and placed in Kimera's shrine at Bumera, where it was cared for by a descendant of Kimera's mother "in much the same way as Wannyana herself had nursed Kimera." Thereafter, the account says, Tebandeke's children no longer died because Kimera's Twin, which had been killing them, had been found and reinstated in the shrine (Kaggwa [1901] 1971: 58). Possibly the idea of a royal Twin symbol originated at this time as a means of protecting royal offspring.

Whatever its origins, the Twin played an important role in the kingship. During the king's lifetime, it was guarded by the Kimbugwe, who was the second-ranking minister of state. The Twin had its own house in the Kimbugwe's compound, which was located outside the palace enclosure to the right side of the palace gates. The Twin was carefully attended to and exerted a certain mystical influence on both the king and the kingdom. It was treated as though it were both a living child and a powerful charm. At the time of the appearance of the new moon, the Kimbugwe took the Twin out of its house and placed it in the doorway so the light of the moon would shine on it, much as Ganda mothers held their newborn children up to the light of the new moon to make them healthy and strong. The next day, the Kimbugwe took the Twin to court and placed it among several other royal charms (*mayembe*) that were brought to the king at this time. An observer described the scene: "His umbilical cord is presented to Mutesa. He rises from his seat to touch the precious talisman solemnly with his royal hand. All the assistants rise: those with swords unsheath them and brandish them, and the soldiers present arms" (Faupel 1962: 7, quoting the Rubega Mission Diary, 25 July 1880).

Speke and Grant note that Mutesa also regularly honored the Twin of his father at the time of the appearance of the new moon. Later during his reign, Mutesa had the Twins of all his royal ancestors brought to him during the first phase of the moon:

> From all corners of Busiro the bearers of the royal umbilical cords descended from their hills. When they arrived, each marched before the king, holding the vase [the Twin] in hand, the handle supported on the left shoulder: "Behold, here is you father so-and-so . . . , your father so-and-so." While saying this, each in the order of succession of the ancestors passed the venerated symbol to the monarch, standing and silent; he pressed it to his heart, as he had with each of his fathers, and the next followed. (Gorju 1920: 112)

The king's Twin also seems to have exerted a certain influence on the monarch's health. At one time during Mutesa I's long illness, his mother brought his Twin for him to hold, presumably in the hope that it might have a curative effect (Cunningham 1905: 190). During this same time, Mutesa was advised by the priests of Mukasa to dismiss the Kimbugwe, whom he had appointed from the wrong clan, and to restore the office of Mugema to the Vervet Monkey clan. Otherwise, the priests said, his Twin might wither away, which would cause his health to worsen (Wright 1971: 5). The royal Twin also accompanied the king's armies in battle, and together with the national gods and royal fetishes it lent mystical support to military campaigns.

The Kabaka and his Twin were inseparable both in life and in death. After the king died, the Twin, together with the royal jawbone, was placed in the concealed "forest" sanctuary of the royal shrine behind the barkcloth curtain. When the king or other royalty visited the shrine, both the jawbone reliquary and the Twin symbol were taken out and placed on the earthen platform (*mwaliiro*) in front of the curtain. On state occasions, the Twin was also carried in procession outside the shrine on the right shoulder of its bearer in the same manner as the living king.

The Twin was the deceased king's spiritual double. During ceremonies at the shrines, people sang songs to honor the Twins that stood before them on the throne-platform; these were the same songs that were sung in honor of newly born twins. Afterward, the attendants "dressed" the Twins in barkcloths, wrapped them in sacred bbombo vines, and held them in the same way that female relatives held royal offspring.

Roscoe, in an attempt to fit the Kabakas into Frazer's notion of the divine king, said that it was necessary that the Twin and the jawbone reliquary be placed together in the shrine "because each object had its ghost; [and] by this union of objects the two ghosts were brought together and a perfect deity obtained" (1921: 152). But this interpretation ignores the fact that the jawbone and the Twin represented very different aspects of the deceased Kabaka. Although both could be referred to as "Kabaka" and in this sense were the same, the jawbone, resting on its bed of clan beads, represented the deceased Kabaka as Ssaabataka, while the Twin represented his childlike double. Moreover, the jawbone reliquary was never taken from the shrine, whereas the Twin symbol was often taken out, carried in procession, and presented to the living Kabaka together with his other powerful fetishes.

Conclusion

During his lifetime, the Kabaka might be said to have had two "bodies": his physical person, which was regarded with considerable fear and respect, and his Twin counterpart. At death, he acquired two more: his jawbone reliquary and his spirit medium. Immediately after death, the king's corpse symbolized the end of his reign and the demise of the kingdom. The corpse was preserved throughout the five-month mourning period, and only after it had been buried could the new king complete his installation. This was an important liminal phase, a symbolic inter-regnum when political adjustments occurred. It was this phase that Mute-sa and his son Mwanga virtually abolished in seeking greater power for the king. During the colonial period, the liminal phase disappeared en-tirely, as the colonial government retained control of the royal corpse and the process of succession. After Mutesa I, the royal jawbone, represent-ing the deceased king, was no longer removed, nor was the spirit medium allowed to impersonate the deceased king or advise his successor. How-ever, Mutesa's wishes did not influence the shrines of the other kings. Without a medium to impersonate the king and without the regular gathering of attendants "to pay court" (*kukiika mbuga*) to the king's spirit, the deceased king's spiritual reality would have faded away with the decaying corpse. This fate the clans would not allow, for the royal shrines were the pride of those clans whose sons and daughters had been kings, royal sisters, queen mothers, prime ministers, and other important offi-cials at court. Hence, except for the Kasubi tomb, where Mutesa and his successors lie buried, the mediumship ceremonies lived on. Today, the royal medium continues to be the focus of these ceremonies, and the royal Twin remains the object of personal care and affection. In this way, the spirits of the kings live on, and the shrines serve as the sacred center of the now defunct kingship.

5

The Royal Shrines

The royal shrines are located in the county of Busiro, part of the ancient heartland of the Buganda. Out of respect for the royal ancestors, the palace of the king always faced Busiro, and a road ran directly from the palace, through the middle of the capital, to the shrine of the king's immediate predecessor. Thus the capital as well as the palace was oriented toward the shrines of the nation's ancestors. The temples of the national gods (*lubaale*) were also strategically located around the kingdom. From the time of its beginnings in approximately the fifteenth century, the kingdom had expanded territorially, mostly at the expense of Bunyoro. By the nineteenth century, Buganda had developed a clearly defined sense of its external boundaries and internal organization.

Geography and Ritual

It has been said rightly that nineteenth-century Buganda was a kingdom with "sharp edges: one was either in it or outside it" (Beattie 1971: 254). Territorially, Buganda was cresent-shaped, stretching some 150 miles around the northern shores of Lake Victoria from the Nile River in the east to the Kagera River in the southwest, near the present-day Tanzania border. Along this arc, the kingdom extended back from the lake some fifty to sixty miles (Frontispiece). Buganda's borders were "sharp" not only because they were visibly marked by rivers and other features of the landscape, but also because they were militarily and politically enforced. Buganda's armies regularly raided its adversaries, the kingdom of Bunyoro to the north and west and the petty chiefdoms of Busoga to the east. By exacting tribute from the small chiefdoms of Buhaya and from the kingdom of Nkore, Buganda also maintained political control over its southern and southwestern borders. Foreign visitors, who came from the south, such as Zanzibari traders and Europeans, could enter Buganda only by permission of the king, and had to wait at the southern border until word was sent from the capital. Military aggression and central administration therefore made Buganda's territorial boundaries clear, and emphasized the existence of an organized state within.

Buganda's borders were also maintained through ritual means. Human and animal victims, called *byonzire*, were taken across the border to Bunyoro and Busoga and sacrificed, both to rid Buganda of dangerous diseases and to "cleanse" Buganda's armies when they returned from military expeditions. The border regions were also protected by the national gods. In northern Bulemeezi county near Buganda's northeastern frontier with Bunyoro and Busoga stood the shrine of lubaale Kawumpuli, the god of the plague (Frontispiece). This temple contained an underground chamber in which the god remained trapped, thereby restricting the plague to this virtually unpopulated region. The temple of the war god Kibuuka (Frontispiece) was located at Mbale in Mawokota county in the western part of the kingdom, which formerly belonged to Bunyoro. According to legend, Kibuuka was a powerful Ganda warrior who was killed by the Banyoro at this site, and after his death he became a god. Kibuuka's priests advised the king about warfare on Buganda's western and northern frontiers and supervised the ritual procedures associated it. The temple of the second war god, Nnende (Frontispiece), was located in the eastern part of the country at Bukerere in Kyaggwe county, next to Busoga. Nnende's priests protected this frontier, which in the late nineteenth century was regarded as Buganda's private "back door" (*mmanyu*), through which large quantities of plundered slaves, cattle, and plantains were regularly brought into the country (Nsimbe 1950: 208). The greater part of the southern boundary of the kingdom was formed by the offshore Ssese Islands of Lake Victoria, called Nnaalubaale, or "Mother of the Gods." Mukasa was the chief god of the lake, and his main temple was located on Bubembe Island (Frontispiece). His priests governed all the traffic across the lake and controlled Buganda's large fleet of war canoes. Strategically placed and heavily subsidized by annual tribute from the king, the temples of Buganda's important national gods—Kawumpuli, Kibuuka, Nnende, and Mukasa—played an important role in maintaining the political and ritual integrity of the kingdom.

The Capital

The royal capital, called the *kibuga*, consisted of a massive concentration of thatch huts on top of a bare hill. Oval in shape, about two miles wide and three miles long, the nineteenth-century capital had a population of about 10,000 people (Gutkind 1963: 15–16). It dominated the landscape for miles around, and was the only such concentration of dwellings in the kingdom. At the beginning of each reign, and periodically thereafter, a new capital was built at a different location for sanitary reasons and sometimes for strategic military purposes. When choosing a site for the capital, the king tried to find a place that would command the roads leading to the ten administrative counties (*ssaza*) of the kingdom.

Like ancient Rome, the kibuga was the center of an efficient network of straight roads that radiated across the rolling hills and through the marshy papyrus swamps. The roads conveyed the royal taxes, in the form of livestock, plaintains, barkcloths, hoes, and laborers, from all parts of the kingdom. The roads also conveyed the king's personal messengers between the capital and the counties and subdistricts of the realm. Most important, the roads enabled the king's armies to assemble quickly for military expeditions at the kingdom's borders. Buganda was blessed with a stable climate and ample crops (mostly plantains), which were cultivated entirely by women. This freed the men for the tasks of manufacturing (large houses, pottery, weapons, and war canoes), political administration, and, above all, warfare. In the absence of international trade, the real basis of Buganda's economy was predation. At approximately six-month intervals, nineteenth-century Buganda regularly plundered Bunyoro and Busoga of cattle, women, and slaves, and exacted tribute from its neighbors to the south in the form of food and manufactured items, such as barkcloth. By the beginning of the nineteenth century, Buganda was "essentially a military machine designed for the exploitation of the wealth of its weaker neighbors, and its intricate political structure was essentially a chain of military command" (Wrigley 1964: 19). The hierarchy of command, centered at the capital, extended from the king at the top through his chiefs and sub chiefs to the peasants at the bottom.

Although the most valuable possessions in Buganda were women (both as wives and as laborers), cattle, and goats, honor (*kitiibwa*) and power (*buyinza*) were viewed as the stuff from which all wealth flowed. The division between chiefs (*bwami*) and peasants (*bakopi*) was marked, but not fixed. Each chief had a following of peasants whose primary loyalty was to him, and this loyalty was rewarded by appointment to office. In principle, no chiefship was beyond the reach of the lowliest peasant. All depended on the favor of one's superiors, and ultimately on the favor of the king, which could be rapidly won or lost. Meteoric promotions and demotions were common, making the whole structure extremely fluid.

The interlocking relationships of honor and power all converged at the capital, whose center was the palace of the king. The Kabaka's "rule" (*kufuga*) consisted of four main activities: judging legal cases (*kusala emisango*), levying taxes (*kusoloza omusolo*), waging war (*kugaba oluta-balo*), and appointing or "giving" (*okuwa*) chiefships. At the palace audience hall called Bulange, the Kabaka met almost daily with his senior chiefs and periodically with his Great Council (*Lukiiko*) of all county and department chiefs. Here legal judgments were dispensed, and people acquired honor and power in the form of chiefships. The Kabaka appointed not only his immediate subordinates, but also most of their subordinates down to the lowest level, thus exercising almost total control over his kingdom. The promotions and demotions that were effected at the palace reverberated throughout the kingdom. Since chiefships were attached to estates and to the peasants who lived on them, the acquisition and loss of a position at court affected the lives of large numbers of people.

The palace was also the educational center of the chiefly class. Chiefs from all the clans sent their brightest sons to serve as pages in the royal court, where they learned the art of politics and government, and rose to important chiefships. "He who attends court," says a Ganda proverb, "knows what's going on" (*akiika mbuga, amanya ensonga*). As the center of honor and power, as well as wealth and education, the capital was what Geertz, referring to the capital of precolonial Bali, has called "the concentrated locus of serious acts." It was the point in Ganda society "where its leading ideas come together with its leading institutions to create an arena in which the events that most vitally affect its members' lives take place" (Geertz 1977: 151). The kibuga was therefore not only Buganda's vital "nerve center," to use Fallers's characterization (1964: 104) but also Buganda's sacred center, a point to which I shall return.

The diagram of the capital, which Kaggwa prepared for Roscoe (1911), shows the capital at Nabulagala Hill (now called Kasubi) as it was in the latter period of Mutesa I's reign, around 1882 (Figure 1).[1] On top of the hill at the southern end of the capital was the large palace enclosure (*lubiri*), an oval area measuring one mile by one-half mile (Roscoe 1911: 200). In front of the palace was an open space, called the *mbuga*, or "forecourt" (2). The term *mbuga* refers to the space in front of a chief's house where his council or court is held. It is from this word that the royal capital derived its name; *kibuga* means, literally, "the large or great mbuga" (Le Veux: 1917: 78; Snoxall 1967: 130). Spatially, the large open area of the mbuga, where the king reviewed his assembled army, separated the royal palace from the chiefs' compounds. These were spread out down the flanks of the hill, imitating the arrangement of the chiefs assembled before the king in council. When the Great Council was assembled at the palace in this fashion, it was said that "the whole of Buganda (*obuganda*) is present" (Kaggwa [1907] 1934: 135). Thus the capital, with the chiefs' houses arrayed in front of the palace, represented in microcosm the whole of Buganda as a corporate polity.

Under Mutesa I, Buganda contained ten counties, or *ssazas*, each governed by a chief (*mukungu*). All the county chiefs were required to maintain compounds at the capital and to reside there for part of the year. Other royally appointed chiefs of special departments (*batongole*) were also required to reside at the capital for part of the time. The mbuga therefore divided the capital into two parts: the chiefs' area, which formed its northern half, and the king's palace, which formed its southern half. The county chiefs' residences were also located nearest to the roads leading to their counties, so that the chiefs' side of the capital formed a geographic microcosm of the kingdom as a whole. This can be seen by observing the location of the county chiefs' compounds on Kaggwa's diagram. For example, the Ssekiboobo, who was the governor of Kyagwe county, lived at the head of the road to Kyagwe (11); the Mugema, who was the governor of Busiro, lived on the road to Busiro (13); the Kasujju, who was the governor of Busujju, lived on the road to Busujju (17); and so on. The capital was therefore a copy of the realm, and the realm a copy of the capital. At the center and apex of the capital was the palace of the king; in front of the palace, the chiefs' compounds; around the capital, the realm; and around the realm, the foreign kingdoms and chiefdoms on which Buganda preyed.

To the rear of the palace enclosure was Lake Victoria, and all the land between the palace and the lake belonged to the king. Two or three private roads ran from the palace to the lake, and in times of trouble the king could escape from his chiefs undetected, board one of his war canoes, and take refuge on an island in the lake. For purposes of security, the back of the palace was surrounded by the residences of the king's wives and by officials personally loyal to the king: the Ssenero (deputy of the Kalali, the keeper of the eastern gate, called Wakole) and his subofficers; the Sseruti (chief beerkeeper of the king); the Mumbowa (executioners [20]); and four priests (Gaboga, Kolokoli, Kyobe, Mobirizi) of important royal charms (*mayembe*) that protected the king and assisted his armies.

The palace entrance imposed a right–left axis on the mbuga, determined by the right and left sides of the king's person when he stood at the palace gates to review his chiefs and their troops before military campaigns.[2] To the right of the gate was the large compound of the prime minister (*Katikkiro* [6]), who was the king's chief minister of state. In front of the Katikkiro's compound stood a small shrine for lubaale Ssemuyima and his guardian (B). This shrine contained the king's walking staff, called Ssemuyima (*muyima* means "sponsor" or "guarantor"). Next to the Katikkiro's compound was Lady Nanzigu's house (8), in which an important royal charm, called Mpeta, was kept. Lady Nanzigu was the wife of Nakibinge, the sixth Kabaka, who died fighting against Bunyoro-Kitara in the sixteenth century. She gave up her son so that the mighty warrior Kibuuka would join the Ganda cause, and one of her descendants was always married to the king. In front of Lady Nanzigu's residence stood a small shrine dedicated to Kabaka Nakibinge (C). Nearby was a temporary shrine for lubaale Mukasa (A). Mukasa was both the guardian of the lake and the guardian of the king's health. Whenever Mukasa's priests called on the king, a small temple-house was built in the mbuga. Farthest to the right stood the Kimbugwe's large compound (7), where the king's Twin symbol was kept.

Outside the palace gates, on the left side, was the royal hearth (*Ggombolola* [1]); its constantly burning flame signified that the king was alive and well. Opposite the hearth stood two other lubaale temples (3): one for Kibuuka, the other for Musisi. Like Mukasa's temple, these were not permanent structures, but were set up for the priests of Kibuuka and Musisi when they visited the capital to advise the king (Kaggwa [1907] 1934: 217; cf. Mackay 1890: 155, 167–68). Kibuuka's temple was situated so that it backed up the ssaza chiefs when they assembled their officers in the mbuga for military review before the king. Musisi, the father of Mukasa, was the earthquake god who was believed to dwell in the center of the earth and to cause earthquakes by his movements. Offerings were made to him lest he disturb the earth and cause women to miscarry. Women who desired children would invoke Musisi and rub their stomachs with earth to become fertile. The temples to Kibuuka and Musisi were paired, perhaps because of their complementary functions: Musisi protected the earthly foundations of the kingdom and its human fertility; Kibuuka protected the king and the military security of the realm. Both shrines stood opposite the palace gates on the (king's) left side, "left" signifying, among other things, women, war shields, death, and destruction. At the extreme left was the large compound of the king's cook (Mufumbiro), who was also a major palace official, and the king's drummer (Kauta), another high official. The spatial structure of the mbuga therefore united the king's most important political and religious authorities before the palace gates.

The capital was basically a secular, administrative center, the political, economic, and cultural heart of the kingdom. Unlike many ancient royal cities, the kibuga was not made in the image of the heavens or according to a divine plan. It was laid out as a microcosm of the earthly kingdom and reflected the administrative order established and maintained by the king and his chiefs. The role of the priests, who lived outside the capital, was to send messages and make occasional visits to the palace to advise the king and his council, mainly about the king's health and times to wage war.

Yet although the capital was a secular city, it symbolized the essence of the kingdom; it was where all "'serious' events," to use Shils's apt expression (1975: 259), took place. Its sociocultural centrality, hence "sacredness" in Shils's sense, was constituted precisely by "its formative power in initiating, creating, governing, transforming, maintaining, or destroying what is vital in man's life" (1975: 258), within the kingdom as whole.

Because it was the royal residence, the capital was bounded by the compounds of the six most important ritual functionaries of the kingship. These were the compounds of the Queen Mother (*Nnamasole* [22]), the Queen Sister (*Lubuga* [4]), the Second Wife (*Kabejja* [5]), the Royal Midwife (*Nabikande* [19]), the Mugema (13), and the Royal Uncle (*Ssaabaganzi* [23]). Small streams separated their compounds from the king's palace because "two chiefs cannot live on the same hill." A stream on the left side of the palace divided the king's enclosure from the palace of his Queen Sister. She was the king's ritual partner during his installation ceremonies and a Kabaka in her own right.[3] Upon the king's death, she became the overseer of his shrine and her title changed to Nnaalinnya. Beyond the palace stood the compound of the Royal Uncle, or Ssaabaganzi, who played an important role in the king's installation. Closer to the palace lived the Second Wife, or Kabejja, who kept the royal charm, called *Nantaba*. The charm was made for the king's wives at the time of his accession. It was said to have the power of attracting the king's favor, and of assisting his wives in conceiving children (Roscoe 1908; 1911: 325ff). On the right side of the palace, another stream demarcated the residence of the Royal Midwife. The midwife, who was the sister of the Queen Mother, presided over all the births and ceremonies of the king's children at the palace. A third stream ran across the northern end of the capital and separated it from the Queen Mother's palace, which stood on its own hill, called Lusaka, after the residence of Kimera's mother Wannyama. At the accession of her son, she too received the title Kabaka and was forbidden to see her son again. Opposite the Queen Mother, on the left side of the capital, lived the Mugema. As the county chief of Busiro, where the dynastic shrines were located, he was responsible for the construction of the royal shrines. He also played a key role in the installation of the king, and in this regard he was known as the "Father of the King." The palace and the capital were therefore surrounded by titled figures who were instrumental in the life cycle of the king (birth, installation, death, ancestorhood) and the perpetuation of the kingship.

Viewed as a whole, the capital may be seen as a set of three concentric circles. The inner circle was the spacious mbuga, where the king's chiefs assembled in times of war. It contained shrines for visiting priests of the national gods and the residences of the king's chief ministers of state. The next circle contained the chiefs' compounds in its northern sector and the king's palace in its southern sector. The outer circle contained the ritual officials of the kingship, one in each of the four quadrants. The inner two circles were thus devoted to the political and religious concerns of the king and the kingdom, while the outer circle was devoted to the ritual foundations of the kingship itself. In this way, the major ritual and political elements of the kingdom were structurally integrated within the spatial framework of the capital.

Royal Shrines

In Mutesa's time, the main road, which formed the central axis of the capital, branched northwest toward Busiro county and to Ssuuna's shrine at Wamala. Busiro, where the royal shrines (*masiro*) stood, derived its name from their presence in this area.[4] Today, most of the shrines are located on either side of the Hoima Road, ranging from ten to fifteen miles west of Kampala (Frontispiece). The king's palace faced in the direction of Busiro in honor of the royal ancestors (Kaggwa [1907] 1934: 127–28), and this orientation determined the axis of the capital. The road joined the two royal centers, the shrines of the ancestors in Busiro and the palace of the living king, the one religious, the other secular, each belonging to a different sphere of the kingship.

The Katikkiro of Ssunna's shrine explained that the interior architecture of the royal shrines is based on the tradition about Kintu's disappearance into a forest at Magonga. It is for this reason that the shrines of his successors contained an inner sanctuary, called the "forest" (*kibira*), where the royal spirits reside. Like Kintu, the Kabakas of Buganda were never said to have died but always to have "disappeared" or "gone away." Afterward, they were installed in the "forest" sanctuaries of their shrines. At death, each Kabaka therefore repeated Kintu's mythical transformation into a spirit, transcended time, and became spiritually available for the benefit of the kingdom.

In 1972, Kintu's shrine at Magonga was a well-built brick house with a tiled roof. It stood next to the forest grove in which he allegedly disappeared and where his spirit was thought to dwell. The shrine itself was empty, except for a small thatched hut in the center where offerings of coins were placed. Coffee berries were kept in the hut and given to visitors in return for their offerings. During my visit to the shrine, the attendant, who was a member of the Leopard clan, stood before the shrine at a respectful distance and announced the names of the visitors: "Here come your grandsons. They have come to visit you. They are from far away at Makerere [University]." Kintu's shrine house is called Ttonda, and the place where it stands is called Nnono (cf. Kulubya 1942: 55). The shrine did not contain any jawbone or Twin symbol belonging to Kintu, who is said to have disappeared without a trace. The forest grove next to the shrine is referred to as Kintu's "palace" (*lubiri*) because it is where his spirit lives. Several small huts and shelters stood near the shrine for the use of women who hold the titles Nnambi (Colobus Monkey clan), Nnaakintu (Pangolin clan), and Nnaakimera (Grasshopper clan). The whole area around the shrine is considered sacred ground; one must remove footwear when crossing it, and bloodshed is forbidden within the shrine's precincts. The Nnaalyinna in charge of the shrine lived nearby in a brick house beside the road.

In 1972, only three of the twenty-three existing shrines were constructed in the traditional, conical/thatched-roof style. Of these, the two largest were located at Kasubi-Nabulagala, where the last four Kabakas are buried, and at Wamala, where Ssuuna II is buried (Plate 1). The third was the small conical shrine of Kabaka Kyabaggu at Kyebando. All the other shrines were more durable rectangular houses having mud-and-wattle walls and corrugated-iron roofs (Plate 2). The great majority were constructed by Mutesa after his return from exile in England in 1955. He built them at the request of the shrine attendants and, in some instances, at the behest of the royal spirits themselves. Most of the shrines were indistinguishable from ordinary village houses. A few still retained the traditional *lubiri*, or "royal fence," and some had a royal entrance gate (*wankaaki*) and council huts (*bigango*). At the entrance was a gatehouse called Buggya-Bukula ("to incite the people to war"), which served the same function as the gatehouse of the living Kabaka's palace, where a guard was always on duty.

A hearth was located in the forecourt of most shrines, usually at the left. The hearth was known as the Ggombolola, the name of the hearth that burned at the palace. At the shrine, the Ggombolola was lighted only on ceremonial occasions when the spirit of the Ssekabaka manifested itself through a medium. The houses of the shrine attendants, including the royal medium, were located in the forecourt within the precincts formed by the royal fence. Behind the shrine stood thatched houses covering the graves of princes and princesses descended from the deceased Kabaka.

Each shrine had its own name or title, which was often the same as that given by the Kabaka to the house of his chief wife, the Kaddulubaale, within the palace enclosure. Thus the shrine represented the king's domestic house where his wives dwelled, and not the Palace of the Kingship (*Twekobe*), which was his official residence and the place where he slept. The names of the shrines referred to the unique qualities of the kingship, or to a distinguishing characteristic of the Kabaka himself. At Kasubi-Nabulagala, the shrine of Mutesa I (and his successors) bore the name *Muzibu-Azaala-Mpanga*, or "It is an unusual person who begets a Cock [Kabaka]," meaning that only a king can bear an heir to the throne. Ssuuna II's shrine had the name *Batanda Bezaala*, "The dignified ones [Kabakas] begat themselves." Kyabaggu's shrine was called *Bunoonya*, "The place which is looked for." Some names became popular and were used repeatedly. Thus the shrines of Kimera, Nakibinge, Mutebi, and Juuko all carried the same title, *Kanyakasasa*, or "blacksmith's forge." This refers to the well-known proverb "Just as the blacksmith's forge has coal burning all the time, yet no ashes accumulate, so it is with the king who always kills his people, yet they still go to him" (Kaggwa [1907] 1934: 28). Another popular name, *Kiryokyembi*, emphasizes the king's mortality. It derives from a proverb meaning that "death kills both peasants and kings alike" (Kaggwa [1907] 1934: 29). Mulondo's shrine bore this title before it was changed to *Mutegalla*, "It [the shrine] never closes." This title refers to the fact that the barkcloth curtain that concealed Mulondo's jawbone effigy was always kept open so that Mulondo's spirit could keep watch over the shrine. The attendants said that Mulondo's jawbone has been stolen several times, but always returned thanks to the Ssekabaka's alertness and far-reaching powers.

The modern rectangular shape has not affected the shrine's ritual symbolism. The front doorway was supposed to (but did not always) face the direction from which the Kabaka came to establish his capital. For this reason, the shrines of some kings faced the shrines of their predecessors, if they were nearby, to honor them. In recent times, the shrines located near Kasubi faced in this direction because Kasubi was regarded as the ritual headquarters of the kingship. The large shrine at Kasubi faces west in the direction of Busiro county, as did Mutesa's palace, where the shrine is now located.

A threshold separated the shrine's front porch from its interior. Upon entering, all removed their footwear, which was left outside on the front porch. A layer of sweet-smelling lemon grass covered the interior floor of the shrine, and sitting mats lay over it. During the ceremonies, it was a rule that the men sat on the left side and the women on the right. This was an explicit reversal of the normal Ganda custom, and it reflected the presence of the royal spirit within the shrine. Because the Ssekabaka was thought to reside in the "forest" and to face the front door, men had to sit on the Ssekabaka's right and women on his left.

A large barkcloth curtain that stretched from the ceiling to the floor divided the interior of the shrine into two rooms. In front of the curtain, directly under the center of the roof, stood a raised platform, called the *mwaliiro* (Plates 3 and 4). In conical-roof shrines, the mwaliiro was located under the dome of the roof between the four (or eight) central roof poles. In less elaborate shrines, the mwaliiro consisted simply of dried grass spread in a rectangular shape on the floor in front of the barkcloth curtain. During the ceremonies, goat skins lay over the front of the mwaliiro to serve as a *kiwu*, or "royal carpet," which lay at the feet of royalty when they held public audience.

A barrier of raised spears, knives, shields, and staffs stood in front of the mwaliiro. This barrier separated the mwaliiro from the open area (*mbuga*) where people sat, and partially obscured it from view. Some of the weapons and staffs were said to have belonged to the Ssekabaka, and they bore the names he had given them. Some of the daggers and knives also had double blades, and some of the shields had double bosses, which may have signified the "twinness" of royalty.

The interior of the shrine resembled the royal audience hall, or *Bulange*, of the living king. Although the proceedings in the shrine were different from those in the Lukiiko, the spatial structure was the same. The proceedings at both the audience hall and the shrine were called *kukiika mbuga*, "to attend court," and both required the same placement of people and the same formal behavior. Hence the same distinctions applied between right and left, male and female, front and rear, and high and low.

In 1862, Speke's traveling companion James A. Grant drew a detailed picture of the Great Lukiiko of Mutesa I (Plate 5). The drawing shows Mutesa seated in his audience hall before his assembled chiefs. Mutesa sits on a raised platform throne (*kituuti*), which is covered with dry grass, leopard skins, and barkcloth. The throne elevated the king above his chiefs, who are seated on the ground in front of him. A wall behind the throne conceals the interior of the audience hall. This is where the king's pages sat together with children of royal blood. A door at the rear enabled the king to enter or leave the hall quickly (*Munno* 1933: 71–74).[5] Grant depicted several princesses and wives seated on Mutesa's left, slightly to the rear, one of whom, perhaps the Second Wife (a favorite of Mutesa), is shown kneeling and offering Mutesa a drink. Against the rear wall to Mutesa's right lean his two spears and shield of office. Grant and Speke sit in front of Mutesa, to his right, having been granted the extraordinary privilege of sitting within the audience hall on chairs almost level with the king's throne. A raised threshold separates the king and his entourage within the hall from the forecourt. Several royal police sit inside the threshold and face the assembly of chiefs. The chiefs sit on the ground in a semicircle around an open space (*mbuga*) and face the king. On the left side of the forecourt stands a small band of drummers and musicians. In the middle, three men assume different postures of respect before the king. The first is a chief who stands, holding a shield in his left hand and a spear in his raised right hand, making a formal gesture of swearing loyalty (*kuwera*). A second man lies prostrate on the ground and twists in the dust in the posture of giving thanks. The third man kneels on the ground and raises his hands in prayerlike fashion. As the transitional zone between the king and the chiefs, the mbuga was governed by a strict set of rules that regulated the intercourse between those on either side of it.

The interior of the royal shrines exhibits the same spatial arrangement. The main difference is that the mbuga of the audience hall around which the chiefs sat is located inside the shrine. Thus the activities at the shrine were held in semidarkness, not outside in the daylight. An aisle made by the roof posts in the shrine leads from the doorway down the center to the mwaliiro. On top of the mwaliiro stands the Twin symbol of the deceased Kabaka, together with the Twins of his principal wife and princes (Plate 4). Here, too, sat the royal medium, or "bearer," when he or she wanted to become possessed by the Kabaka's spirit. The mwaliiro was thus the "empty throne" of the deceased Kabaka.[6]

People sat on the floor facing the mwaliiro and left an open space in front. They sat as though they were sitting before the living king, whose presence they seemed truly to have felt. In the words of one Ganda scholar, "The dignified array and adornment of everything inside this shrine [Kasubi] awakens a transcendent, quasi-numinous atmosphere . . . " (Lugira 1970: 40). Men sat on the throne's right and women on the left, separated by the central aisle. Behind the throne hung a barkcloth curtain that concealed the rear portion of the shrine. This was the inner sanctuary, the "forest," where the royal spirit dwelled. As one attendant said, while pointing to the barkcloth curtain, "This is where the 'Lion' [the Ssekabaka] went. He is in there like the wind, and he can hear anybody." The king's Twin symbol was also kept in the forest, and in some shrines the Kabaka's jawbone was located there as well. When the ceremonies began, the barkcloth curtain was parted in the middle so that the Kabaka's spirit could leave the forest and possess the medium and enter the court.

The royal shrine thus mediated between the realm of the living and the realm of the dead (Figure 2). One sphere, which I shall call the mbuga or "court," was made up of the Ssekabaka's Lukiiko, the shrine officials descended from the king's original court; the other sphere, the hidden "forest" sanctuary, contained the spirit of the royal ancestor and his sacred relics. Forests in Buganda were regarded as dangerous places, full of wild animals. No one lived there, and people ventured into them only to hunt or to hide from the rest of society. The sacred and dangerous placenta of twins was also buried in the forest to keep it away from human beings. In structuralist terms, it might be said that the relation of the "forest" section of the shrine to the court section is as nature to culture; that is, the forest sanctuary represented nature in its most extreme form as the dangerous sphere of hidden nonhuman powers, in contrast to culture, represented by the officials of the Ssekabaka's court. Mediating between the two, the royal shrine united the spirit of the royal ancestor with the living members of his court.

Ceremonies

The New Moon

Although ceremonies at the royal shrines might be held at almost any time (even daily, according to Roscoe), in the past people usually "paid court" (*kukiika mbuga*) to the royal ancestors on the day following the appearance of the new moon.[7] The first light of the new moon seems to have signified a renewal of life after a period of darkness when the lunar cycle was momentarily interrupted. Kintu is said to have instituted these ritual days of rest, called *Bwerende*. According to Zimbe, it was a time of celebration and giving thanks:

On the day the new moon appeared, people rejoiced, took out their magic charms (*jjembe*) and requested that their lives might be prolonged and praised their gods for having enabled them to see the new moon. The following day was Bwerende. They did not do any sort of work but congratulated one another upon having been able to see the moon again and wished one another to see it again. (1939: 13; cf. Kaggwa [1907] 1934: 1)

On this day, celebrations were held throughout the country at the temples of the gods, the royal shrines, and the palace of the king. At the palace, the king spent the day of the new moon paying his respects to his great charms (*jjembe*) for having seen him through another month. Some of the charms protected the threshold of the palace; others surrounded Mutesa's bed and protected him when he slept (*Munno* 1933: 172). Each jjembe was brought to him, and he touched it with his hands. Mutesa also honored the Twin symbols of his ancestors on the same day, receiving them from their bearers and pressing them to his heart.

Behind the king stood the Kimbugwe, the guardian of the king's Twin symbol. On the previous night, the Kimbugwe anointed the king's Twin with butter and placed it in the doorway of his compound to be exposed to the light of the new moon. The king spent the night alone in his palace and did not sleep with his wives. The next day, he observed the prohibition against work and passed the day examining his charms; he also shaved his head, as did everyone else at the palace. These acts were associated with the mourning period, and they suggest that the moon may originally have been thought to have "died" during its dark phase.[8] In any case, at the time of the new moon, the idea of passage through a period of darkness and transition reminded the people of death, and this was explicitly referred to in people's greetings (Zimbe 1939: 13). When the moon became visible again, the kingdom celebrated the renewal of life and reestablished contact with the spiritual world of the gods and royal ancestors, thereby reaffirming the spiritual health and unity of the kingdom.

The Songs

In 1972, the ceremonies at the shrines were performed less frequently, owing to the dispersion of the shrine authorities and to their reduced number. Some of the shrines lacked mediums, and ceremonies could not be conducted without them. One attendant explained that this sometimes happened because the Ssekabaka himself did not care to choose a new medium, perhaps because he did not take any interest in the royal ceremonies when he was alive. But it was assumed that a new medium would eventually be chosen and the ceremonies would resume. In most cases, attendants said that except for a brief period during the second exile of Mutesa II in 1966, when some of the shrines came under attack from government soldiers and attendants were forced to leave, ceremonies were performed more or less regularly for as long as they could remember. In 1972, the attendants tried to hold the ceremonies as regularly as possible, preferably at the time of the new moon. Widespread conversion to Christianity does not appear to have seriously affected the activity of the shrines; indeed, most of the royalty in charge of the shrines were baptized Christians.

The monthly ceremony began early in the morning because, I was told, the kings liked to manifest themselves during the coolest part of the day. The shrine's drummer beat loudly on the royal drum to call the people and to welcome the Ssekabaka. The shrine officials were dressed in their best traditional clothing. Women wore colorful formal dresses (*busuuti*), and men wore long white robes (*kkanzu*) over which barkcloth wrappers were tied; men knotted the wrappers over the right shoulder, women across the chest. A garland of bbombo vine, which is sacred to deceased twins, was tied over the right shoulder of some men and around the waist of some women. A fire burned in the hearth inside or outside the shrine. People entered the darkened interior and sat down in the posture of respect (legs tucked up neatly to the right) and faced the mwaliiro. The aisle leading from the door to the mwaliiro separated the men sitting on the left from the women on the right, and there was a central space for dancing, pouring beer, and drumming.

One of the most popular songs for this occasion was one that was sung at ceremonies for the birth of twins:[9]

> The owner of the house [the shrine] is father of all.
> CHOR: He does not discriminate against his relatives;
> All the children who have come belong here.
> Owner of the house, oblige yourself.
> CHOR: *Ssaalongo* [Father of Twins], oblige yourself,
> We are bringing your twins;
> Make a sound with the drum.
> CHOR: *Ssewasawa*, the father of children,
> Ours, Nannyondwe.
> The royal drums are heard at Ndawula's [shrine].
> CHOR: Ndawula, Ndawula, brother.

Ndawula is the name of the seventh Kabaka, who lost his eyesight and regained it while hiding in a forest. Later, he was discovered by members of his court and brought triumphantly back to the palace All ceremonies might be said to recall this legendary incident when the spirits of the kings come out of their "forest" sanctuaries to greet the members of their court.

> Ndawula, Ndawula, Ndawula's is where they are drumming.
> CHOR: Ndawula, it's where they are drumming, at Ndawula's.
> Convey my greetings to my friend Ndawula.

Other songs implore the Bassekabaka to manifest themselves. The kings are sometimes called the "favorite ones," and the people are anxious to see them "invade" and "settle down" on their mediums and "greet" the assembly.

> He is invading, he is invading.
> CHOR: Let the owner invade, if he had a spear, he would.
> He is invading, he is invading, Mawanda is invading.
> CHOR: The owner [of the house], oblige yourself.
> He has settled down on him, your king.
> CHOR: The owner of the house wants you to go [and see him].
> CHOR: See, the iron [spear] made him speak at Nabulagala.
> Make an alarm, the Kabaka is there.
> He greeted the elders of the [elephant] tusk.
> CHOR: He greeted them.
> He greeted the cultivators.
> I am proudly singing, my favorite one, I favor you.
> CHOR: How are you? I have given meat to the children.
> We came for conversation. You, Waswa [Senior Twin], where are the twins?
> I am calling [Prince] Kizza Kalemeera, the carrier of the hoe.
> Where did my favorite one go?
> I am worried about my favorite one, [Prince] Lumansi.
> How is he? I did not see him, he had closed, my favorite one.

When the ceremonies begin, the Twin symbols are placed on the throne-platform and the barkcloth curtain is opened to expose the "forest." The opened curtain alerts the Ssekabaka so that he will come out and "climb over the head" (*kulinnyuka ejjoba*) of his medium. It is a climactic moment, not to be missed. Afterward, the curtain will be closed and the ceremony will end.

> They are climbing, the children of (Prince) Ggolooba at Mpinga.
> CHOR: The elders are climbing, I shall come and see.
> I didn't see him. I found he had closed [the curtain].

Possession

Informants agreed that possession took place when the medium sat on the mwaliiro platform, although in the ceremonies I witnessed, this was not done. As the center of the shrines, and as the place of transition between the inner "forest" and the outer "court," the throne-platform was obviously the suitable place for the Ssekababa to possess his medium.

The mediums were chosen by the Bassekabaka themselves, and usually only one served at a shrine. Mediumship was not an inherited office, and anyone might be chosen. I did not encounter any mediums of royal blood, and the large majority were women. Apparently, some Ssekabaka preferred to choose people from distant places. At Bulondo a woman spent five days in a state of trance outside Mulondo's shrine before she was discovered. This, I was told, attested to the superior power of the Bassekabaka to draw mediums from great distances, unlike the lubaale, who had to rely on local people.[10]

Once someone became possessed at a shrine, he or she was taken to the shrine of the Ssekabaka's grandfather for testing and approval. In addition to answering correctly questions about the personal life of the Ssekabaka, the medium had to speak in a voice resembling that of the dead king and to manifest the king's mannerisms and facial expressions, presumably while possessed by the royal spirit. The medium also had to know how to dance properly, to gesture with the spear, to utter the royal greetings, and generally to behave in a royal manner. A medium who passed these tests was officially "married" to the Ssekabaka and henceforth lived at or near the shrine as his "wife." If the medium had relatives some distance away, permission to leave the shrine to visit them had to be obtained from the Nnaalinnya or Katikkiro of the shrine.

Unlike the mediums of the gods, the mediums of the royal spirits I witnessed did not use stimulants (tobacco or alcohol) to induce possession, although Roscoe describes a medium who "smoked a special pipe, and gazed into the fire, until at length he began to speak in the tones of the late king" (1921: 151). Merely opening the "forest" and singing songs was apparently enough to bring the royal spirit "onto the head" (*ku mutwe*) of the "bearer." Ankle bells and rattles, which were sometimes used in lubaale possession, were also absent. In the cases I observed, the trance state was mild, at best; the mediums may simply have been impersonating the kings through gesture and greetings.

When the medium began to dance, he or she took up the Ssekabaka's spear. As indicated in one of the songs above, the spear was essential to the performance and the medium's dance could not begin without it. The thrusting of the spear resembled the gesture known as *kuwera*, "to display loyalty," made by warriors before the king. In the context of the shrine ceremonies, the gesture seemed to express the power and authority of the Ssekabaka. An honored visitor might also find himself the object of vigorous spearing, much to the amusement of the people. Those in attendance responded by greeting the spirit in the royal manner, "Businze, obusiro naffe bwatusinga," literally, "He has conquered, obusiro [the Kabaka] has conquered us!" The Ssekabaka, in turn, may respond by returning the greeting, "Businze, businze!"

After the ceremony, some of the princes and princesses went up to the bearers and sat in their laps, embracing them and exchanging affectionate greetings. Since the mediums "were" the Bassekabaka, the royal offspring were sitting on the laps of their "grandparents" and conversing with them.

Ssuuna's Shrine

A more elaborate ceremony was performed at the opening of a new or rebuilt shrine. This was called the ceremony of "entering the house" (*kuyingira enyumba*), and it included several rites: the cutting of the thatch over the porch (*kusala ekisasi*), the procession of the Twin symbols (*kukonja abalongo*), the greeting of the Ssekabaka (*kuloma*), the running display of the mediums (*kukaazakaaza*), the confirmation of the resident medium by the blood of a slaughtered goat (*kubaaga*), and the feasting by the women of the clan. This series of rites was performed at the opening of Ssuuna's rebuilt shrine at Wamala (Plate 1) on August 4 to August 6, 1972.

The dedication was announced on the radio several days in advance, and the organizers were called to meet at the house of Ssaabalangira Paul Lukongwa in order to make arrangements. The ceremony was a three-day affair, and attracted royalty and ritual attendants from the shrines of the other kings. Prince Lukongwa and the assistant Conservator of Antiquities, Patrick Y. Bulenzi (a Muganda), officially opened the ceremonies with speeches and a ribbon-cutting. When Prince Lukongwa, an old and respected gentleman, arrived at the shrine, he immediately became the center of attention. People came forward, knelt down, lowered their heads, and greeted him respectfully by gently clasping his hand in theirs and by speaking in a high-pitched or a subdued voice. In his opening remarks, the Ssaabalangira recalled that Ssuuna II had been the twenty-ninth Kabaka of Buganda. In this way, he drew attention to the antiquity of the kingship, which had, until recently, been the central institution of

Ganda society. He also pointed out that Ssuuna had been the first Kabaka to adopt Islam. Thus he recalled the progressiveness of the Baganda,
for they had been the first in Uganda to be converted to Islam, which was
now being aggressively promoted by Idi Amin. The Ssaabalangira's words
expressed what everybody felt: the dedication of the shrine was a celebration of Bugunda's national pride. By contrast, the conservator, who represented the Uganda government, emphasized that Ssuuna's shrine was of
historical significance for all of Uganda, which now embraced a variety
of ethnic groups.

The Sentongo, a subchief of the Mugema, opened the shrine in the
traditional manner by trimming the thatch over the front porch. As soon
as this was done, the Twin symbols of about sixteen Ssekabaka were
dramatically carried into the shrine on the right shoulders of their bearers. Ssuuna's Nnaalinnya led the procession, followed by a bearer carrying Ssuuna's Twin (Plate 7). The bearers took the Twins inside and placed
them out of sight behind the barkcloth curtain (Plate 3). The mediums
and bearers then gathered in double ranks in front of the mwaliiro. Each
identified himself or herself by name and recited the lengthy genealogy of
his or her office, all raising the pitch of their voices in honor of Ssekabaka Ssuuna. As each one finished, people responded with vigorous ululations, showing their pride in the work of the mediums.

When the mediums and attendants left the shrine, they proceeded to
run back and forth along the path to the entrance gate while flourishing
their spears. The crowd cheered them on with resounding ululations. This
performance, called *kukaazakaaza*, resembled the triumphant conclusion
of the coronation ceremonies, when the new king was displayed on the
shoulders of his bearer who ran before the crowd.

Several hours later, the mediums again assembled in front of the
shrine, this time to witness the confirmation of Ssuuna's female medium.
Someone slit the throat of a black goat, and the medium stepped over
(*kukuza*) its blood. This, I was told, was an ordeal to test the genuineness
of the medium. If she were falsely impersonating Ssuuna II, she would
die by the goat's blood. Although a woman, the medium wore a *kkanzu*,
the men's traditional white robe, which reinforced her identification with
Ssuuna II.

Inside the shrine, the mediums and attendants assembled again in front
of the mwaliiro and formally greeted Ssuuna. Then they sang and danced
before the people, waving their spears and impersonating the royal spirits. During the ceremony, people came forward and knelt before the
mwaliiro and deposited token offerings of money in baskets placed there
for this purpose.

A final rite, called *kusiba enkweyo*, was performed the next day. The women of the Lungfish clan of Ssuuna's mother brought a feast of goat's meat, beer, and coffee berries, and they sang songs in celebration of the opening of Ssuuna's new house.

Ancestors, Gods, or Kings?

Since the Ganda term for the ceremonies at the shrines, *kukiika mbuga*, "to pay court," does not distinguish between paying court to living kings and paying court to dead ones, it would be misleading to call these ceremonies "ancestor worship" or an "ancestor cult," and thus to separate them from the wider phenomenon of courtly behavior. Failure to comprehend this point can lead to the view that the deceased Kabakas became deities or gods at death, as Roscoe supposed, and that dead kings assumed utterly different social roles from living kings. The problem, according to the anthropologist Igor Kopytoff, is that the term "ancestor" invites a basic misperception:

> The term "ancestor" sets up a dichotomy where there is a continuum. By conceptually separating living elders from ancestors, we unconsciously introduce Western connotations to the phenomena thus labelled and find ourselves having to deal with paradoxes of our own creation and with complex solutions to them.
> . . . African living elders and dead ancestors are more similar to each other than the Western living and dead can be, . . . an elder's social role does not radically change when he crosses the line dividing the living from the dead, and [hence] . . . African "ancestorship" is but an aspect of the broader phenenomenon of "eldership." (1971: 140)

It would be misleading, though, to insist that the royal ancestors were sociologically the same as living kings — that is, that a king's social role did not markedly change after he died and took up residence in a shrine. First of all, the Luganda word *muzimu* (plural, *mizimu*), "ghost" or "ancestor spirit," belongs to a different class of nouns than words for living persons — for example, *muntu*, "person," or *bantu*, "people" — indicating that ghosts and ancestors belong to a nonhuman category of being (cf. Brain 1973). Even though the Baganda prefer the term *Ssekabaka*, which belongs to the noun class of persons, to the term *muzimu*, both words may be used in reference to deceased kings, thus blurring the distinction between the dead and the living. A similar duality obtains in the lexicon of the royal shrines. The proper term for "royal shrine" is *masiro*, which applies only to the shrine, but the Baganda also refer to it as a "palace" (*lubiri*), again blurring the distinction between dead and living kings. In fact, one way of defining *masiro* in Luganda would be to say that it is the lubiri of the Ssekabaka. Indeed, the masiro was intended to be a physical replica of the palace of the living king, although it served a very different function. The activities at the shrines were primarily ceremonial, while those at the court were primarily political, yet the term *kukiika mbuga* does not distinguish between them.

The resolution to the problem is not to deny the appropriateness of the terms "ancestor" or "ancestor cult," as Kopytoff proposes, but to recognize that the royal ancestors played a dual role in Buganda. They were both the objects of worship and political actors in their own right, and it would be incorrect to place them exclusively in one sphere or the other. The dead kings were "ancestor spirits" (*mizimu*) in the sense that they belonged to a separate spiritual and ceremonial realm, and they were "kings" (*Bassekabaka*) in the sense that they continued to be involved in the political life of the kingship. Thus during the reign of Mutesa I, his deceased father, Ssuuna II, had two shrines: one at Wamala, near Busiro county, where the other royal ancestors dwelled; and one in the capital where Mutesa paid his respects (Figure 1 [1]).

In 1972, the question I asked my informants was not whether the Bassekabaka should be regarded as ancestors (*mizimu*) but whether they should be regarded as gods (*lubaale*), in view of their power to answer people's prayers and grant blessings. In the past, Zimbe notes, "people thought that the deceased kings were lubaale" (1939: 14). Today, many diviners are in fact possessed by lubaale, whom they refer to as "princes" (cf. Taylor 1958: 212; Orley 1970: 18).

My inquiries met with two different interpretations, which appeared to correspond to differences between royal and nonroyal points of view. On the one hand, nonroyal attendants at the shrines said that the Bassekabaka were similar to the lubaale in that both granted people's requests. One attendant went further and said that "there is no real difference between the Bassekabaka and the lubaale because both give similar help to people. They also appear similarly when they are 'on the heads' of the mediums and the diviners." Although the majority recognized that the lubaale and the royal mediums behaved differently, most nonroyal informants agreed that both granted requests for the same things: children, money, and health.[11]

Royalty, on the other hand, firmly denied that the Bassekabaka were efficacious in this way. While recognizing the tendency among the common people to believe otherwise, the princes and princesses minimized the agency of the royal spirits. Ssaabalangira Lukongwa, an educated Roman Catholic, put it this way: "People usually ask the Ssekabaka for things, such as property and children, but they forget the fact that they cannot get anything because the Kabaka is an ordinary human being, just like anybody else." An educated Nnaalinnya put it more explicitly: "Before the introduction of religion [dini] by the Europeans, the Baganda believed in the Bassekabaka as their lubaale." But in her view, "requests can never be granted by the Bassekabaka because they are not lubaale, even though uneducated people believe that they are." Going further, she rejected the powers of the lubaale as well: "Neither the lubaale nor the Bassekabaka are able to help people in any way. This is because they are all spirits [mizimu] of people who once existed. And human beings cannot give such blessings to other human beings." Although this royal point of view may well be the result of Christian influence and Western education, it may also reflect the opposition between the monarchy and the lubaale priesthood that developed under Mutesa I, who sought to limit the role of the lubaale in the affairs of the kingship.

Indeed, there may always have been a difference between nonroyal and royal points of view. The nonroyal attendants owe their association with the shrines to their forebears who held palace appointments. Over the years, close association with the shrines may have led the attendants to link some of the characteristics of the lubaale cult to the Bassekabaka. The deification of the royal ancestors may also be an expression of the attendants' loyalty to throne. Royalty, however, may simply have continued to regard their ancestors as family spirits (mizimu) – specters with rather limited spiritual powers – while maintaining a clear separation between them and the lubaale with which the kingship was often in conflict.

Whatever the historical situation may have been, the royal authorities of today reject the view that the royal ancestors belong in the same spiritual and sociological realm as the lubaale. The Bassekabaka constitute an exclusively royal cult; only royalty and descendants of palace officials may attend ceremonies at the shrines. The ceremonies also appear to be primarily acts of homage and devotion, not divination, which is the primary purpose of the lubaale cult. Personal requests may sometimes be made to the royal ancestors, and messages from the ancestors are sometimes given through the mediums, but in the latter half of the twentieth century both occurrences appear to have been infrequent.

Finally, the royal ancestors and the lubaale were thought to belong to different ritual domains. At every shrine, I asked whether there was a lubaale temple nearby, and I was consistently told that there was not. In the area that I came to know best (containing about a dozen shrines), I was certain that this was the case.[12] The attendants usually explained that the lubaale temples were prohibited by the royal officials or by the Bassekabaka themselves. According to one attendant, "This is because the Bassekabaka have the power to refuse anything they do not like. They think it disrespectful to have other gods [*lubaale*] while they exist." But the same informant also said that a lubaale temple might be allowed to exist if the Nnaalinnya in charge of the shrine permitted it. However, the Ssaabalangira, who regarded himself as the principal authority, held a stricter view. "The Kabaka and the Ssaabalangira cannot permit anyone to have a temple in the area of the royal shrines." In his view, the two spheres were as incompatible as two different religious faiths. "Even if people ask for things from the Bassekabaka, you cannot ask them from the lubaale, because it is not believed that a person can attend a service at two or three different types of churches; for example, a Catholic cannot go to a Protestant church or a mosque." The first informant, who believed in the efficacy of the Bassekabaka, used the same analogy, but held a more flexible view.

> People make requests to the Ssekabaka for children, but if a person has a lubaale at home, his request might not be considered [by the Ssekabaka], for both the Ssekabaka and the lubaale are spirits. Thus you cannot decide to stop going to your particular church to worship and go to a mosque or another kind of church. If you do request something from your lubaale and get a response, then you can go to the Ssekabaka [for something else].

In other words, while the two spheres should not be brought into competition, they are not totally incompatible.

Sacred Center

It seems appropriate to conclude this chapter by examining the significance of the royal shrines in terms of Eliade's notion of sacred space. Eliade's concept depends on the well-worn dichotomy between the sacred and the profane, as formulated by Emile Durkheim, a dichotomy that many anthropologists believe to be analytically unsound (Goody, 1961; Evans-Pritchard 1965: 64–65; Stanner 1967). Recently, Luc de Heusch has pointed out that it is the Latin language that opposes *sacer* and *profanus*, and any account that relies on this opposition is marred by Indo-European ethnocentrism (1985: 4). Durkheim, following the Latin meaning, identified the sacred as that which is set apart and prohibited. Later, Rudolf Otto defined it as the "holy," the "numinous," and the "wholly other." Thus the concept made its way into the phenomenology of religion as an ambivalent, mysterious, and suprahistorical power, utterly separate from and opposed to the profane world and the source of everything religious.

Nevertheless, despite its ethnocentric character, the sacred–profane dichotomy still has considerable value. It is, of course, a widely recognized mode of symbolic classification, like the dichotomy between right and left. But it also risks becoming a prefabricated cliché unless its scope and character are carefully defined according to the materials to which it is applied.

One of the difficulties here is that, unlike right and left, sacred and profane are not always explicitly distinguishable. Many languages, such as Luganda, do not have words that can be translated as "sacred" or "profane," and people are not necessarily aware of the existence of such a dichotomy in their culture. This circumstance makes matters more complex, but it does not count against using the sacred–profane opposition as an analytic scheme. Perhaps the often used analogy between an analytic scheme and the grammar of a language (of which the speakers may be similarly unaware) is worth repeating. Thus to use the sacred–profane opposition as an analytic concept is to attribute it to the structure of the thoughts and imagery of the people under study—not to their conscious apprehension.

It should be clear that the sacred–profane opposition is not always absolute and systematically pervasive (without contextual variations), and sometimes refers to things aspectually rather than totally. Thus when employing this opposition, it is necessary to focus primarily on context, and to limit the dichotomy to certain facets of thought and imagery. The terms "sacred" and "profane" do not cover everything in Ganda culture, nor is this distinction the most important form of dualistic classification in Ganda thought.

At the beginning of *The Sacred and the Profane*, Eliade asserts that the "first possible definition of the *sacred* is that it is *the opposite of the profane*" (1961: 10). The rest of his book is, of course, an elucidation of this statement. Here I shall concentrate on his remarks about sacred space. He describes it as an "irruption," a "break" in the homogeneity of space, a "revelation of Reality," opposed to the "nonreality of the vast surrounding expanse." Sacred space involves the discovery of a "fixed point," a "center," an *axis mundi* that connects the celestial and terrestrial realms. As such, sacred space provides a cosmic "orientation," making it possible to "found a world" patterned after mythical and cosmogonic

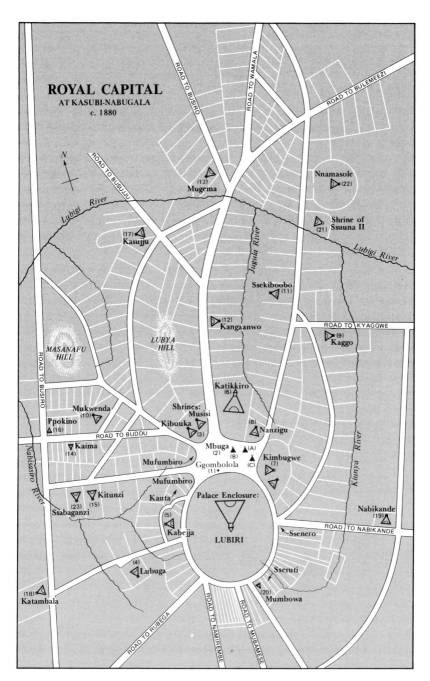

FIGURE 1. The royal capital.

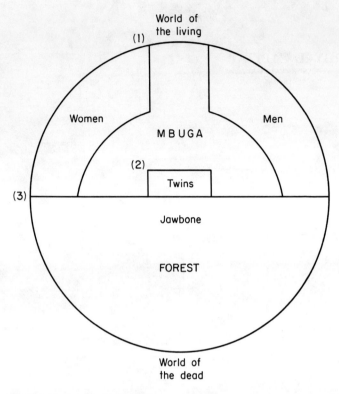

FIGURE 2. The royal shrine.

PLATE 1. The shrine of Ssuuna II at Wamala.

PLATE 2. The shrine of Kimera at Bumera.

PLATE 3. Inside Ssuuna's shrine facing the mwaliiro. Note the barrier of spears and shields and the barkcloth curtain.

PLATE 4. Inside Mawanda's shrine. Note the animal-skin carpet (*kiwu*) in the foreground, barkcloth curtain, doorway behind the curtain, and Twin symbols standing on the throne-platform (*mwaliiro*).

PLATE 5. Grant's drawing of Mutesa I sitting in his audience hall (*Bulange*) and presiding at the royal council.

PLATE 6. A bearer (*mukonggozi*) gesturing with her spear during a ceremony at the shrine of Kabaka Mulondo.

PLATE 7. The royal Twin symbols being carried into Ssuuna's shrine.

PLATE 8. Officials holding wrapped Twin symbols at Kabaka Mulondo's shrine.

archetypes. By contrast, profane space is "neutral," "homogeneous," and "relative," even "chaotic" and "nonreal." It is the meaningless vastness of the temporal domain, devoid of any "true" order or ontological orientation, and always threatened by "non-being."

In these passages and elsewhere, Eliade constructs a model of the sacred–profane opposition that applies to many traditional and ancient societies, especially those of India and the ancient Near East. But it would be a mistake to take this form of the opposition as a universal archetype. Indeed, Eliade's own studies show how many different forms this opposition may take.

In regard to the royal shrines, the sacred–profane dichotomy may be more appropriately defined as a relationship between complementary forms of reality within a basically dualistic structure. In this scheme, the opposition is not between the absolute and the relative, order and chaos, or reality and nonreality, but between two different modes of being whose separation and complementarity make up the wider reality of the kingship.

Fundamental to the cosmology of many Bantu-speaking peoples is the division between the world of the living and the world of the dead. In many respects, the world of the dead is the opposite of the world of the living, and each shares some of the structural properties of the other. In Buganda, the realm of the dead consists of the family ghosts (*mizimu*), hero gods (*lubaale*), and royal ancestors (*Bassekabaka*), all of whom were once living human beings. The sacred world is thus an extension of the world of the living via its negation. However, in contrast to Eliade's view, the aim in Buganda was not to escape the "nonreality" of the profane realm in order to enter the sacred, or even to seek primary orientation in terms of the sacred. The aim was to keep the two spheres in proper relation, and thus to maintain a balance between them. Both spheres, the living and the dead, contributed positively to the structure of the whole. The key to this system was not the sacred alone, but the relationship between the sacred and the profane.

The royal shrine expressed the separation and unity between the living and the dead within its very architecture; the shrine was both a model of and an instrument for this relationship. The purpose of the shrine was to contain and conceal the spirit of the deceased king, and to make it accessible, in a restricted way, to the world of the living. There was nothing sacred about the site where the shrine was built; it was constructed on the site of the king's palace, and then made sacred by the "entering the house" ritual when the royal jawbone was placed in it.

"Sacrality," says Jonathan Z. Smith in a recent study, "is, above all, a category of emplacement" (1987: 104). In the case of Ssuuna's shrine, I was fortunate enough to observe its transformation into a sacred place. Although Ssuuna's body, with its jawbone attached, already lay in a tomb within the new building, it was not until after the thatch-cutting rite that the building became truly the house (*enyumba*) of Ssuuna's spirit, and therefore his shrine. As if to emphasize this point, the bearers of the royal Twins, including Ssuuna's, waited until the thatch-cutting ceremony was completed before bringing the Twins into the shrine and introducing themselves to Ssuuna. Smith rightly notes that a "ritual object or action becomes sacred by having attention focused on it in a highly marked way." Hence, he asserts that ritual "is not a response to 'the Sacred'; rather, something or someone is made sacred by ritual (the primary sense of *sacrificium*)" (1987: 104–5).

It would be going too far, however, to adopt Smith's ritualist theory and hold that something is sacred only by virtue of its place in a ritual setting. According to Smith, "there is nothing that is inherently sacred or profane. These are not substantive categories, but rather situational ones" (1987: 104). The "*sacra*," therefore, "are sacred solely because they are used in a sacred place; there is no inherent difference between a sacred vessel and an ordinary one" (1987: 106).

While this theory may be acceptable to the outside observer, it does not necessarily represent the perspective of the believer. For the Baganda, the royal relics, the jawbone and Twin, were inherently sacred, and this is why they were made into ritual symbols. To be sure, the jawbone relic was created to serve a ritual function within the shrine, but its sacrality did not originate in that context. It was called the "Kabaka" before being placed in the shrine because it represented the dead king. The same is true of the royal Twin that contained the spirit of the king's placenta; the perceived sacredness of the royal umbilical cord made it a suitable ritual object. Thus, wherever the royal Twin was present, whether standing in the shrine or displayed outdoors on the shoulder of its bearer, the situation was converted into a ritual one. Even the Twins that Roscoe brought back to Cambridge, now sitting in museum storage boxes far from their indigenous ritual settings, are still properly regarded as sacred objects because they represent the royal ancestors. They possess a permanent symbolic value that is attached to them as elements of Ganda culture, no matter where they are.

For Eliade, it is clear that the notion of a sacred center depends heavily on the idea of the sacred as a substantive category. "Man becomes aware of the sacred," he writes, "because it manifests itself, shows itself" to us (1959: 11). As I have indicated, there was nothing substantive about the sacredness of the royal shrines; they were sacred solely by virtue of their ritual function. Eliade's notion of a sacred center is also tied to the symbolism of cosmogonic origins, *axis mundi*, and celestial orientation (1959: 37), a set of symbols that is entirely foreign to the royal shrines.

Nevertheless, an essential feature of Eliade's sacred center is the notion of a breakthrough, the "image of an opening," which is the primary feature of the royal shrines. For Eliade, a sacred center is "where the break in plane was symbolically assured and hence communication with the *other world*, the transcendental world, was ritually possible" (1959: 37). It is "where space becomes sacred, hence pre-eminently *real*" (1959: 45), making possible an "ontological passage from one mode of being to another" (1959: 63). A sacred center is also an "opening" to sacred time, where "man can pass without danger from ordinary temporal duration to sacred time" (1959: 68), which is "indefinitely recoverable, indefinitely repeatable." Finally, a sacred center is an *imago mundi*, constructed on the basis of a mythical archetype established at the time of the beginnings.

Insofar as the royal shrines possess these attributes, they are sacred centers in Eliade's sense, and their universal religious features are thereby evident. The shrines incorporated a mythic paradigm, established by Kintu when he "disappeared" into a forest at the time of the beginnings. Kintu's forest realm became the model of the shrine's sacred zone, the hidden inner sanctum, where Kintu's descendants dwelled after they died. Hence, the shrines were an *imago mundi*, representing the division between the living and the dead, which was fundamental to the Ganda cosmos. Prominently placed on the hills of Busiro, which the royal capital always faced, the shrines were the sacred dimension of the kingship. They contained the relics and spirits of the royal ancestors, and made the latter accessible through mediumship rites. When the ancestors spoke within the shrines, time was transcended, and the past momentarily became the present.

As I walked from one shrine to another, an additional feature of the royal shrines struck me: the temporal sequence of dynastic chronology was transposed into a spatial sequence, and thus temporality was obliterated (cf. Smith 1987: 113). Here, standing along a path a few hundred yards from one another, there were shrines of kings who lived centuries apart, their temporal distance overcome by their spatial contiguity. Time was suspended. I could "walk" across the centuries and behold the reigns of kings permanently frozen in fixed memorials, the chronology of the past made simultaneously present within the precincts of Busiro, the kingdom's sacred dynastic center.

In keeping with their function as "openings" to the spiritual world, the shrines remained geographically separate from the capital, the center of secular political life. The world of the shrines was virtually the mirror image of the royal capital. "Ritual," Smith notes perceptively, "is, above all, an assertion of difference" (1987: 109). Within the shrines, it was ritual, not politics, that prevailed; not the prime minister but the Queen Sister was in charge. Instead of legal cases and political affairs, people brought spiritual requests for health and prosperity. When the Kabaka "spoke" it was through his medium, not his prime minister, and his words were generalized messages and formalized greetings, not legal decisions and administrative pronouncements. The songs were sacred songs for the Kabaka's symbolic Twin, not praise songs for the living monarch.

Although dedicated to dead kings, the shrines constituted an elaborate denial of their mortality. The dead kings still reigned, but in another realm, and their officials still held their posts through generations of replacements provided by the clans. "Ritual," to quote Smith again, "is a means of performing the way things ought to be in conscious tension to the way things are" (1987: 109). The historical kings lay moldering in their tombs, but in the shrines they lived on in spiritual form as idealized, enthroned monarchs. Each shrine was the pride of the clan whose "son" became king, ruled and died, and then reappeared in a different realm, separate from that of his successor. The shrines were not merely attempts to imitate the royal court; they represented an effort to create the court of a spirit king, who ruled in a ritual fashion for an eternity. In 1972, the shrines I visited commemorated kingship in its purely ritual dimension. During the ceremonies, the people sang praises to the king's Twin, the king appeared "on the head" of his medium and delivered ritualized pronouncements, and the members of the court basked in his presence and paid their respects through conventionalized greetings and praises.

This was not a presentation of the kingship as it "ought" to be in contrast to the way it actually was, as Smith's idealist theory of ritual might suggest. It was the celebration of the eternal essence of kingship, the spiritual dignity of Buganda's dead kings. Like every kingship, the essence of the Kabakaship was the fact that it made one man the symbol of ultimate order and meaning, the sacred center of Buganda. Within the shrines, that temporary status was converted to an eternal one expressed by a combination of *sacra*, the jawbone, Twin, and royal medium, which were the focus of the ceremonies. Collectively, the shrines celebrated the

Kabakaship as an eternal office held by different clansmen. Each shrine expressed the pride of a clan that produced a king, and collectively the shrines were the glory of the whole nation. Here, within the shrines, an "opening" was created for the mystical dignity of each dead Kabaka to manifest itself to the world. Thus the secular palace of the living king respectfully faced Busiro, where the collective spirits of ancestors reigned eternally.

The shrines, then, were the sacred pivot of the Kabakaship: they contained its historical legacy, the dynastic traditions by which Buganda understood itself and the justification of its institutions, and they contained its eternal essence, the mystical dimension by which the institution of the Kabakaship transcended the death of kings. The unique function of the shrines was to assert, through the differentiating power of ritual, the "coincidence of opposites" between the temporal character of the kingship embodied in the person of the living ruler and its eternal nature embodied in the relics and mediums of the deceased kings.

6

Regicide and Ritual Homicide

Regicide and homicide were common features of the Ganda kingship, at least in the eighteenth and nineteenth centuries. According to the dynastic chronicles, most of the kings of this period were either murdered by usurping princes or killed by supernatural powers. Kings also killed their subjects with impunity, both at the time of their installation and during their reign. In 1862, Speke was the first to describe the executions at Mutesa's court, and such reports became commonplace in later accounts. Frazer of course thought that regicide and homicide were essential to the institution of kingship in order to preserve the king's divine soul. More recently, the anthropologist Luc de Heusch, an advocate of Frazerian ideas, has asserted that "in Africa, human sacrifice is most often a means of deferring the sacrifice of the [sacred] king" (1985: 215–16). But, as we have seen, the Kabakas of Buganda were not divine beings; they possessed no sacred powers, nor did the installation killings transfer any sacred vitality to them, as Frazer and Roscoe supposed. The Kabakas killed their subjects, sometimes in great numbers, but not for the purpose of mystically revitalizing themselves. Why, then, did acts of regicide and ritual homicide regularly occur in precolonial Buganda?

Regicide in Historical and Mythical Perspective

The dynastic history covers the reigns of thirty kings from Kintu (ca. fourteenth century) to Mutesa I, who died in 1884. According to these accounts, the first two kings, Kintu and Chwa Nabakka I, disappeared from Buganda and were never seen again. It was this oral tradition that led Frazer and Roscoe to speculate about ritual regicide in the early kingship (Chapter 1). But the dynastic accounts say nothing about regicide, ceremonial or otherwise. In the early 1970s, the historian David Cohen proposed that the alleged disappearance of these kings "may very well mark the beginning of a pattern of royal suicide" (1972: 109). But he gives no evidence, and the traditions themselves contain no report of such a practice. They say that Kintu fled the throne because he inadvertently killed his prime minister and wished to avoid the shame of judgment by his chiefs. He went into a forest at Magonga and disappeared into a tree trunk, where his spirit still dwells (Kaggwa [1912] 1949: 9; 1971: 6–7; Nsimbi 1956b: 222–23). His son and successor Chwa disappeared some years later while searching for Kintu. Although the founding myth tells of Kintu's killing the indigenous ruler Bbemba, regicide did not become a rule of succession, for neither Kintu nor Chwa were succeeded in this fashion.

A more promising approach to the problem of the disappearance of Kintu and Chwa is to note the similarities between this tradition and the Nyoro traditions about the disappearance of the Chwezi founders of the kingdom of Bunyoro-Kitara. The Nyoro accounts say that the Chwezi left because they lost the respect of the people, much as Kintu fled from the throne to avoid the shame of being found guilty of murder by his chiefs. Another story, collected by Stanley, says that Kintu departed Buganda in disgust because his drunken sons were killing one another and threatening to kill him (1878 I: 347). Historians suppose that the stories about the departure of the Chwezi rulers reflect their actual displacement from the Bunyoro-Kitara throne by the new dynasty of Bito kings who invaded and took over the kingdom. The same might be said of the evanishment of Kintu and Chwa, whose line seems to have been replaced by a new dynasty introduced by Kimera.

Another tradition associates the disappearance of Kintu and Chwa with the absence of jawbone relics. According to several informants, the fact that the jawbones of the later kings were preserved shows that they "were strong and would not disappear like Kintu and Chwa." Since the traditions attribute the custom of preserving the royal jawbone to Kimera, the fact that the jawbones of Kintu and Chwa were not preserved is consistent with the supposition that Kimera introduced a new dynastic line, and with it the custom of preserving the royal jawbone that is associated with the kings of Bunyoro-Kitara (cf. Oliver 1959).

As for the successors of Kintu and Chwa, the chronicles say that only three of the next nineteen were killed. During this formative period, the royal and clan accounts agree that the king was looked on by the clan heads (*Bataka*) as the first among equals. A balance of power seems to have existed between the Bataka and the Kabaka such that the throne was not an object of political contention, and kings lived out their reigns. Of the three kings killed, two are said to have been good rulers overthrown by ambitious princes; the third, a bad ruler, was killed by a spell cast by a prince. Most kings of this period are said to have died at middle age or older; others succumbed to illnesses or unspecified causes.

In the eighteenth century, however, regicide became the common method of succession: seven out of eight kings were murdered by princely usurpers. The only exception, Kabaka Namugala, abdicated in favor of his brother Kyabaggu, whom he feared would kill him. The increased power of the monarchy appears to have created an unstable situation. Important county chiefships, formerly held by the aristocracy of Bataka were increasingly taken over by the throne and given to royal favorites. A new order of chiefs, called the *batongole*, was also created. These chiefs, whom Lloyd Fallers has called "the king's men" (1964: 93), were loyal only to the throne and enabled the monarchy gradually to acquire the territorial authority formerly held by the clan heads. Throughout the eighteenth century, the Bataka seem to have backed rebellions in order to put princes from their own clans on the throne.

The practice of regicide was finally halted in the late eighteenth century by Kabaka Semakookiro. Acting on the advice of the priests of Mukasa, who helped bring him to the throne, Semakookiro killed all but three of his sons. Semakookiro's successors continued the practice of liquidating princely rivals, thereby reducing the risk of rebellion and greatly enhancing the power of the king. With no political rivals, the nineteenth-century Kabakas became a law unto themselves and turned Buganda into an ordered despotism, a form of government that was quite rare in precolonial Africa.

From this brief review of the dynastic history, it seems clear that regicide in Buganda was fundamentally a political matter, a means of replacing the king, not a ritual requirement of succession. This is confirmed by the fact that regicide occurred most frequently in the eighteenth century when the powers of the monarchy were expanding at the expense of the clan aristocracy.

James Vaughn, however, has suggested that the ideology of king killing in Africa is not quite as simple as it appears. The distinction between political and ritual regicide, Vaughn notes, was introduced by Evans-Pritchard in criticism of Frazer. Evans-Pritchard argued that the Shilluk practice of regicide, an example that was central to Frazer's theory, was entirely due to political tensions within the kingdom. Shilluk assertions that they killed their kings when they became old or ill, which Frazer's disciple Charles Seligman reported so confidently to Frazer in 1911 (Frazer 1911–1915 IV 17ff), were interpreted by Evans-Pritchard as a fiction for justifying the killing of kings when power struggles erupted during times of political unrest. Thus Evans-Pritchard dismissed Seligman's reports of Shilluk ritual king killing, saying that Seligman was "evidently determined to find a clear example in support of Frazer's theory" (1971: 162).

Nevertheless, it remains a moot point whether regicide among the Shilluk was a political action with ritual justification or a ritual imperative with political consequences (Young 1966: 151). Vaughn argues that in the case of institutional regicide, the political dimension cannot in fact be separated from the ritual; the two are fused, as he discovered among the Margi Dzirngu of northern Nigeria:

> On the one hand, there is the political, Evans-Pritchardian view held by the competitors [in the Margi kingdom] and their supporters (and the political anthropologist), while on the other hand, there is the more detached Frazerian view of the commoners, a view which discerns a pattern of behavior and views *thilda* [regicide] as an institution for the removal of failing kings. One might argue for either one or the other as being more realistic. That is basically what the argument in anthropology has been about, but I am convinced that it is not a question of one or the other, rather it is necessary to see that they should never be separated. They are the same. (1980: 132)

That is, in kingdoms where regicide was an accepted means of replacing kings, there was always a symbolic dimension to king killing that was as important as the political motives that brought it about. Among the Margi, the palace intriguers killed the king for their own political advantage. But the rest of the society viewed the murder as an expression of the monarch's "failure" to rule.

In Buganda, the dynastic accounts generally explain regicide as an act of revenge against kings who used the power of their office to murder princes or chiefs. Such abuses of power provoked princes, backed by chiefly supporters, to kill the king and accede to the throne. It is also true that the person who killed the king during such a revolt was recognized as a great hero (Roscoe 1911: 347). In other words, from the point of view of the royal chronicles, the Kabakas who were killed by princely usurpers usually deserved their fate; they had abused the power of the throne, and their death was both fitting and required.

This attitude was enshrined in Buganda's origin myth, the story of Kintu's killing the tyrannical ruler Bbemba the Snake. As we have already seen (Chapter 3), the story of Kintu's conquest by regicide, which was enacted in the installation rites at Buddo Hill, was probably invented in the eighteenth century when regicide became the common method of succession. By means of the Kintu myth and its ritualized enactment, regicide was built into the ideology of kingship. Every new king was portrayed in Frazerian fashion as a slayer who in the course of time would himself be slain.

Even after Semakookiro had effectively abolished the practice of regicide, the death of a king was viewed by most Baganda as the result of royal abuse of power, the king's "hubris," as Michael Kenny recently called it (1988). Although princes could no longer rebel and kill the king, gods and spirits were thought to punish royal despotism. Thus, according to the chronicles, Semakookiro died of an illness sent by the ghost of a priest whom he had murdered (Kaggwa [1901] 1971: 100–101). His successor, Kabaka Kamaanya, died (ca. 1826) from an illness attributed to both ghostly vengeance and the wrath of the god Mukasa (Kaggwa [1901] 1971: 110–11). Kamaanya's son, Ssuuna II, died around 1856 of smallpox because he allegedly disobeyed the advice of the priest of the war god Nnende (Nsimbe 1956b: 134). Earlier, Ssuuna had been struck by lightning allegedly sent by the thunder god Kiwanuka because Ssuuna had abused one of his priests. Ssuuna's son, Mutesa I, died in 1884 after a prolonged illness, most probably gonorrhea, which was believed to have been sent by the ghost of one of the wives Mutesa had killed (Roscoe 1901: 127). In 1879, Mukasa's priest had told Mutesa that his illness was the result of his having taken away the powerful office of the Mugema from the Vervet Monkey clan and his having appointed a favorite from the wrong clan to be the guardian of his Twin (Wright 1971: 5). The implication was that Mutesa had become ill because his political ambitions over the clans had offended Mukasa.

From the eighteenth century onward the Kabakas of Buganda therefore came and left the throne according to the example expressed in the Kintu myth. Each successor to the throne vacated by a ruler who had abused his power would himself become an ambitious and "cruel" ruler who died the victim of an avenging prince or supernatural power.

Ganda ideology therefore resembled Frazer's theory of kingship. Frazer's point was not (as Vaughn suggests [1980: 140]) that kings, like all mortals, must ultimately die, but that the nature of kingship is such that it demands the life of its incumbents, whether or not they submit willingly. In Buganda this view took on a Faustian dimension: princes chosen to be kings were given great power which they inevitably abused, and this cost them their life.

Frazer of course thought that kings were killed in order to transfer their immortal souls to their successors. Unfortunately, unlike Evans-Pritchard, Frazer never distinguished between political and ceremonial king-killing. But Frazer did grasp the point that regicide as a method of replacing kings was somehow intrinsic to the institution of kingship and that the important question concerned the "meanings" that different societies gave to it. For the Baganda, it was explained and justified by the origin myth, and from the eighteenth century onward every act of succession was an explicit enactment of this tradition.

Unlike Frazer, the essayist René Girard sees regicide as a means of stemming society's inherent tendency toward violence. In Freudian fashion, Girard postulates an original, precultural state of humanity in which excessive violence threatened to destroy society until the warring factions united and channeled their aggression onto a human "surrogate" whom they collectively murdered. Henceforth, ritual sacrifice became the guarantor of social order by re-creating and renewing society through periodic acts of sanctioned killing; the practice of slaying a few selected victims prevented violence from running wild. "The sacrifice," Girard writes, "serves to protect the entire community from *its own violence*; it prompts the entire community to find victims outside itself" (1977: 8). Girard argues that in African kingdoms this inherent social tendency toward violence was directed at a fundamentally powerless, "external" figure at the top, a Frazerian god-king. The system was periodically renewed and strengthened each time the king was killed.

> Behind the pageantry of African monarchies lurks the specter of the sacrificial crisis, suddenly resolved by the unanimity arising from the generative act of violence. Each African king is a new Oedipus, obliged to play out his own myth from beginning to end, because ritualistic theory sees in this enactment the means of renewing and perpetuating a cultural order that is constantly on the brink of destruction. (Girard 1977: 106)

In Girard's view, regicide in Africa was an instrument for controlling inherent societal violence and thereby renewing the wider political order. "The elements of dissension scattered throughout the community are drawn to the person of the sacrificial victim and eliminated, at least temporarily, by its sacrifice" (1977: 106).

But from the Ganda point of view, the violence that threatened to undo the nation came not from society in general but from the king himself. As a balanced relationship between the segmentary authority of the clans and the centralized authority of the king, the kingdom risked becoming destabilized by excessive violence from the throne. In Buganda, royal violence was an expression of the king's authority: the more the Kabaka killed, the more power he obtained. This was the point of the Kintu myth. Bbemba's chiefs were justified in asking Kintu for help because the tyrannical Bbemba had murdered and plundered his subjects. The ideology expressed in the myth supported chiefs in rebellions against excessively violent kings. In the eighteenth century, this principle was used effectively by princes and coalitions of chiefs, backed by certain clan heads, to obtain control of an increasingly powerful monarchy. In doing this, however, the chiefs did not imagine the king to be an "innocent" deity, as Girard proposes, but a man like themselves, an all-too-human competitor within the system. Although the king was treated as an exalted personage while on the throne, this did not prevent his being murdered during a rebellion and replaced by a more desirable candidate.

If the Kintu conquest myth functioned as an example of the inevitable violence of succession, at least since the eighteenth century, to what extent can it be said that Kintu himself functioned as an example of kingly behavior?

Here we encounter an interesting contradiction. On the one hand, the story of Kintu's abrupt departure from the throne after killing his faithful Katikkiro, Kisolo, showed that even the noble Kintu finally fell victim to the royal penchant for violence. This story, which is part of the Otter clan tradition (Kaggwa [1912] 1949: 8–9; Nsimbi 1956b: 222–24), makes Kintu the virtual paradigm of the violent eighteenth-century king who came to the throne by regicide and subsequently abused his power. On the other hand, there is the well-known tradition about Kintu's abhorrence of bloodshed (Stanley 1878 I: 346; Roscoe 1911: 214; Zimbe 1939: 10), a tradition that was still evident at his shrine at Magonga in 1972. According to a story recorded by Stanley, Kintu was a pacifist king whose benevolent rule was brought to an end by the debauchery of the princes, making Buganda a "horrid, cruel land" (1878 I: 357). Stanley's informant Sabadu, one of Mutesa's junior chiefs, related that Kintu's sons began to kill one another after they discovered how to make intoxicating wine from plantains. Kintu's despair was so great that he and Nnambi finally left the kingdom:

> See, my sons whom I brought into this world have become wicked and hard of heart, and they threaten to drive their father away or kill him, for they say I am become old and useless. I am like a hateful stranger amongst my own children. They shed the blood of their brothers daily, and there is nothing but killing and bloodshed now, until I am sick of blood. It is time for us to get away and depart elsewhere. Come [Nnambi], let us go. (Stanley 1878 I: 347)

That this story was widely known is evident in a letter written by the CMS missionary Alexander Mackay and sent to Mutesa in 1881. Mackay, together with his missionary companion C. W. Pearson, tried to dissuade

Mutesa from carrying out a mass execution. They told him, among other things, to "remember what KINTU said about blood-shedding," for, as Mackay pointed out in another letter, "Kintu, the founder of Uganda, disappeared because the land had become so full of blood" (1890: 190, 192).

Thus we have two rather different portraits of Kintu. One indicates that he left the throne in shame because he murdered his Katikkiro; the other says that the actions of his violent and murderous sons caused him to leave in despair. But instead of assuming, as John Yoder does, that one story represents the "official" image of Kintu and the other an unofficial "variant" (1988),[1] it is more appropriate to note that both portray the kingship as an inherently violent institution. One implies that the violence of kings stemmed originally from Kintu; the other blames it on his sons. The former perspective may represent a "clan" point of view, for the clans suffered many losses at the hands of the powerful eighteenth- and nineteenth-century kings. The latter may represent a royalist view, certainly one that the frequently targeted eighteenth-century Kabakas could identify with. Both stories clearly reinforce the view that violence and the kingship were intrinsically intertwined.

Human Sacrifice and the Dead King

A number of killings took place when the Kabaka died. After the announcement of the king's death, the royal hearth outside the palace gate, whose flame signified that the king was alive and well, was extinguished. The Musolooza, the keeper of the fire, was immediately strangled so that he could go to the underworld and tend the fire for the dead Kabaka. Five months later, when the funerary officials placed the king's mummified corpse in its tomb, a number of royal wives and servants were also killed. The servants had charge of the king's kitchen, beer, water, drinking well, cattle, milk, clothing, and bedchamber. Both the wives and the servants were clubbed on the head outside the door of the tomb, women on the left and men on the right. Their bodies were left where they fell, protected by a strong fence to keep out wild animals.

According to Kaggwa and Roscoe, these people were killed so that they could serve the king in the afterlife (Roscoe 1911: 106–7; Kaggwa [1907] 1934: 10). Only the king merited this kind of funerary sacrifice. It was both a statement of his unique status and a means of providing him with wives and servants in the next world. Kaggwa explains why so many were killed: "Let one [of them] be killed, and he will come back, and we will [have to] give him the others" ([1907] 1934: 10). In other words, if only one of the king's servants were killed, the officials would ᴗe forced to kill the others because the spirit of the one who was killed would demand (on the king's behalf) that the others be sent as well. It is understood that such a demand would have to be acceded to lest the royal spirit punish the responsible officials. Although Kaggwa uses the verb "to kill" (*kufa*) in reference to these homicides instead of the word "to sacrifice" (*kutamba* or *kwenzira*), he explains them according to a typically Bantu conception of sacrifice: the giving of something that is owed to the spiritual world. In Bantu-speaking societies, ritual sacrifice is often regarded as a matter of paying debts to the spiritual world in order to maintain the separation between it and the human world. Sacrifice is disjunctive and ensures that the spirits make no demands on humans, which, if unfulfilled, would cause misfortune (de Heusch 1985: 10–11).

At the end of the mourning period for the dead king, a different kind of human sacrifice took place. The new king wounded with an arrow a man who was taken to the border of Bunyoro, Buganda's traditional enemy, and killed. The victim's body was then burned in a fire made from the center post of the king's tomb. According to Kaggwa, this man was called the "'fowl' that was burned at the death of the king" ([1907] 1934: 13; cf. Roscoe 1911: 109). This rite was similar to the ceremony called "destroying death," which ended mourning for a commoner, in which a chicken was killed and roasted over the center post of the deceased's house. In the case of the king's death, a human being was substituted for the chicken. The substitution followed the Ganda rule of sacrifice in which the sacrificial victim represented the social status position of the sacrificer. According to Kaggwa, peasants (*bakopi*) killed chickens and goats; chiefs (*bawami*, *bakungu*) killed cows; and kings (*bakabaka*) killed human beings ([1907] 1934: 234). Although Kaggwa describes this rule in the context of discussing sacrifices in cases of illness, it applied to all occasions in which sacrifices were made.

Roscoe says that the human funerary "fowl" was a scapegoat (*kyonzira*) that took away the pollution associated with the dead king.[2] In this respect, it was similar to other sacrifices of human beings at the Nyoro border that rid Buganda of the pollution associated with warfare, the birth of twins, and diseases within the country, and cast it on enemy territory.

The killing of the human funerary "fowl" also had historical and political significance. According to Zimbe, who described Mwanga II's accession in 1884, the victim was a Nyoro boy. He was killed, Zimbe says, to avenge the death of the eighth Kabaka, Nakibinge, who was killed fighting the Banyoro in the sixteenth century. Zimbe adds that the taking of the boy's life showed that the new Kabaka was "grown up (*akuze*) and could kill a human being" (1939: 83–84). The county chief who lived near the border region then took the victim to the frontier and led a ritual raid against Bunyoro. The killing of the scapegoat "fowl" therefore served to put Bunyoro on notice that after the five-month mourning period, when foreign wars were prohibited, the king was now securely installed and ready to defend the country. Additionally, the rite announced the king's intent to undertake warfare against Bunyoro, something that was an annual event (Roscoe 1911: 346).

The royal funerary process ended with an orgy of killing, called *kiwendo*, or "mass execution," which inaugurated the shrine of the deceased king. Such killings also occurred whenever a royal shrine was rebuilt or on the rare occasions when the king visited the shrine in person. In 1880, Mutesa reportedly had 2,000 people killed at Ssuuna's shrine after it was rebuilt (Mackay 1890: 185). The victims, who were peasants (*bakopi*) traveling to the capital and transporting goods in the service of their chiefs, were captured by the royal police as they approached the narrow bridges leading to the capital. Roscoe wrote that these people were killed "to join the ghost of the king" (1911: 112). For the same reason, Ssuuna, after decorating the jawbone relics of his father and several other kings at Wamala, had a large number of people killed so that they would "keep my father's fire burning at Wamunyene [Wamala]" (Kaggwa [1901] 1971: 134).

The Baganda regarded the underworld as a very cold place. The dead were wrapped in yards of barkcloth to keep them warm, and graves were lined with barkcloth and covered over the top with thatch or plantain leaves to keep out the cold (Roscoe 1911: 486). The king's tomb was filled with barkcloths for the same reason. Once during his reign, Mutesa visited the shrine of his father at Wamala and ordered numerous people killed to keep him warm. The following account describes the scene:

> The king entered the courtyard [of the shrine] and when a portion of his following had entered, gave orders to close the gate and all who remained outside were to be seized and killed. Again, on leaving the tomb the door was closed on a signal from him and all who remained inside were killed. So that even his friends were not safe. (*Uganda Journal* 13, no. 1, March 1949)

While these killings supplied servants to the spirit of the dead king, as Roscoe and Kaggwa point out, they also indicated the importance of the relationship between the king and the spirit of his predecessor. Mutesa frequently consulted Ssuuna's ghost at a small shrine that had been built near the palace. According to Roscoe, Mutesa "stood in awe of his father's ghost and constantly made offerings to him" (1911: 112), and he took his wives with him to sing praise songs to the late king. Mutesa also dreamed that his father warned him about the disloyalty of some of his chiefs, so all newly appointed chiefs were required to visit Ssuuna's shrine (Figure 1 [21]) and pay their respects before taking office. Mutesa's intense dependence on Ssuuna for the security of his throne apparently found expression in the thousands of people slain in Ssuuna's name at Wamala.

Although the Baganda do not refer to these killings as sacrifices, it is important to grasp their symbolic significance. Otherwise, they appear to be only a practical means of offering servants, as gifts, to the royal spirit. In Luganda, there are four closely related words: *kyonzira* (sacrificial victim, offering), *kiwonga* (offering), *kitambiro* (execution, sacrifice), and *kiwendo* (mass execution). *Kyonzira*, *kiwonga*, and *kitambiro* refer to killings (of animals or human beings) that are dedicated to the gods or required by ritual injunction, whereas *kiwendo*, "mass execution," may be commanded by the gods or by the king alone, as in the case of convicted criminals or people killed at the shrines. *Kiwendo* refers simply to the act of mass execution, while the other terms refer to the religious intent of ritual execution. The anthropologist Valerio Valeri has argued that the essence of sacrifice lies not merely in its instrumental function of gift-giving but more importantly in its symbolic function of representing "the deities, the sacrifier, their relationship, and the results required — in other words, the entire relationship, its partners, and the process that brings about the result" (1985: 67). Valeri's semiotic theory focuses on the awareness (or understanding) of the persons performing the sacrificial action. The killing of hundreds of people at Ssuuna's shrine apparently expressed Mutesa's personal sense of loyalty to his father's ghost and displayed his own convictions about his powers as Kabaka. The CMS missionary Mackay pointed to both factors when he indicated that Mutesa ordered the executions as an exercise of power "after the example of his father" and that the mass killings were "expiatory offerings" to Ssuuna's spirit (1890: 184–85). Valeri, in his attempt to explain the psychological and symbolic function of sacrifice, surmised that sacrificial killings had both conventional and nonconventional effects on the consciousness of the persons performing them (1985: 73–74). First, in ordering the killings Mutesa could see himself in his father's image as a powerful king maintaining order and authority within his realm by executing his subjects. Second, the killings seem to have evoked an assurance in Mutesa that his father's powerful spirit would continue to support him and protect the throne. By his action, Mutesa showed the nation that he "understood" his role as king and that he placed a high value on his father's ghost for his continued success on the throne. Such a holocaust provided ample confirmation of Mutesa's autocratic rule, lest any of his chiefs begin to think otherwise.

Valeri has also drawn attention to the psychological impact of sacrificial violence: "It creates a strong impression and therefore a memory" (1985: 69). In 1862, Speke discovered that Ssuuna's shrine at Wamala, which Mutesa had inaugurated with human sacrifices not long before, was held in such awe that people were forbidden to look in its direction (1863: 276). In Luganda, the verb *kutya*, "to respect," "to honor," also means "to fear," "to be frightened," and its noun derivatives, *kitiibwa* and *ntiisa*, mean "honor" and "fear," respectively. No doubt, the dreaded massacres at Ssuuna's shrine did much to reinforce its sanctity as a monument that inspired both awe and fear in the hearts of the Baganda.

Ritual Homicide and ''Eating the Kingship''

In addition to the killings associated with the dead king, a number of homicides took place during the installation of a new one. Such killings were not sacrifices to the gods or the royal ancestors, and they had no magical power. They are referred to simply as "killings" or "deaths" (*kutta* or *kufa*), and they took place during the final "confirmation" (*kula*) phase of the king's accession rites. In the 1930s, long after such killings had passed into memory (Ssuuna refused to perform them at his accession around 1826), Lucy Mair was correctly told that they were "an assertion that the new king had entered on his reign and acquired the power of life and death over his subjects" (1934: 179).

All such killings were symbolic expressions of the king's unique authority: the right to kill on behalf of the throne. During his installation, the king was repeatedly told that he should exercise the power to kill. The Mugema, after clothing the king in a leopard-skin cloak, admonished him not only to exercise justice and to put down rebellion, but also to kill whoever despised him, for "the peasants are like sorghum; whoever judges them, owns them" (Kaggwa [1912] 1949: 21). The Kasujju gave the king a knife and said, "whoever rebels against you, you shall kill with this knife" (Kaggwa [1912] 1949: 47). The injunction to kill was broad in scope. The king was to kill to uphold the laws of the society, to maintain national security and welfare, and to enforce the code of behavior toward his person. The third rubric covered the rules of courtly etiquette, such as the prohibition against sneezing or coughing in the king's presence. Such matters were deemed as important as the laws of the state, for behavior toward the king's person was regarded as an expression of one's allegiance to the throne that he represented. Thus Mutesa sometimes condemned his wives to death because they coughed while he was eating (Grant 1862; Speke 1863). The king was understood to hold the power of life and death over every living thing in Buganda. When hunters speared animals, they were supposed to say "on behalf of the Kabaka" (*kulwa Kabaka*), for the Kabaka "ruled over all things, not only the people but over the animals as well" (Zimbe 1939: 8).

As if to dramatize this principle, the king engaged in a royal hunt at the time of his installation, and later a man was strangled on the king's behalf and his body concealed in a papyrus swamp (Roscoe 1911: 197). In a second hunt, which took place several months after the king's accession, the king killed a leopard and a bushbuck and then speared a man slightly. The man was taken away and strangled and his body hidden under papyrus roots (Roscoe 1911: 209–10). The leopard's hide was sewn together with a lion skin and made into the royal carpet (*kiwu*) that was placed before the throne. The carpet, made from the skins of two fierce predators, symbolized the king's power. As the primary agent of capital punishment, the Kabaka was called the "lion" of his people. For the Baganda, violence was intrinsic to the kingship as the central institution of justice and political order.

Roscoe, following Frazer, understood the installation killings entirely in terms of magical instrumentality: "These men were killed to invigorate the king" (1911: 210). As we have seen, Roscoe picked up the notion of royal revitalization from Frazer, but neither Kaggwa nor any other source indicates that this represented the Ganda view. Roscoe, however, did point out an important parallel between other ritual killings and the sacrifices performed at the installation of a chief. "Commoners," he noted, "were required to spear an ox, which was killed and eaten, when they became heirs to valuable property" (1911: 210; cf. Kaggwa [1907] 1934: 203–4). This was not to "invigorate" the successor but to complete the succession by making a killing that was appropriate to a newly achieved office. In Buganda, the successor to a chiefship is completely identified with the office; he is said to have "eaten" it because he encompasses it totally. The succession sacrifices were thus conventional (or "performative") acts, empowering the person with the office and control over everything that went with it (cf. Valeri 1985: 75). Chiefs owned cows and killed some of them in succession to office; kings owned human subjects and killed some of them in their rites of succession.

Succession killings took place at the estates of the important clan heads Nankere and Walusimbi. According to Semu K. L. Kakoma, who was a member of the sublineage to which Nankere belonged, "the king killed [*kutta*] people because he finished the *kula* ceremony" that made him king (Kakoma, Ntate, and Serukaga 1959: 18). Although Kakoma uses the verb "to kill," not "to sacrifice," the purpose of these killings was entirely symbolic; they were not indiscriminate murders but ritually pre-scribed executions. By killing people on the estates of the most powerful clan heads, the Kabaka gained supreme authority over all the land, even over the territory governed by the most senior clan chiefs.

On his way to Nankere's, the king engaged in a hunt to show that he was about to complete his succession. Then Nankere administered an oath that gave the king the right to kill anyone who refused to obey. The king thereupon struck one of Nankere's sons with his fists. The boy was taken away and killed, and his back sinews were made into anklets for the king so that he would "have a long life" (*okuwangaala*) (Roscoe 1911: 210; Kaggwa [1907] 1934: 22–26, 142; Kakoma, Ntate, and Serukaga 1959: 15–22). We have seen in Chapter 1 that these anklets contained medicine to protect the king from madness (*eddalu*). They also had a symbolic significance: decorated with tiny glittering beads, they signified the king's superiority over the indigenous clan heads (including Nankere and Walusimbi), who wore anklets made of cowrie shells and seeds (Kaggwa [1907] 1934: 25). The killing of Nankere's son for the benefit of the king also signified Nankere's subservience to the throne. In compen-sation for the sacrifice of his son, Nankere was one of the few chiefs granted immunity from capital punishment, an immunity that included the members of his lineage as well. According to the royal chronicles, in the seventeenth century a chief who held the office of Nankere refused to let one of his sons be killed at the accession of Kabaka Sekamaanya. After his succession, Sekamaanya killed this chief together with many of his clansmen (Kaggwa [1901] 1971: 36–37). The killing of Nankere's son was therefore a dramatic means of empowering the king with superiority over this senior clan at the time of his final accession rites.

Other killings occurred at the estate of Walusimbi, the head of the indigenous Civet Cat clan, where the king took his final oath of office. Here again, the king was admonished to "rule the people with mercy and punish those who rebel against you" (Kaggwa [1907] 1934: 24). The first killing took place while the king played a game of spinning tops with Walusimbi. The object of the game was to knock over the opponent's tops and capture them. By defeating Walusimbi, the king displayed his superiority. When the king called for more tops to play with, the person who ran to fetch them was speared to death (Roscoe 1911: 211–12; Kaggwa [1907] 1934: 260). Then the king went to the nearby estate of Kauzumo, who was the chief of the royal police. Here the king's cooking pots were smashed in order to rid the king of any evils (*bibi*) and diseases. According to Kaggwa, Kauzumo asked the king's followers, "You dirty-cheeked folk, didn't you paint the king black [with soot]?" ([1907] 1934: 25). Anyone who answered was seized and killed. Roscoe reports that the victims were boys who had been sent ahead with the cooking pots and were said to have "soiled" the king's path (1911: 212). By killing these boys, the chief of police gained the authority to kill for the welfare of the Kabaka. The king then went to Kavumba, the estate of Lady Nakku, who was the daughter of Walusimbi, and ordered the building of a ritual hut. The first to bring grass for the hut was killed and beheaded, and his head was hung on the roof of the house. This man was known as Semujizimuto, "he who 'hit' his elder with grass," which meant that the first one to bring grass "hit" the Kabaka (Kaggwa [1907] 1934: 25). Lady Nakku served the king a feast inside the hut, and the king spent the night with her to complete his succession.

At this point, it may be asked why it was necessary for the king to kill some of his subjects in order to complete his succession. Would not the killing of the two "royal" animals, the lion and the leopard, be deemed sufficient to express the king's power over his subjects? The skins of these predatory beasts, later displayed in front of the king's throne, clearly symbolized the Kabaka's absolute authority. On this matter it may be surmised that metaphorical expressions were insufficient; only the actual killing of human beings would do. In precolonial Buganda, a person's life was valued primarily in terms of the welfare of the group to which he or she belonged. The welfare of the kingdom was the ultimate norm to which all human life was subject, and the king was the personification of this norm. Only the taking of human life could adequately "confirm" the king's succession to this supreme status and show that he had "eaten the kingship" (*kulya obwakabaka*) and "eaten Buganda" (*kulya obuganda*). Thus it seems clear that these killings were not merely symbolic accompaniments to the king's accession; they were instrumental to its occurrence. They were like performative utterances in which the saying of certain words both expresses a meaning and performs an action. Valeri has put it this way:

[W]hen a rite of passage is declared successful, and as a result the sacrifier is incorporated into a new group (for instance the group of adult males), it is conventionally supposed that he has "understood," and therefore taken as a guide for his new actions as an adult, the concept of that action as personified by the god. (1985: 74)

In Buganda, the installation sacrifices were not performed as offerings to a god; they were performed as empowering acts that transformed a prince into a king. Henceforth, the Kabaka would take these killings as his ultimate "action" guide in administering the kingdom. The transformative effect of these killings is indicated by the word *kula*, which was given to the rites at the estates of Nankere and Walusimbi. *Kula* means "to grow" or "to mature," and in these rites the Kabaka was "grown" fully into Kabakaship, and only then was he called "Kabaka."

Ssuuna abolished these sacrifices at the time of his accession (ca. 1856), and they were not, of course, revived during the colonial period. Instead, during the accession ceremonies of the young Daudi Chwa in 1914, Nankere presented a ring to the Anglican bishop of Buganda, who placed it on the king's left hand with the words: "Receive this ring as a token of the lasting bond between yourself and your people" (*Okutira Engule* 1914: 6; cf. Kaggwa [1907] 1934: 114; Snoxall 1937: 286). Thus Nankere's sacrifice of a son to the kingship was converted into the gift of a ring, blessed by the Church of England.

The King's Health and the Peace of the Realm

After the king acceded to the throne, he exercised to its fullest extent the power to kill for the sake of the kingship. If the priests of Mukasa, Kibuuka, Nnende, or other gods warned the king that Bunyoro was sending diseases to Buganda, the Kabaka would call for sacrifices to avert the threat (Roscoe 1911: 342; Kaggwa [1907] 1934: 233). The royal police would seize a man and a boy or a woman and her child who were afflicted with opaqueness of the cornea, whitened fingers on the left hand, or swelling on the head. These people were arrested on the roads to the capital and taken under military escort across the Nyoro border, together with animal victims: a cow, a goat, and a fowl. After the victims' legs were broken so they could not return, the military escort carried out a punitive raid on Bunyoro and returned with captives and cattle.

In Roscoe's view, these sacrifices (a specific category called *kyonzira ekibamba*), were scapegoats, an interpretation that seems correct (cf. Gorju 1920: 250). The human victims' physical defects apparently were regarded as signs of evil influences (*bibi*) that came from Bunyoro and were sent back to Nyoro territory with the victims. According to Mair, such killings were purifications that were meant to "set the land right" (1934: 233). The fact that the victims represented all three categories of Ganda society—king (human beings), chiefs (cow and goat), and peasants (fowl)—meant that all of Buganda was protected.

The welfare of the king was of supreme importance to the nation, as was his right to impose capital punishment. These notions were fused together in the king's right to order mass executions (*kiwendo*) of both criminals and innocent victims. Sometimes when the king fell ill, or when extensive littering of the roads with excrement or the seduction of princesses indicated that too many young men were residing in the capital, the gods told the king to order a mass execution for the purpose of protecting the king's health and/or preventing rebellion (Mackay 1890: 185, 197; Roscoe 1911: 331–38; Kaggwa [1907] 1934: 141–46, 233).

Mair estimates that such mass executions occurred about once every ten years (1934: 179), although Alexander Mackay's account indicates a greater frequency during the later years of Mutesa's reign when he was ill. Upon the advice of the gods, the king issued the decree to arrest and execute (*kiwendo*) anywhere from 200 to 500 persons. Peasants arrested on the roads leading to the capital were added to the people already held in detention for various crimes, such as disobedience to the king, plotting rebellion, incest, theft, and adultery. When the required number was reached, the police sounded their drums to signal the end of the arrests, and the king informed the priests of Kibuuka or Nnende. The police then led the prisoners outside the capital in procession to the several execution sites, some of which were located in the surrounding hills, and others at greater distances.

The journey to the execution sites was a public demonstration of the king's power. The royal executioners plundered and looted along the way and arrested people at random. The progress of the processions was deliberately slow and took several days. Every day, the Kabaka heard pleas from the relatives of the prisoners. Sometimes important chiefs and their relatives, if their crimes were not serious, were ransomed by gifts of women or cattle. In this way, the king might pardon as many as 100 people. While many were guilty of committing actual offenses, others (mostly peasants) were innocent of any crime. They had been arrested only to make up the requisite number demanded by the gods. In principle, however, all were guilty; and if any were freed by the king, it was because they were pardoned (*kusonyiwa*), not because they were found to have been innocent.

During Mutesa's reign, there were thirteen execution sites. Each was dedicated to a god, and some had priests and temples attached to them. The sites were known as *ttambiro*, or "places of execution." Although Roscoe refers to them as "sacrificial places" and describes them in his chapter on religion, there is no evidence that the executions performed there were sacrifices to the gods (cf. Mair 1934: 189). Kaggwa explains that to ensure that the ghosts of the victims would not take revenge on the Kabaka or the police, victims were told that the gods Kibuuka and Mukasa had ordered their deaths ([1907] 1934: 145). This procedure would not have been necessary had the sacrifices been offerings to the gods. The executions were legitimated by the gods and took place on their land, but were performed to protect the health and welfare of the king.

Inconceivable as it may seem, the victims of a kiwendo accepted their fate in the interest of the national welfare. According to Roscoe, witnesses reported that the victims seldom protested and "went to death (so they thought) to save their country and race from some calamity, and they laid down their lives without a murmur or struggle" (1911: 338). Valeri points out that in precolonial Hawaii, the guilt of the victim was also essential to human sacrifice, and sometimes transgressions were intentionally provoked in order to secure victims. In Buganda it was sufficient to have been arrested by order of the king. Valeri comments, "Violence can be exerted against them because they have threatened the values that constitute society. Their sacrifice 'purifies' and reproduces society because it reestablishes its values against those who have threatened the social order with their violence" (1985: 69), whether real or fictional.

Mair points out that unlike the executions that occurred regularly at the temple of the war god Kibuuka, the mass executions decreed by the king were done explicitly "to show the power of the king" (1934: 233). Richards concurs, and emphasizes Buganda's uniqueness in this respect: "Many African chiefs are formally praised for their ferocity to enemies, but the insistence that the Kabaka can and should destroy his own subjects is, I think, unusual" (1964: 191, n. 46).

The Kabaka's many praise titles clearly emphasize the king's arbitrary power to kill. For example, he is likened to a queen termite that eats her drones, to the blacksmith's forge that beats and shapes iron, to the blacksmith's hammer that crushes anything it hits, to a cook with plenty of firewood (meaning that he could kill as many people as he wished), and to a long-toothed predator that eats all the animals (Mukasa 1946a; Nsimbe 1956b: chap. 2).

"All this has to be admitted," comments Mair, but "the question of precisely how the cruelties which are known to have been perpetuated by the last independent kings were reconciled with the conception of the 'good king' as expressed at this accession is one that cannot be answered" (1934: 182). The answer to Mair's question is found in the rituals of succession. Here the king-to-be was clothed with a leopard skin and depicted as a leopard who preyed on his people; he was given a knife and told to kill anyone who rebelled. A "good king" conquered his rivals, put down disloyal chiefs, and vigorously enforced the rules of respect for the throne. In this way, he maintained order and peace in his realm and protected his subjects.

Fallers suggests that popular consent to the king's arbitrary fierceness can be explained by the "payoff" that his chiefs enjoyed in plundering the estates and assuming the offices of those who had fallen into disfavor. He also points out that there was a payoff for the nation as a whole, a "psychic satisfaction which came with national aggrandizement at the expense of their neighbors" (1959: 21; cf. 1964: 6). Nonetheless, although certain chiefs benefited by sudden promotion to office and the nation benefited from regular supplies of war booty, the foundations of the king's arbitrary powers were not economic and psychological; they were political and ideological. Richards puts it this way:

> He [the Kabaka] was the source of the whole system of authority on which the political structure of Buganda rested. He was the ultimate sanction for the legal rights of every section of the community and preserved the balance between them. The prosperity and general well-being of the country, as well as its prestige in the eyes of neighboring peoples, was thought to be due to him. (1964: 278–79)

In Buganda, to be without a king was equated with lawlessness; more specifically, it meant civil war, which was the actual state of affairs on the death of a king. As the lynchpin of the political system, the personal arbiter of law and order, the king and the kingship were one. The more the king exercised the powers of the kingship through capital punishment, the more respect and vitality he appeared to possess. Uniquely in Buganda, perhaps, a king's killing of his subjects was one of the throne's inherently sacred expressions of order, power, and prosperity.

In 1860, the explorer Richard Burton was told that when Zanzibari visitors to Buganda remonstrated Kabaka Ssuuna for committing mass killings, he declared that he "had no other secret for keeping his subjects in awe of him" ([1860] 1961 II: 190). Some years later, the missionary explorer David Livingstone recorded the Ganda comment that "if Mtesa didn't kill people now and then, his subjects would suppose that he was dead" (Waller 1874: 223). Such killings were therefore displays of royal vitality, not a means of transferring "mystical" vitality to the king, as Frazer might suppose. In later years, when Mutesa was in a state of declining health, the CMS missionary Robert W. Felkin reported that he often heard the remark, "If Mutesa were well you would soon see some executions" (Wilson and Felkin 1882 II: 23), implying that periodic killings were signs of royal vigor.

In 1862, James A. Grant noticed that Mutesa had to exhibit a certain degree of ferocity when sentencing people to death or imposing punishment: "[T]he existing law of this country obliges him to assume the fierceness of a lion when he has to execute or punish criminals, events of frequent occurrence, and often for very trivial offenses" (1872: 272). Felkin reported that when Mutesa was shown a picture of Queen Victoria, he asked not only how she lived, what she wore, and how many servants she had, but also whether she killed many people (Wilson and Felkin 1882 II: 18). In Mutesa's mind, killing one's subjects was a clear measure of a monarch's power, an index of royal charisma. Mutesa's capital was not only the administrative center of the nation, but also a vast theatrical arena in which the Kabaka was "the master image of political life," as Geertz puts it for the king Bali (1980: 124). The mass killings that he ordered were part of the drama in which the Ganda political life was acted out.

From Mutesa's point of view, capital punishment was also the primary deterrent to public lawlessness. Mutesa once explained to Alexander Mackay that he was justified in having sixty people killed and burned because someone had speared one of his cattle. "In this country," Mutesa explained, "anyone who commits a crime which would cause others to die, that person we kill very quickly, and burn by fire in order to put fear into others who might do likewise" (Mukasa 1938: 67; trans.: 73). Killing the king's cattle was an affront to the kingship, a subversive act, that had to be severely suppressed in the interests of maintaining royal authority. Mutesa appears to have assumed that there was an inherent tendency toward lawlessness in Ganda society that could be controlled only by the display of kingly violence. Every execution was therefore an act of justice, sanctioned by the gods, for the purpose of preventing greater violence.

Such institutionalized violence, Valeri indicates, also creates a psychological impact. "It associates the moral laws that are reproduced in [human] sacrifice with fear and pain and therefore helps to perpetuate them" (1985: 70). In Buganda, as Livingstone's informant put it, if mass executions stopped, people would assume that the king was dead. Then lawlessness and violence would truly abound, as it did during the interregnum period when princes fought for the throne. By contrast, the king's reign was known as "peace" (*mirembe*), and it was dramatically maintained by periodic displays of the king's violence upon his subjects.

Consider in this light Mackay's description of the methods of execution:

> Some will have their throats cut, while others will be tortured to death — their eyes put out, nose and ears cut off, the sinews of their arms and thighs cut out piecemeal and roasted before their eyes, and finally the unhappy wretches burnt alive. Others, again, are tied hand and foot, dry reeds and firewood heaped over them, and then the whole ignited. . . .
>
> Death is almost invariably the punishment for adultery, as also theft on a large scale. The culprits are executed by having their throats cut, just as goats are slaughtered. In some cases they are taken to a distance from the capital, generally to the side of a swamp. Their bodies are then smeared over with butter, or frequently with the gum of the incense tree, and they are hung up alive over a slow fire till dead, the executioner and his slaves meantime sitting by, smoking and drinking, and jeering at the wretch in agony. (1890: 185, 198)

Michel Foucault has called this type of corporeal punishment "coded action," a symbolic expression of the monarch's power brutally etched onto the body of the criminal. It made "the body of the condemned man the place where the vengeance of the sovereign was applied, the anchoring point for a manifestation of power, an opportunity of affirming the dissymmetry of forces" (1979: 55). Both in eighteenth-century France and in nineteenth-century Buganda, such executions were at once acts of punishment and displays of royal supremacy that were crucial to the maintenance of public order.

Mutesa also killed people in front of foreign visitors to show his power. A few days after Speke's arrival in 1862, Mutesa, who was greatly impressed with Speke's skill with firearms, asked Speke to shoot four cows in front of his chiefs. Afterward, the king gave a loaded rifle to one of his young pages and told him to kill a man in the outer court. This done, the page returned with a smile on his face (Speke 1863: 290). Mutesa's point seems obvious: "Speke, you may be able to kill animals easily, but only I can kill my subjects with impunity. Let that be a lesson to you and all my chiefs!"

Mutesa reserved some of his most blatant displays of power for two military envoys from General Gordon, the commander of Egyptian forces in Khartoum, on behalf of the Khedive of Egypt (cf. Alpers 1964). Mutesa feared that the Khedive was making plans to conquer Bunyoro and attack Buganda, and he was determined to convince Gordon's envoys that he was a strong ruler who demanded respect. When the first envoy, Charles Chaillé-Long, arrived at Mutesa's court, he was made to witness the decapitation of thirty lubaale priests (Chaillé-Long 1875: 107–8; 1876: 106–7). The point was not lost, even though Chaillé-Long wrote that the executions were performed in his honor. Later, Chaillé-Long reported that Mutesa held absolute power and authority in his kingdom. The following year, Gordon's second emissary to arrive in Buganda, Colonel Ernest Linant de Bellefonds, accompanied Mutesa's party on a hunting trip. To demonstrate his shooting prowess, the Kabaka aimed his rifle at a woman in the distance who was carrying a vase on her head. He fired, missed the vase, and blew off the woman's head (Bellefonds 1876–1877: 64). Stanley, who represented no threatening military power, was never subjected to such displays.

Public killing, then, was both a legal and a symbolic matter. It disposed of people who broke the law, and it effectively dramatized the king's authority, thereby affirming the kingship. To be sure, the practice of killing subjects could be carried too far. A king who executed important chiefs or was otherwise overzealous in exercising his power was said to be cruel and found himself a victim of regicide, from either human or supernatural agents. Nevertheless, throughout the nineteenth century periodic displays of death within the vicinity of the capital were an accepted phenomenon. Although appalling to Christian and Muslim visitors, such displays expressed the vitality of the kingship, and they renewed that vitality in the people's minds. "Strange to say," wrote Mackay, "in this most lawless land, there is a never-ending amount of *musango* [trial] going on" (1890: 187). Indeed, the Baganda prided themselves on their system of courts. Mackay also noted that Mutesa had a "real sense of *justice*, without respect of persons." However, "to show the power of the king" by means of mass executions was not, as Mackay believed, evidence of lawlessness and royal bloodlust but a demonstration of the system of justice that maintained the peace of the realm (*mirembe ku bwakabaka*).

By the late nineteenth century, the number and scope of the executions had gotten out of hand. The kings, their police armed with guns obtained from Zanzibari traders, had become increasingly ruthless in the exercise of their power. Writing in 1907, Kaggwa observed that "the killing of people in Buganda was the worst of its kind. It had no limitations as the Kabaka ordered the execution of his brothers and even his own sons – the princes" ([1907] 1934: 147). Kaggwa also notes that "the chiefs used to kill their own people, whoever committed an offense was ordered to be killed" ([1907] 1934: 147). Even though this was done in the name of the king's justice, the ideals of the governmental system were severely eroded.

Converts to Islam and Christianity also fell victim to the mania for mass execution. In 1876, Mutesa burned to death seventy Muslim converts, mostly young palace pages, because they rejected his lax standards of Islamic law. Ten years later, Mwanga II burned to death over thirty Christian pages because they disapproved of his practice of sodomy, which he was said to have learned from the Zanzibaris. New challenges to the king's authority were met by increased killings, especially of chiefs and princes. In this period, as one historian has put it, "execution was an occupational hazard at the Kabaka's court" (Low 1971a: 28).

Eventually, the Muslim and Christian chiefs rose up and overthrew Mwanga. After a period of bitter civil war, the Christian chiefs, headed by Kaggwa and aided by the British, emerged victorious and established a government headed by a puppet king, Daudi Chwa II. Thus ended the mass executions "to show the power of the king." Once again, the Kintu myth was reenacted as chiefs revolted against a tyrannical king and placed a successor on the throne.

7

Buganda and Ancient Egypt: Speculation and Evidence

In 1911, the Egyptologist E. A. Wallis Budge drew attention to the many similarities he saw between the myths and rites of ancient Egypt and those of sub-Saharan Africa, including Buganda. On this basis, he concluded that Egyptian beliefs "are of indigenous origin, Nilotic or Sudanic in the broadest significance of the word" (1911 I: vii). Two years later, the anthropologist Charles G. Seligman, a disciple of Frazer, published his now notorious Hamitic theory, in which he claimed both a cultural and a racial connection between Egypt and sub-Saharan Africa. Using ethnography from East Africa, including Roscoe's accounts of Buganda and Bunyoro, Seligman argued that the divine kingship of ancient Egypt derived from a prehistoric, Caucasian/Negro culture, which he called "Hamitic." This culture, he believed, had given rise to many East African societies, including the kingdom of the Shilluk in the southern Sudan and the kingdoms of Bunyoro and Buganda farther south. He also attempted to show that certain elements of Egyptian royal symbolism had later spread up the Nile and left their mark on Bunyoro and Buganda (1913; 1934). Seligman was joined by other scholars who utilized Ganda ethnography in an attempt to describe a widespread sacral kingship "pattern" or "culture circle" that was linked to ancient Egypt and even to Mesopotamia (Baumann, Westermann, and Thurnwald, 1940; Bulck 1959; Irstam [1944] 1970; Hadfield [1949] 1979).

With their far-reaching claims, Budge and Seligman contributed significantly to the burgeoning interest in the relationship between ancient Egypt and sub-Saharan Africa. As recently as 1966, a standard history of Africa stated that the institution of divine kingship developed first in ancient Egypt and later became the key feature of Sudanic civilization

and Egypt's "legacy to so much of the rest of Africa," including Bunyoro
and Buganda (Oliver and Fage 1966: 37ff; cf. Arkell 1961: 177).[1] Today,
however, historians largely dismiss the Egyptian explanation of the origins of kingship south of the Sahara. A major textbook on African
history puts it this way: "[T]he best present hypothesis suggests that many
aspects of sacred kingship were independently invented in several places"
in the African continent, not only in Egypt (Curtin et al. 1978: 49; cf.
Posnansky 1966).

Nevertheless, while rejecting the concept of "divine kingship" as an
adequate category, P. L. Shinnie points out that of all the sub-Saharan
societies for which Egyptian influence has been claimed, Seligman's case
for Buganda and Bunyoro still looks somewhat convincing (1971).[2] Contemporary Egyptologists, for their part, are no longer interested in the
question of Egyptian parallels or influences south of the Sahara, perhaps
because of the doubtful interpretation of Egyptian texts and archaeological remains that this debate has involved.

Although Buganda's role in the discussion of Egyptian relationships to
sub-Saharan Africa has been peripheral, it is worth examining for two
reasons. First, the evidence that Budge and Seligman offered from Buganda and Bunyoro has never been critically evaluated. In 1949, the
ancient Near Eastern scholar Henri Frankfort called for ethnologists to
"test the strength of the evidence" that Seligman presented for the "astonishing similarities in material and spiritual culture between ancient Egypt
and some of our African contemporaries" (1949: 95). These "astonishing
similarities" warrant reexamination in view of the new ethnography on
the Ganda kingship presented here. Second, some scholars have accepted
part of Seligman's argument, minus its racial (and racist) element—that
Egyptian civilization derived from a common, East African cultural substratum (Frankfort 1949; Curtin et al. 1978: 49). The contemporary African and African-American critique of Egyptology has also revived this
aspect of Seligman's thesis, along with his view that divine kingship, as
Frazer defined it, constituted the foundation of all African kingdoms, in
both ancient Egypt and the rest of Africa (Diop 1974: 138; 1978: 153).
Directly or indirectly, the ethnography of Buganda and Bunyoro has
played a role in each of these discussions.

Budge's Evidence

In his book *Osiris and the Egyptian Resurrection* (1911), Budge argued
that Egyptian religion originated from indigenous African beliefs rather
than from those of the ancient Near East or Europe. In putting forth this

view, Budge refused to be swayed by the opinion of his contemporaries that Egyptian civilization could only be the product of the white race. It is worth quoting a statement of this early-twentieth-century opinion because it was so widespread and carried such force in its day. One of its advocates, the renowned American Egyptologist James Henry Breasted, held that black Africans not only were isolated from Egypt by the Sahara Desert barrier, but also were "unfitted by ages of tropical life for any effective intrusion among the White Race, [thus] the negro and negroid people remain without any influence on the development of early civilization" (1926: 113).[3] As Martin Bernal has recently pointed out, there was a concerted attempt by European thinkers to completely dissociate black Africans from "the cradle of civilization." Later, when Egypt was no longer seen as the source of Western philosophy, its African affinities could be reconsidered (Bernal 1987: 30–31). Without mentioning the racial prejudices of his contemporaries, Budge argued that the similarities between ancient Egypt and tropical Africa showed that everything about ancient Egypt, especially its religion, could be understood only in the context of sub-Saharan Africa, and that "the Egyptian religion was of African . . . origin" (1911 I: xiv).

Budge pointed out five similarities between Buganda and ancient Egypt: the preservation of the royal jawbone, the preservation of the royal umbilical cord, the performance of lunar ceremonies, the identification between the king and a bull, and the identification between king and nation.

Budge cited several texts as evidence that the jawbones of Egyptian kings were removed and preserved. One is a list of the parts of Osiris's dismembered body. According to Egyptian myth, Osiris, the first king, was killed and dismembered by his younger brother Seth. Most lists of Osiris's dismembered parts mention only fourteen, but two refer to sixteen, and they include Osiris's jawbones. Budge cited another text from the pyramid of the Fifth Dynasty king Unas that says, "O Unas, thy two jawbones which were separate have been established" (Pyramid Text No. 37). Two other texts from the *Book of the Dead*, Spells 99 and 136B, say that the jawbones of the deceased have been returned to him.

Although Budge admitted that no other Egyptian text explains these allusions to royal jawbones, he suggested that they might make sense in the context of Ganda royal ritual. The Baganda, he noted, "cut out the jawbones of their dead kings and preserved them in honour, and the passage in the text of King Unas suggests that the Egyptians must have treated the jawbones of their dead kings in primitive times in a somewhat similar manner" (1911 II: 92). But the equation here is entirely unwarranted. R. O. Faulkner's modern translation of the pyramid text in question indicates that it concerns a ritual procedure performed on the deceased during the "opening of the mouth" ceremony: "O King I fasten for you your jaws which were divided—*pps-kf* [an instrument for 'opening the mouth']" (1969: 8). As for the texts from the *Book of the Dead*, they refer to the restoration of Osiris's body parts, not to the removal of the deceased's jawbones. Budge himself recognized that these texts were obscure, and he attributed the practice of jawbone removal to the predynastic period of Egyptian history, because the Osiris cult prohibited the mutilation of the human body. Unfortunately for Budge, predynastic burials give no indication that the jawbones of the dead were removed or otherwise interfered with.

Budge also thought that the ancient Egyptians preserved the umbilical cords of kings. He referred to a commentary on Spell 17 in the *Book of the Dead*, written for a scribe named Ani. The text says that the umbilical cord was cut off at birth as an act of purification and seems to imply that this had been done to Ani. According to another text, four goddesses cut off the umbilical cords of three ancient kings at the time of their birth and preserved them in a stone box. On this basis, Budge concluded that

> it is therefore clear that under the ancient Empire, and long before, the Egyptians were in the habit of preserving the umbilical cords of kings and great personages. What they did with them the texts do not say, but the customs of the Uganda and Unyoro throw some light on the matter, for the Baganda and Banyoro have been in the habit of preserving the umbilical cords of kings for untold generations. (1911 II: 94)

But in the absence of any textual explanation, or any evidence of preserved umbilical cords in predynastic or dynastic tombs, it must be recognized that Budge's supposition is unfounded.

Budge also suggested that Osiris was originally an African deity whose birthplace lay somewhere in Upper Egypt. To support this assertion, Budge turned his attention to the relics of the Ganda war god Kibuuka, which Roscoe had recently obtained for the Archaeological and Ethnological Museum in Cambridge. He noted that Kibuuka's relics were kept in a small bag that had been placed on top of a wooden stool. The bag held Kibuuka's jawbone and genital organs encased in barkcloth and decorated with cowrie shells. Seeking a possible parallel, Budge noted that the seat on which Osiris is often shown to be sitting in the *Book of the Dead* resembles a sepulchral coffin, and he suggested that it may have contained Osiris's missing phallus, detached and lost by the murderous Seth. Budge also indicated that the *Book of the Dead* alludes to the phallus of Osiris and that a model of it was worshiped in the Osiris temples. He concluded that the phallus of Osiris played a prominent part in Egyptian beliefs concerning the resurrection (1911 II: 96). The similarity that Budge proposed between Osiris and Kibuuka on the basis of Kibuuka's relics, however, is entirely circumstantial.

Budge also thought that the Ganda new moon ceremonies were evidence of a belief in the divinity of the moon, similar to the Egyptian belief in Osiris as a moon god. But in Buganda, the moon was not regarded as divine nor was it worshiped. Rather, its appearance at the beginning of a new lunar cycle was the signal for people to thank the national and local gods for sustaining them through another cycle and for the king to inspect his magical charms (*mayembe*).

Budge pointed out that one of the titles of the Egyptian king was "Bull," and that the king was praised by being likened to a "young bull" or a "mighty bull." He indicated that the bull god Apis was regarded as an incarnation of Osiris, and he described some examples of cattle rituals among certain Nilotic and Bantu societies of East Africa. In this context, Budge referred to Speke's account of Mutesa sitting on his throne with the head of a black bull on the ground before him (1911 I: 402). To Budge, this indicated that the king of Buganda was symbolically associated with a bull. However, there were no such associations in Buganda, where the Kabaka was likened to a lion, never a bull. This is not surprising, since the Baganda were not a cattle-herding people. Speke took note of the fact that one of the bull's horns was knocked off and placed next to the head (1863: 290). In Buganda, animal horns were used as containers of medicines (*mayembe*), and the bull's head may have been taken to Mutesa for the purpose of obtaining a horn for medicinal use. On this occasion, Mutesa in fact asked Speke if he would concoct some medicine from instructions in a book that he handed to him.

Finally, Budge pointed out that in ancient Egypt the king was regarded as identical to the kingdom, and he quoted Speke's statement that "Uganda is personified by Mutesa; and no one can say that he has seen Uganda until he has been presented to the king" (Budge 1911 II: 162). In Buganda, the Kabaka did personify the nation. But as Budge should have realized, the symbolic identity between the king and his realm is characteristic of all kingdoms, not just those south of the Sahara.

Budge recorded hundreds of other examples from other sub-Saharan societies, sometimes pointing only to general parallels with ancient Egypt. After describing a number of funerary rites, including those in Buganda and Bunyoro, Budge noted that in the Osirian tomb "we see the three essentials of the African tomb, the place for offerings, the pit, and the chamber for the dead" (1911 II: 85). Here, Budge either failed to recognize that such features are to be found the world over or, more likely, never bothered to investigate the matter. In any case, he concluded by observing that from "the statements contained in the above descriptions of modern African funerals the reader will see that the similarity between them and the funerals of ancient Egyptians is too close and too wide-spread to be the result of accident. The indigenous Egyptians being Africans buried their dead like Africans" (1911 II: 115). In fact, the burden of Budge's argument, which fills two large volumes, can be phrased more generally and no less accurately in these terms: the indigenous Egyptians, being Africans, developed an African religion. Nevertheless, Budge's conclusion was important in view of the prevailing theory that the sources of Egyptian civilization lay in Mesopotamia or Europe.

Still, Budge's argument poses some major problems. The first concerns the definition of the term "African." In what sense was Egyptian religion uniquely African? This question never occurred to Budge, who was satisfied with only the most general resemblances. The second problem concerns the matter of superficial comparison: the similarities Budge discovered between ancient Egypt and sub-Saharan Africa can be found elsewhere in the world, especially among ancient and traditional kingdoms. Budge's argument therefore turns out to be little more than a case of "trait hunting," the finding of superficial resemblances between cultures, the most extravagant example of which is Frazer's *The Golden Bough*. Frazer, however, recognized the limitations in Budge's work and asserted that they could not be attributed to "any closer relationship than the general similarity in structure and functions of the human mind" (1911–1915 VI: 161).

Seligman's Racial Theory

For Frazer and his contemporaries, the primary stumbling block in establishing an affinity between ancient Egypt and sub-Saharan Africa was not cultural—it was racial. Here is how Frazer put it:

> [E]ven if the resemblance in this respect [the worship of dead kings] between ancient Egypt and modern Africa should be regarded as established, it would not justify us in inferring an ethnical affinity between the fair or ruddy Egyptians and the black aboriginal races, who occupy almost the whole of Africa except a comparatively narrow fringe on the northern seaboard. Scholars are still divided on the question of the original home and racial relationship of the ancient Egyptians. It has been held on the one hand that they belong to an indigenous white race which has been always in

possession of the Mediterranean coast of Africa; and, on the other hand it has been supposed that they are akin to the Semites in blood as well as in language, and that they entered Africa from the East, whether by gradual infiltration or on a sudden wave of conquest like the Arabs in the decline of the Roman Empire. On either view a great gulf divided them from the swarthy natives of the Sudan, with whom they were always in contact on their southern border. (1911–1915 VI: 161)

It was one of Frazer's disciples, Charles G. Seligman, who took over the discussion of the ancient Egypt–black Africa link and placed it on a racial footing. Like Budge, Seligman discovered certain striking resemblances between ancient Egypt and the kingdoms of Buganda and Bunyoro. In doing so, however, he earned the condemnation of later scholarship by identifying the institution of divine kingship in Egypt and the rest of Africa with the white race.

Seligman, who trained as a physician before turning to ethnography, based his theory on certain physical features of the peoples who speak the Hamitic languages (now reclassified as Cushitic, Omotic, Berber, and Chadic languages) of East Africa, some of whom have light skins, narrow heads, and narrow noses, and are tall in stature. In Seligman's view, the early Hamites were a culturally superior immigrant race of Caucasians who intermixed with the indigenous Negroes and became the "civilizers" of Africa. The "incoming Hamites" Seligman wrote, "were pastoral 'Europeans' — arriving wave after wave — better armed and quicker-witted than the dark agricultural Negroes" ([1930] 1966: 100). According to Seligman, the most distinguishing cultural feature of the Hamites was the institution of divine kingship. Following Frazer, he limited the term "divine king" to rulers who were responsible for the fertility of the earth and domestic animals, and ended their lives by being killed (either actually or symbolically) or by killing themselves (1934: 5–6).

Seligman believed that the Egyptians were a prominent branch of the Hamitic race. Everywhere in East Africa, he argued, the Hamites intermixed culturally and racially with the local peoples; they became racially black, and produced the current populations and characteristic cultures of this region (1913; [1930] 1966).

Drawing on contemporary ethnographic information from the southern Sudan and East Africa, some of it his own, and utilizing archaeological and written evidence from ancient Egypt, Seligman attempted to discern the major traits of early Hamitic culture. He listed the following features: pastoralism, divine kingship, matrilineal descent, circumcision and clitoridectomy, marriage among near kin, totemism (or animal cults), care of the placenta (regarded as a second child), belief in a sky-dwelling rain god, cult of the dead, burial in a contracted position, and rain-making rites associated with divine chiefship/kingship (1913: 682–83).

Seligman seems to have recognized that these few traits, scattered among various societies in East Africa and found together in none, constituted a slim foundation for his theory of a unified and dominant Hamitic culture. His explanation was that the Hamitic (that is, Caucasian) influence was everywhere "dulled" by African blood so that its progress reached different stages among different ethnic groups. The ancient Egyptians, he believed, showed the closest resemblance to the original Hamites because Hamitic blood ran "almost pure" in their veins, whereas the "drag" imposed by the large amount of African blood in the mixed Negro–Hamitic populations varied in degree (1913: 679).

Of course, the cultural elements that Seligman attributed to Hamitic "blood" can be attributed to his racial assumptions. Taking the Egyptians as his standard, he picked out those social and cultural traits among various East African peoples that most closely resembled those of the Egyptians, and he attributed these traits to the Caucasian racial features that he perceived in the physiognomy of certain East African peoples. Such features were supposedly "measured" by cranial indexes, nasal breadth, body height, and the like. As Evans-Pritchard, one of Seligman's students, noted many years later, "no one today would uphold the Hamitic theory as it was held by Seligman" (1971: 150). According to Evans-Pritchard, "Seligman would always muddle up the categories of race and language, an error which can only lead to confusion. He was also a firm believer in Nordic superiority (as his student I had to read a lot of literature in support of the belief)" (1971: 150).

For scholars such as Henri Frankfort, however, it was not necessary to accept Seligman's version of the Hamitic hypothesis to be convinced by ethnographic evidence that Egyptian culture arose out of a "great East African substratum" ([1948] 1978: 6). Here the concern was not with racial descent but with cultural continuity (1949: 95). Frankfort argued that, purged of its racial and racist component, Seligman's notion of a prehistoric cultural substratum, which united ancient Egypt with the Upper Nile and East Africa, was the most plausible theory yet advanced to explain some of the seemingly remarkable parallels between ancient Egypt and African societies. Hence, he correctly called on ethnologists to test Seligman's evidence. In response to criticism, Frankfort also pointed out that "it is obvious that such a substratum, if it ever did exist and if it could still be recognized at this distance in time, could only appear in the form of scattered survivals among people now differentiated thoroughly in respect of culture, language and race" (1949: 95).

Although Seligman emphasized the evidence from the Shilluk of the southern Sudan, whom he regarded as the most Hamitic of the East African peoples, evidence from Buganda figured prominently in his theory. Seligman described five features of Egyptian kingship that he believed exhibited affinities with Buganda: the preservation of the royal placenta, royal brother–sister marriage, royal renewal rituals, the preservation of the royal corpse, and the royal falcon symbol. The first two features he attributed to the Hamitic heritage that, he claimed, the aristocratic bearers of Ganda kingship shared with ancient Egypt. The rest he ascribed to later diffusion of Egyptian ideas up the Nile at the time of the New Kingdom (ca. 1525–1070 B.C.).

In 1911, before publishing his Hamitic theory, Seligman became fascinated with the similarity between an Egyptian royal standard topped by a cushionlike object, and the Ganda Twin symbol that contained the king's umbilical cord (Seligman and Murray 1911). The Egyptian standard, which is referred to as "the Khons of the king," is one of a set of standards usually shown being carried before the king by a beardless man. Because of its slightly bilobed shape and its association with certain hieroglyphics, Seligman, together with several leading Egyptologists, concluded that the standard represented the placenta of the king. More recent scholarship, however, has established that in the rare instances where the standard is mentioned, it was probably understood as the king's *nhn*, a root associated with youth, and may also be linked to the royal city of Hierakonpolis (Posener 1965). Apart from the name Khons, which appears on relief sculptures and text drawings, the standard is not described or referred to anywhere in Egyptian literature. It has also been established that the hieroglyphic character that was thought by Seligman and others to represent a placenta could not be one (Curto 1959).

In Buganda, the placenta is referred to as "the child which is behind"; it is also called a twin, and it possesses its own spirit. After childbirth, the placenta, or stillborn twin, was carefully buried at the root of a plantain tree or in the floor of the house. This procedure was followed in the case of all births, royal and nonroyal alike. The spirit of the placenta then became attached to the stump of the child's umbilical cord. The umbilical cords of royalty were rolled tightly into a barkcloth cylinder, and a long loop handle was attached to the top. This became the Twin (*mulongo*) of the prince or princess, and when a prince became a king, his Twin was decorated with beads. The king's Twin was kept by a royal official, called the Kimbugwe, who carried it on state occasions. After the king's death, the Twin was placed in the royal shrine together with the king's jawbone. Seligman, with a view to interpreting the Egyptian placenta standard, suggested that the Ganda umbilical cord "represented" the placenta. Thus he wrote that "the umbilical cord, representing the placenta, was carried in state by a high officer" and that "the placenta was considered the twin of the king" (Seligman and Murray 1911: 169). Having conflated the umbilical cord with the placenta, the "child behind," Seligman concluded that "there is the closest correspondence between the ideas of the Baganda relative to their king's placenta and that of the Egyptians, so that it may well be that the beardless man who is shown . . . carrying the placenta standard is a high official corresponding to the Baganda *kimbugwe*" (Seligman and Murray 1911: 169). This statement is merely an elaborate interpretation that can no longer be supported by the Egyptian texts. Although other Egyptologists subsequently took up Seligman's interpretation, they admit that nothing is known about how the Egyptians treated the umbilical cords of kings, and they posit a connection only on the basis of a distant racial or cultural identity between the Buganda and ancient Egypt (Blackman 1916: 206; Frankfort [1948] 1978: 70–71).

Another supposedly Hamitic trait was the practice of royal brother–sister marriage. Accepting the prevailing view that such marriages occurred in ancient Egypt, Seligman asserted that they also occurred in Buganda: "Clan exogamy was strictly observed except in the case of the ruling prince, who, on becoming king, was ceremonially married to one of his half-sisters, who shared the coronation ceremonies" (1913: 651). But Seligman again misconstrued the Ganda ethnography. In Buganda, as we have seen, the king succeeded to the throne with a half-sister, called the Lubuga. She was a daughter of the king's father by a different mother (Roscoe 1911: 191). It is unclear from Roscoe and other sources whether the Lubuga belonged to the same clan as the king, who took his mother's totemic clan, although Mutesa II says that his Lubuga was from a different clan (Mutesa 1967: 86). Seligman, however, failed to recognize that the office of the Lubuga was not an exclusively royal institution but a feature of the clan succession system that the royal accession rites imitated. Moreover, contrary to Seligman's assumption, the Lubuga was never regarded as the king's wife in the conjugal sense, and there is no evidence that they had sexual intercourse. During the installation ceremonies, the heir was required to step over the legs of his Lubuga as a symbolic act of intercourse. The royal Lubuga was not, in fact, permitted to marry anyone or to have any children. The institution of the royal Lubuga was not, therefore, a case of incestuous, brother–sister marriage.[4]

As noted above, Seligman regarded the treatment of the royal placenta and the practice of brother–sister marriage as Hamitic traits that Buganda shared with ancient Egypt by virtue of their common Hamitic past. Equally important, from Seligman's point of view, was evidence of later Egyptian influence, dating, he believed, from the period of the New Kingdom. Seligman thought that the Kabaka's final installation ceremony (*kula*) in Buganda was the "equivalent" of the Egyptian royal Sed festival, and he claimed that the Ganda rite was derived from Egypt via the diffusion of Egyptian ideas up the Nile into the Lake Victoria area. Seligman based his views on Roscoe's account. As we have seen in Chapter 1, Roscoe mistakenly assumed that the kula rite was performed several years after the king had been enthroned, and he interpreted it in Frazerian terms as a ritual of "prolonging" the king's life. If the kula had been as Roscoe described, then it would have resembled the Egyptian Sed, at least in purpose, for the Sed was clearly a post-installation ceremony of royal renewal (Frankfort [1948] 1978: 79). But the kula was actually performed at the conclusion of the installation process, and its purpose was not to renew the king's vitality (by human sacrifice) but to fortify him against disease. Nevertheless, Seligman fastened on Roscoe's revitalization interpretation and regarded the ceremony as a "vicarious form of killing the king or as a substitution in which the ruler instead of being killed was invigorated" (1934: 53). This rite, he thought, derived from the Hamitic practice of regicide, a practice he believed was performed in predynastic Egypt.

Frankfort, however, has pointed out ([1948] 1978: 369, n.28) that the details of the Sed and the kula differ in every respect but one: the shooting of arrows in the four cardinal directions, an act that the pharaoh performed during the festival. The same act, Seligman argued, was repeated in the ritual of "shooting the nations," performed by the king of Bunyoro at his installation and at New Year ceremonies. According to Roscoe's account, the arrows were shot with a special bow, called Nyapogo, that was restrung with human sinews at the time of each installation:

> When it had been restrung it was handed to the king with four arrows, and he shot these, one towards each of the four quarters of the globe, saying "Ndasere amahanga kugasinga" (I shoot the nations to overcome them), and mentioning as he shot each arrow the names of the nations in that direction. (1923: 134)

An account of this ceremony by the Nyoro historian J. W. Nyakatura confirms Roscoe's description exactly and concludes by noting that this action "meant that every rebel [prince] who came from any of these directions would be killed with an arrow" (1973: 199). The symbolic purpose of the ceremony, then, was to ward off the danger of rebellion from any quarter, especially one that was supported by one of Bunyoro's neighbors.

The significance of the pharaoh's shooting of arrows in the Sed ceremony is much less clear. The Sed was a rite of royal renewal held thirty years after the king's accession, although few kings lived that long, and it was sometimes performed repeatedly during a king's reign at more frequent intervals. Even though the Sed was celebrated from earliest dynastic times to the Ptolemaic period, little is known about its many ritual and symbolic elements (Martin 1984). At one point in the ceremony, the king crossed a field in four directions, following the points of the compass, and shot arrows in each of the four directions. Then the king was enthroned four times, each time facing one of the four directions. Frankfort indicates that this action may be what is referred to in a Ptolemaic text from Edfu: "I have passed through the land and touched the sides" ([1948] 1978: 86).

The significance of the ceremony, Frankfort suggests, was the king's assertion of dominance over the land of Egypt as the lawful ruler ([1948] 1978: 86; cf. Martin 1984). There is no indication that the rite was explicitly meant to ward off rebellion, although it may have been implied. This question, however, is a minor one compared with the problem of tracing the historical transmission of the festival from Egypt to Bunyoro. For the sake of argument, it might be assumed that the Sed festival survived in Egypt until the end of the kingship and that it lived on in the Egyptianized kingdom of Meroe in Nubia until its demise at the end of the fourth century B.C. The earliest date that can be ascribed to the Chwezi, the alleged founders of the kingdom of Kitara (later Bunyoro), is the fourteenth century A.D. (Posnansky 1966; Cohen 1972). This leaves seventeen or eighteen centuries unaccounted for, with no evidence of the "shooting of arrows" rite being performed by any people between Nubia and Bunyoro. Thus even if Egypt is assumed to have been the source of the ceremony, it is impossible to trace its transmission to Bunyoro (cf. Shinnie 1971: 450).

Moreover, given the naturally aggressive significance of royal arrow-shooting, the source of such a rite in Bunyoro does not in fact require an explanation. Nineteenth-century Hindu kings in India also engaged in arrow-shooting rites to symbolize their military prowess (Pillai 1940: 574–75; Breckenridge 1978: 86). Thus it seems clear that Seligman's claim that the Nyoro ceremony "can scarcely be other than of Egyptian origin" must be regarded as unfounded. Nor is there any substance to Seligman's idea that regicide occurred in ancient Egypt (Frankfort [1948] 1978: 47; cf. Griffiths 1980: 107).

Surprisingly, Seligman's thesis about the "shooting of nations" in Bunyoro has been taken up by the historians Roland Oliver and J. D. Fage. They argue that it was evidence not only of Egyptian influence, but also of the Egyptian origins of divine kingship in all of East Africa (Oliver and Fage 1966: 37ff). Like Seligman, Oliver and Fage assume that Egyptian ideas were transmitted through Meroe to the south. But they do not show how this transmission occurred, nor do they recognize the differences between the Sed and the Nyoro rite or consider the likelihood of indigenous origins.

Finally, Seligman proposed that both the practice of preserving the Kabaka's corpse and the eagle symbol of the Kabakaship were importations from Egypt.

In Egypt, the royal corpse was preserved so that the spiritual aspects of the dead king, the *Ba* and the *Ka*, would have a place to reside during the afterlife. The concepts of the Ba and the Ka were not uniquely royal, and they were the foundation of the mummification procedures employed by wealthy commoners as well. In Buganda, the motive for preserving the royal corpse was entirely different. The corpse was pressed and dried over a fire so that it would not decompose during the five-month mourning period when the new king was in seclusion and not yet fully installed. The body was entombed after the new king completed the installation process. Later the jawbone was removed and placed in a shrine. The jawbone was believed to be the bodily component to which the spirit (*muzimu*) of the king was attached. Preservation of the whole corpse was not required for the muzimu to survive in its shrine. In light of this, it would be difficult to explain why the Baganda should have adopted the Egyptian custom of preserving the whole royal corpse, only later to abandon it in a tomb that had no ritual significance. It seems obvious that the Egyptian ideas that explained and justified mummification — the notions of the Ka and Ba — never found their way to Buganda. There is also the problem of tracing the transmission of mummification practices from Egypt to Buganda, for there is no evidence of body preservation being practiced in the Egyptian manner by peoples situated in between. Indeed, Egyptian mummification procedures involved the evisceration of the corpse and desiccation by natron salts (from west of the Nile delta), the latter being an Egyptian technique not employed elsewhere in Africa.

As for the royal eagle symbol in Buganda, Seligman claimed that it derived from Egypt, where the falcon was the symbol of the king and the god Horus. For Seligman it was "obvious that the eagle and falcon might be confused" in the process of the transmission of this symbol from Egypt to Buganda (1934: 12, n. 1). In Buganda, the eagle was one of three animal symbols of the kingship, together with the lion and the leopard. The last two were also totemic animals associated with different clans, and the eagle was the secondary totem of the Lion clan. According to the Lion clan accounts, Kintu established the eagle, along with the lion and the leopard, as symbols of the kingship (Roscoe 1911: 128). Each was a predatory animal and symbolized the power of the king to kill, which was the chief sign of royal authority. In Egypt, the falcon was the symbol of both the ruling king and the god Horus, the mythical son of Osiris, whom the ruling king represented. As Horus avenged the death of Osiris and enabled him to become resurrected in the afterlife, so the living king restored the dead king to life as Osiris. The Horus falcon symbolized the living king in his role as the restorer of his dead predecessor. The falcon could symbolize other gods as well—for example, the sun god Ra in his rising form. Even granting Seligman's point about the possible confusion between eagle and falcon, it is impossible to explain why the eagle should have been adopted as a royal symbol in Buganda without any of its other Egyptian connotations. A more probable explanation for the eagle as a royal symbol in Buganda is the eagle's predatory nature, which is shared by the two other royal animal symbols, the lion and the leopard.

The conclusion that has to be drawn from all this is that a historical connection between Buganda and ancient Egypt cannot be construed on the basis of the similarities Seligman proposed. If kingship in Buganda and Bunyoro had once been part of a unified kingship complex to which ancient Egypt belonged, surely Buganda and Bunyoro would have retained some elements identical to those of ancient Egypt. But none are to be found. It is also worth noting that archaeological research has not turned up a single object in the Interlacustrine region or elsewhere south of the Sahara that derives from the lower or middle Nile Valley (Shinnie 1971; Blanc 1978: 59), nor is there any decisive evidence that there were contacts anywhere between Egypt and Africa south of Meroe. Indeed, the attempt to prove that multifarious objects and ideas had their genesis in Egypt was a goal of the now long-discredited Diffusionist School, which saw in Egypt the origins not only of African culture but also of a wide range of cultural elements throughout the world.

As for the prehistoric origins of Egyptian civilization, a number of Egyptologists and historians of Africa agree that Egypt's cultural roots lie within the indigenous, prehistoric context of the Nile Valley (Curtin et al. 1978: 49; Mokhtar 1981). Between 8000 and 5000 B.C., a mixture of African and Middle Eastern peoples slowly migrated into the Nile Valley as climatic changes caused the Sahara region to dry up. They settled within the secure ecological zone close to the river and developed a culture based on agriculture and herding along the riverbanks. What is known about the material and social forms of this early predynastic period cannot be duplicated, except in the most general way, by ethnographic data from contemporary sub-Saharan societies.

The racial identity of this ancient Nile Valley culture, assuming it was homogeneous, is not easily determined. The concept of race, especially as nineteenth-century anthropologists employed it, is now recognized to be scientifically vague and heavily ideological in character, so much so that current anthropologists have abandoned it (Montagu 1964; Stocking 1968). Skull measurements, once the key to racial taxonomies, have been shown to be worthless, and Seligman's notion of a prehistoric "Hamitic" racial complex, linking ancient Egypt to the rest of East Africa, has also been discredited (MacGaffey 1970). To be sure, as one African-American scholar has observed, the "reconstruction and interpretation of Egyptian history has always been carried out from some socially conditioned perspective" (Drake 1987 I: 143). Such was the case for nineteenth- and early-twentieth-century racist Egyptologists. Such is also the case for the African and African-American scholars who wish to prove that Egyptian civilization was black from predynastic times.

In cultural terms, it is reasonable to suppose on the basis of current evidence that Egyptian civilization had its origins in the rich predynastic cultures of Upper Egypt and Nubia, whose African origin is undisputed. To this extent, it can be said that Africa was the "cradle" of Egyptian civilization, a theory that Diop has labored to advance (1974). To what extent Mesopotamian influence, strongly evident from late predynastic and First Dynasty remains, accounts for the unification and establishment of dynastic Egypt is more difficult to determine. Certainly, the idea of political unity under kingly rule need not be sought from outside sources; it may well have stemmed from internal pressures among local polities (cf. Baines n.d.), and hence Mesopotamian influence need not have been crucial. As for the possibility of much later historical connections between ancient Egypt and the kingdoms far to the south around Lake Victoria, the impetus for state formation in this region can be dated no earlier than the thirteenth century A.D. (Cohen 1972), an enormous temporal distance from ancient Egypt. Moreover, all the evidence, both archaeological and ethnohistorical, indicates that state formation in this area was a local phenomenon, a series of conquests by pastoralist invaders from the north that occurred many centuries after Egyptian influence had died out in the Nubian area of the Nile Valley.

This is not to deny the fact that important similarities do exist between Buganda and ancient Egypt, some of which are quite striking. Both kingdoms created myths about a hero king who founded the kingship, died, and lived on in spiritual form; both regarded the institution of kingship as a religio-political system that embraced the living as well as the dead rulers; both required the new king to bury his predecessor and to install his spirit in a shrine or tomb so that it could live on in the realm of the dead; both assumed that the spiritual aspect of the dead king could survive only in relation to the king's corpse (or some important part of it); both constructed shrines that served as "palaces" of the royal spirits where offerings could be made; both made use of a symbolic doorway, or opening, within the shrine as a device for communicating with the royal spirit.

But this set of ideas is not uniquely African, and parallels to it can be found in royal myth and ritual around the world. Whereas the roots of Egyptian kingship clearly lie in the prehistoric Nile Valley culture of the fifth and fourth millennia B.C., the cultural origins of Ganda kingship lie within the far distant Lake Victoria area during the fourteenth century A.D.

Nevertheless, comparisons between Buganda and ancient Egypt can be of considerable interpretive value. Indeed, this was the primary reason Budge and Frankfort turned to them. Budge put it this way:

> The general untrustworthiness of the information about Egyptian Religion supplied by classical writers being thus evident, it is clear that, if we wish to gain exact knowledge about the subject, we must seek for it in the study of the native literature [African ethnography], which is comparatively large and full. (1911 I: ix)

For Frankfort, African ethnography was similarly useful in order "to penetrate behind the words of our [Egyptian] texts" ([1948] 1978: 6). To give further justification for their comparisons, both scholars proposed that Buganda and Bunyoro belonged to the "great East African substratum out of which Egyptian culture arose" (Frankfort [1948] 1978: 6).

This idea must now be set aside. Such a hypothetical "substratum" was obviously not as widespread in East Africa as Seligman and Frankfort supposed, and it did not endure unchanged for thousands of years so that its remnants can now be unambiguously identified. If ancient Egyptian kingship is to be regarded as the baseline of East African culture, its remnants simply cannot be recognized in Buganda and Bunyoro.

This is not to say, however, that comparison between ancient Egyptian and sub-Saharan societies is not a valuable interpretive technique. For example, in attempting to construct a model of Egyptian religion prior to the New Kingdom, John Baines begins with the assumption that it concerned such practical matters as life-cycle transitions (birth, puberty, marriage, death), personal afflictions, and divination, all of which are characteristic of religious life in contemporary sub-Saharan societies (1987). Baines also finds it useful to contrast the role of royal ritual in New Kingdom Egypt with such ritualized polities as the precolonial Swazi kingdom (n.d.). The point is that although historical continuity between ancient Egypt and sub-Saharan Africa cannot be presupposed, comparative analysis may still yield productive results. The problem with the comparative work of Budge, Seligman, and Frankfort is that it was so entangled with historical, anthropological, and interpretive issues that it was less than illuminating.

CONCLUSION

The Kabakaship
as the Symbolic Center

In *The Golden Bough* Frazer displayed at length his genius for seizing on the right subject—the myths and rituals of kingship—in the wrong way. Ambivalent about Christian belief in a crucified messiah and fascinated with the classical and ethnographic literature on kingship, especially accounts of regicide, he interpreted this literature against the background of the late-nineteenth-century theories of cultural evolution. He thought he had found the origins of the institution of kingship—indeed, of all religious belief—in rituals concerned with the fertility of nature. Such "magical" rites, he theorized, lay at the foundations of kingship wherever it existed and hence formed the roots of civilization and religious belief all over the world.

Initially, Frazer must have been disappointed with the work of his disciple John Roscoe, for Roscoe's pioneering ethnography of the Baganda described in detail a king who was neither a divinity nor a priest but a secular ruler. Nevertheless, instead of rethinking his theory of divine kingship, Frazer proceeded to force it on Roscoe's data, and in *The Golden Bough* he made the Kabaka into a modified version of his "man-god" paradigm. Fortunately for Frazer, Roscoe undertook further (although less substantial) fieldwork among the neighboring kingdoms of Bunyoro and Nkore, where he described kings who were better suited to Frazer's paradigm and seemed to bolster Frazer's theory. The result was a theory that captured the attention of other anthropologists and ethnologists, sending them down the wrong path in search of Frazerian "traits" and a sacral kingship "pattern" or "culture circle" within Africa, possibly linked to ancient Egypt or even Mesopotamia.

Other scholars, however, realized that while many kings were believed to be divine or sacred in some way, not all were priestly and few were ritually killed. It also became clear that Frazer's version of the comparative method was a sham and that his evolutionary theories were hopelessly ethnocentric.

Yet, because kingship was the central institution among civilizations all over the world, the study of it continued to flourish within a variety of scholarly contexts, such as biblical studies, Egyptology, ancient Near Eastern archaeology, Sanskrit and Indological studies, and African ethnography. In each of these disciplines, the term "divine kingship" broke loose from its Frazerian moorings and came to serve as a metaphor to explore questions about dynastic mythology, state formation, installation rituals, political legitimacy, and symbolic expressions of power in centralized states both large and small, literate and nonliterate (cf. Feeley-Harnik 1985). It no longer signified a set of traits or a ritual pattern centered on fertility rites and ritual regicide.

In the African context, Evans-Pritchard's attack on Frazer reduced the king's divinity to a mere political construct. This, together with the colonial effort to transform African kings into colonial administrators, helped to shift interest to the king's political and managerial role. In contrast, Thomas Beidelman's emphasis on the symbolic role of the Swazi king emphasized the need to examine the mythic and ritual values that defined both the king and the kingship. As Beidelman saw it, the king's ritual behavior expressed central cosmic values, and neither the king nor the kingship could be comprehended without according them primary significance.

The more recent perspective proposed by Shils and Geertz takes this position a step further by arguing that the symbolic forms by which kings justify themselves constitute the very grounds of their reality and enables them to rule. Hence, Geertz points out that "thrones may be out of fashion, and pagentry too; but political authority still requires a cultural frame in which to define itself and advance its claims, and so does opposition to it" (1983a: 143). Kings as well as revolutionaries need the cultural foundation provided by the symbolism of the political center. "The central zone," says Shils, "partakes of the nature of the sacred" because it is "the center of the order of symbols, of values and beliefs, which govern the society. It is the center because it is ultimate and irreducible" (1975: 3). Here, Shils tries to go beyond the conventional distinction between the sacred and the profane and discern the sort of sacredness that constitutes the center of every society. This is not a Durkheimian reduction of the sacred to the social but an attempt to see the center of the social as grounded in conceptions of transcendent power. This is why Michael Kenny, in trying to examine the strongly "iconistic" character of the Kabakaship, notes that "the two elements of the political and divine are hard to separate," since the kingship was a "transcendental symbol of political identity" for the whole kingdom (1988: 596, 606). Shils elaborates on this point:

> The centrality [in any society] is constituted by its formative power in initiating, creating, governing, transforming, maintaining, or destroying what is vital in man's life. That central power has often, in the course of man's existence, been conceived of as God, the ruling power or creator of the universe, or some divine or other transcendent power controlling or markedly influencing human life and the cosmos within which it exists. (1975: 259)

Although Shils does not draw attention to it, this perspective when applied to the study of divine kingship means that it is no longer a matter of examining kings according to a list of universalistic traits defining their divinity or ritual roles but an investigation of the symbolic and ideological foundations on which the kingship rests. Whether or not certain kings are perceived as divine, their charisma or sacrality consists of the verbal, material, and ritual images that link them to the "totality" of things, to whatever a society regards as ultimate truth and reality.

Such a view also appears to provide some common ground between anthropologists and historians of religions, much as Frazer's theories did, leading to a shared perspective. Evidence of such a perspective can be seen in relatively recent encyclopedia entries under the heading "Kingship." In the *International Encyclopedia of the Social Sciences* the anthropologist John Beattie writes that

> for the majority of their subjects all kings are symbols: they symbolize the kingdom they reign over and its people, its prosperity and security, even its very existence. . . . In a certain sense, then, all kings are "divine"; but some kingships are more divine than others. (1968: 388)

Consistent with this view is the more recent statement by the historian of religions Cristiano Grottanelli in *The Encyclopedia of Religion*:

> The most important aspect of kingship, stressed by different cultures in different ways, is the king's centrality and his role as a symbol of totality. Monarchs are symbolically, and indeed actually, the center of society organized as a state. They are considered mediators between both the various parts and interests that make up the social order and between the human and extra-human worlds. The king holds the social "cosmos" together. Thus his rule is, like that of the supreme being of many religious systems, a symbol of totality. (1987: 313)

Although both encyclopedia entries contain certain Frazerian elements, they do not approach the phenomenon of kingship in terms of a trans-cultural concept of divinity or ritual pattern. Rather, they recognize that both the office and the person of the king are sacred because of their intimate ties to symbols of social and cosmic centrality. Moreover, it is apparent that because societies conceive of this centrality in rather different ways, comparative studies must be aimed at discerning the differences within the overall configuration. To do this, researchers need to focus on specific features within the context of a people's political arrangements, world view, and ritual system.

I therefore conclude by briefly summarizing the important ways in which the Kabakaship was the central symbol of power, legitimacy and prosperity within nineteenth- and early-twentieth-century Buganda.

The Kabakas as the center of myth and history. Ganda myth begins by portraying Kintu, the royal founder, as a patriarchal figure who enters Buganda as a stranger, marries, begets children, thwarts Death, and ensures the collective survival of the Baganda through time. Implicitly, this story also explains the origins of Ganda exogamy rules, marital rites, patrilineal descent, patriarchal authority, affinal relationships, and the threefold structure of the universe: sky (gods), earth (human beings), and underworld (spirits of the dead). Kintu is also the focus of dynastic traditions about the origins of the kingship. In this context, he is represented as a foreign clan leader who enters Buganda and establishes the Kabakaship by killing the indigenous ruler. He then founds the clans and gives them their totems. From this point onward, Ganda history unfolds as a series of narratives about the deeds of the kings, all conceived as direct descendants of Kintu. The royal history was preserved not by a court chronicler but by clansmen attached to the royal shrines. While the clans and sublineages kept their own histories, it was the kingship that provided the overarching narrative of the past by which the Baganda understood themselves and their relationship to the peoples around them. Taken as a whole, this dynastic myth-history provided the perspective by which the Baganda understood themselves and their place in the universe.

The Kabakaship as the center of power, legitimacy, and prosperity. In Buganda, all roads led to the capital. The Kabaka's palace stood at the center, on the crown of a hill, with the chiefs' compounds spread out before it. The capital was a microcosm of the kingdom, laid out so that it reflected the administrative order of Buganda as a whole. This arrangement mirrored the spatial organization of the king's court, the king seated on his throne and his chiefs seated respectfully before him. The royal court was the central arena of power where all "serious" acts of the nation took place and where important knowledge was to be gained.

The Kabaka, as the key player in this arena, was the font of all power, prestige, legitimacy, political order, and material wealth. He was the commander-in-chief, the supreme judge, the distributor of war booty (slaves and cattle) and tribute goods, the controller of most chiefly appointments, the chief tax collector, the owner of all the land, and the wealthiest man in the kingdom — in short, the source of everything vital to the Baganda. The fertility of the land and the state of the crops were not indices of the Kabaka's vitality and power. His charisma was not tied to these natural phenomena because they were not of central social or religious concern. At the agricultural level, there was little fluctuation in the semi-annual rains, and the land was always generously productive. Rather, the Kabaka's charisma was expressed in the sociopolitical arena: successful warfare, the numerous promotions and demotions at court, large-scale public executions, and human sacrifices at the shrines of the royal ancestors. These acts were central to Buganda's conception of its prosperity and well-being, and the Kabaka was uniquely responsible for them.

When the Kabaka died, the kingship collapsed and the nation was thrown into chaos until a successor was elected and installed on the throne. In the installation rites, the kingdom was literally reestablished through the new king's enactment of the deeds of the founder kings and his investiture with the symbols of office by the clans. The symbolic construction of the new king constituted the reestablishment of the kingship.

The Kabakaship as the center of the civil religion. As the source of all major appointments, the Kabaka selected the priests of the national gods, Mukasa, Kibuuka, and Nnende. Although these powerful deities acted in the service of the monarch, their priests took orders not from the kings but from the gods, and kings felt divine wrath when they disagreed with the gods' will and attacked the priests. As the chief patron of the gods, the Kabaka had no ritual duties except to provide annual tribute of women, cattle, sheep, and goats to the temples. The Kabaka himself was responsible for building and inaugurating the shrine of his predecessor by large-scale human sacrifice. The Kabaka also kept a number of charms, together with their officials, in and around the palace for the protection of his person, and it was his duty to review them monthly, together with his Twin and the Twins of the royal ancestors.

The royal shrines, although geographically separate from the capital, were linked to it by a central roadway and by ritual ties. They constituted the sacred sphere of the kingship in contrast to the secular capital, and the royal palace always faced in their direction out of respect. Mediums, possessed by the royal spirits at monthly ceremonies, regularly advised the king on matters of state and helped to protect him from his enemies. As the dwelling places of the royal ancestors and the repository of royal relics and dynastic history, the shrines symbolized the "eternal" nature of the Kabakaship through time, despite the death of kings. They were also the pride of the many clans whose "sons" became kings, and they stood for the enduring unity of the nation as a whole.

The Kabaka's charisma. The Kabaka's many praise titles indicated his exalted position at the pinnacle of Ganda society. None referred to any sacred qualities or powers. All signified the Kabaka's supreme authority and expressed the people's acceptance of it; all expressed the king's uniqueness — his differences from and superiority to ordinary people, even the highest chiefs.

He was *Ssaabasajja*, "Greatest of Men," literally, "father or head of all men." This title analogously equated the Kabaka's authority with the authority of a father to punish — or even to kill — his children. The Kabaka's subjects owed him absolute obedience and total respect, like children owe their father. He was also *Bbaffe*, "Our Husband," a title indicating that the Kabaka was both the master of all men and husband or master of all women. Another title was *Ssaabalongo*, "Head of the Fathers of Twins." Fathers of twins were especially honored, and the Kabaka was held to be father of them all (for every king had a symbolic Twin) and hence superior to ordinary fathers of twins and deserving of the highest public esteem. The Kabaka was also *Ssaabataka*, "Head of the Clan Heads." This ancient title originally referred to the Kabaka as *primus inter pares* among the clan heads, a position that the eighteenth- and nineteenth-century Kabakas surpassed when they usurped most of the clan heads' authority and became virtually autocratic rulers.

Many titles and proverbs referred to the Kabaka's arbitrary powers by analogy with predatory animals, the blacksmith's forge, and destructive objects. The Kabaka was *Nnamunswa*, "Queen Termite," because the queen was believed to eat the termites of her hill; he was *Mpologoma*, "Lion," whose roar evokes fear and respect; he was *Ssemanda*, "Blacksmith," a title that referred to the sayings "Charcoal both breaks and welds axes" and "Blacksmith's fire melts in order to mold iron"; he was *Magulu nyondo*, meaning "Heavy One Who Crushes Everything." The constant use of such praise titles expressed not only the Kabaka's position as the most powerful and respected person in Buganda, but also the people's approval of his status and thereby helped to maintain it.

The foundation of these titles lay in the installation ceremonies that invested the Kabaka with the powers of the kingship. The royal symbols that expressed these powers were mostly violent and militaristic: lion and leopard skins, spears, knife, war shield, and royal drums. The words of investiture consisted of the king's vows to defend the throne by killing foreign enemies and rebellious subjects. The acts of succession were also violent and alluded to the violent deeds of the founder kings, acts of regicide and homicide, and the hunting of game. Each was enacted in rituals that legitimated the new king, empowered him with the rights and duties of his office, and reestablished the kingship. Hence, the virtual identification between the Kabaka and the Kabakaship that he had "eaten."

It is a ritual principle that whatever is sacred is hidden from view and elevated in height. So it was with the Kabaka. He was unapproachable by all except important chiefs, and even they had to be announced and wait their turn for an audience. The palace gates were constantly guarded. The king's pages ran back and forth taking chiefs to the waiting enclosure and conveying messages to the king. The Kabaka left his palace only rarely — for example, when hunting or reviewing his troops. The royal fire, which burned constantly in front of the palace gates, signified that the Kabaka was alive and well. Within the palace, the Kabaka ate his meals alone, for no one was allowed to observe him consuming food. Outside the palace, the king never walked on the ground but was carried on the shoulders of a bearer, and no one could look at him on pain of death. At court, people sat respectfully on the ground and knelt when addressing the Kabaka. If they received a royal favor, they clapped their hands, threw themselves on the ground, and uttered thanks repeatedly while twisting from side to side. All important chiefs lived at the capital for part of the year, and each morning they paid their respects to the Kabaka at the palace. As the names of the chiefs were called out, each responded by saying, "Osinze!" ("You have conquered!"). Such acts of courtly behavior were ritual expressions of status hierarchy on which the king's power depended.

As this brief review of royal myth, ritual, and symbolic expressions indicates, the majesty of the Kabakaship was made, not born. The Kabakaship, like all systems of central authority, was a cultural creation, not just a political product, and to understand it requires a humanistic focus on symbolic forms. Frazer, misguided though his methods were, rightly perceived that the substance of kingship lay in its symbolic dimension. African ethnography supplied him with many of his best examples, of which the Kabakaship was perhaps the most problematic. By examining closely its symbolic forms in their historical context, we may have come to understand it better and, perhaps, to have seen more deeply into the study of kingship as well.

Shrines and the Kinglist: Did Mutesa Cheat?

As early as 1862, Speke's companion James A. Grant noted that the Ganda recollection of past kings was kept "carefully on record" by the numerous royal shrines that were "protected and preserved by the Crown to the present day" (1862: 207; 1872: 272). Taking this point a step further, the Catholic missionary and historian Julien Gorju commented that the shrines were "palpable proof of the validity of the royal chronology" (1920: 112). In 1959, Roland Oliver visited most of the shrines and body tombs and concluded that their existence "affords the strongest possible evidence" in support of the orthodox kinglist of Kaggwa and Roscoe (1959: 133).

Other historians have been less confident. Christopher C. Wrigley asserts that the evidence provided by the shrines and tombs for the Kaggwa and Roscoe kinglist is not an "insuperable obstacle to the determined skeptic" (1974: 129). He argues that the Kabakas might easily have created new shrines (and new tombs) whenever they wished to expand the kinglist and that the shrine custodians, seeking royal prestige for their clans, would have eagerly cooperated. Following this line of thought, the historian David Henige has wondered whether Mutesa I might have converted some of the shrines built originally for the relics (Twin symbols) of nonruling princes into shrines for kings, especially those belonging to early princes (whose status might have been forgotten). In this way, Mutesa would have lengthened the kinglist in order to impress Zanzibari traders and European visitors with a more ancient pedigree (Henige 1980). This is a plausible suggestion because in the Mumyuka district of Busiro alone there were thirty-four shrines for princes (Musoke 1935).

In this connection, Henige has emphasized the discrepancy between the number of kings recorded by Speke and Grant in 1862 and the number recorded in 1875 by Stanley, the next European visitor to write down the kinglist. Speke listed the names of seven kings prior to Mutesa I (Grant said there were eight but did not name them), while Stanley listed thirty-one, including two early princes,

Kalemeera and Wampamba (1878 I: 344–81).[1] Since all subsequent lists are in substantial agreement with Stanley's, including Kaggwa's orthodox list, the discrepancy between Stanley's list and Speke's list, amounting to twenty-four kings, is significant. If Speke and Grant's list was accurate, then Mutesa can be charged with greatly inflating the number of kings when he named them to Stanley in 1875. As Henige points out, this would mean that Mutesa had to "rummage around and find other shrine and [body] tomb sites" to back up his lengthened list, for the appropriate shrines and tombs seem clearly to have been in existence when Kaggwa collected his information from elderly informants in the late 1890s. If so, Henige argues, then "the value of the Ganda tombs as independent physical evidence authenticating the oral kinglist is nil" (1980: 251).

The question, of course, is whether Speke and Grant obtained an accurate kinglist. Speke failed to mention the source of the kinglist in his account, perhaps supposing that it was unimportant, but Grant recorded in his diary that the source was a man named Kengo (1862: 207). Speke refers to the same man, whose name he spells as K'yengo, as a minor official at Mutesa's court. Since neither Speke nor Grant say that they checked this list with other sources, including Mutesa (as Stanley did), it seems that K'yengo was probably their only informant.

There was no court historian in Buganda. The only officials trained to recite the royal genealogies were the custodians of the royal shrines who lived in Busiro. They were trained from youth to recite the kinglist by using sticks of wood as counters, each stick representing a single Kabaka. They also learned to recite the names of important royal wives and children, and the major chiefs of each Kabaka (Kaggwa [1907] 1934: 136), many of whom possessed jawbone shrines of their own. When Speke and Grant visited, only the decorated jawbone of Mutesa's father was brought to him during the new moon ceremonies (Grant 1862: 207; 1872: 272). At this time, except for the Mugema, who was the governor of Busiro county and supervisor of the shrines, most of the chiefs who lived at the capital would not have had a detailed knowledge of the royal genealogy. Knowledge of the kinglist among the chiefs may well have been limited to the name of the founder and seven or eight generations of kings. As it happened, this is the kind of list that Speke obtained from K'yengo. Sometime thereafter, Mutesa arranged for the bearers to bring all the royal Twin symbols to him at the time of the new moon, and in this way Mutesa and his senior chiefs became acquainted with the full dynastic genealogy.

Speke relates the story of Kimera's coming to Buganda (to found the kingdom), and then lists eight names without further comment: Kimera (19), Mawanda (6), Kateregga (9), Kyabaggu (5), Semakookiro (4), Kamaanya (3), Ssuuna II (2), and Mutesa (1) (1863: 246). For convenience, I have placed numbers after the names to indicate their generational level according to Kaggwa's list. As is apparent, Speke's list runs sequentially through five generations, from Mutesa to Kyabaggu, then skips to the ninth generation, then back to the sixth, before reaching Kimera, who Speke was told was the founder of the kingdom. Comparison with Kaggwa's list shows that Speke's informant, K'yengo, reported the names of the most important kings of each generation and left out the lesser ones: Kagulu (6), Kikulwe (6), Mwanga I (5), Namugala (5), and Jjunju (4). K'yengo also left out all the names of generations seven and eight and reversed the order of the two names before Kimera. This is the kind of fragmentary knowledge that might be expected from a minor chief at Mutesa's court. Since Speke was interested primarily in the relative age of the Interlacustrine kingdoms, not in kinglists as such, it is also possible that he asked for a simple list of kings by generations. In any case, it is clear that Speke understood the list that he received to be a generational one, and hence his comment that Kimera left Bunyoro "eight generations back."

When Stanley arrived thirteen years later, Mutesa was about thirty-six years old and fully in command. Six years before Stanley's visit, Mutesa exhumed the bodies of eight of his immediate predecessors from their tombs at Merera and reburied them at the shrines with their jawbones. Henige comments that Mutesa's "manipulation of the tombs" possibly casts doubt on the contemporary body-tomb sites as evidence supporting the official kinglist. However, in 1959 Roland Oliver went to Merera and was able to confirm the existence of seventeen tombs and to account for the absence of five others, making a total of twenty-two kings. He was unable to locate the tombs of the seven other kings, owing to the absence of the cemetery's guardian. Most of these belonged to the eight kings whom Mutesa reburied. One of them was Mawanda, whose tomb Oliver located, and he was told by one of the local residents that it was empty. Given the overall consistency of Oliver's findings, it appears reasonable to assume that Mutesa did not tamper with the tombs, but only with the bodies that he exhumed and reburied next to the shrines, leaving the tombs in place as empty memorials.

Henige suggests, however, that because the number of kings reported by Grant — eight — matches the number of bodies that Mutesa reburied, there may have been only eight kings in the kinglist at the time Speke and Grant arrived. Otherwise, Henige implies, Mutesa would have reburied more than eight bodies. One solution Henige proposes is that Grant (and by inference Speke) may have been "mistaken and, having become aware of Mutesa's exhumations, had concluded wrongly that the small number of tombsites [opened by Mutesa] actually involved all the previous *bakabaka*" (1980: 251). But Kaggwa says that Mutesa's reburials took place in 1869, seven years after Speke and Grant's visit ([1907] 1934: 28–63), a date that is consistent with other evidence Kaggwa gives. Furthermore, Mutesa reburied nine kings, not eight as Henige assumes. In addition to his eight immediate predecessors, Mutesa dug up and assembled the bones of Kimera, "joined them with his jawbone," and buried them at Lunyo in Busiro county (Kaggwa [1907] 1934: 28). Perhaps Mutesa's exhumations and reburials were limited to the bodies of his eight immediate predecessors because skeletal decay prevented his finding any more remains. An exception was obviously made in the case of Kimera, whom Mutesa regarded as the founder of the dynasty and wished to honor. Although a few of his bones were said to have been found, it seems unlikely that these bones were Kimera's. The kings Mutesa reburied, then, are the following: Kimera (19), Mawanda (6), Mwanga I (5), Namugala (5),

Kyabaggu (5), Jjunju (4), Semakookiro (4), Kamaanya (3), and Ssuuna II (2) (Kaggwa [1907] 1934: 28–63). With the possible exception of Kimera, there can be no doubt about the existence of these kings, the earliest of whom died in the eighteenth century. Given the climate and soil conditions in Buganda, it would be remarkable if Mutesa had found more skeletal remains to treat in a similar fashion. This might explain why Mutesa did not rebury the remains of Mawanda's brother kings, Kagulu and Kikulwe.

If we speculate with Henige for a moment and suppose that Mutesa's nine reburials did, in fact, represent the total kinglist in 1862, this would mean that Mutesa later built eighteen new shrines (and body tombs) and outfitted them with custodians and false genealogies or converted the same number of princely shrines into kingly ones, and that he did so in order to impress Stanley, whose arrival he had no reason to expect and who was never in fact shown the shrines and body tombs. It would also imply that the clan-appointed custodians of the shrines remembered Mutesa's nine reburials of 1869 but somehow forgot his subsequent building of eighteen new shrines or conversion of princely shrines. The memory of such an enterprise, which would have required the complicity of eighteen clans, could hardly have been suppressed, either during Mutesa's reign or afterward. Although the new shrines would have brought prestige to some of the clans (who would have gained kings in their genealogies), most of the thirty-odd clans would have been left out. Given the wide participation of the clans in the kingship and their competition for the throne, the memory of such an undertaking on the part of the dissatisfied clans would have been especially vivid. As it happens, the clan authorities whom Kaggwa and Roscoe consulted were in complete agreement on their contributions to the dynastic history, and no clan head has subsequently raised any objection to Kaggwa's list of post-Kintu kings. At most, there exists some uncertainty about the sequence of kings in the middle generations of the kinglist (Wrigley 1974), but not about their identity and number. Thus the shrines and the relics they contain clearly support the kinglist obtained by Stanley in 1875 and recorded by Kaggwa and Roscoe in 1901.

NOTES

Introduction

1. *Baganda* (sing. *Muganda*) are the people; *Buganda* is the kingdom; *Luganda* is the language; *Kiganda* is the adjective for things that are done by or belong to the Baganda. In accordance with customary usage, I retain the prefixes (such as *ba, mu, bu, lu*), dropping only the prefix *ki* in the adjectival form. Thus I speak of Ganda instead of Kiganda beliefs and customs. I have also modernized the spelling of personal names, such as Apolo Kaggwa (formerly Kagwa), in keeping with current scholarly practice, but have retained the old spelling of the names of Kabakas Mutesa I and II and Daudi Chwa.

2. Extensive bibliographies may be found in Fallers (1964), Rowe (1966), and Kiwanuka (1971a).

3. Oliver's list was reprinted in *The Kings of Buganda* without acknowledgment.

4. This popular form of address was used only by the British press. In Uganda, Mutesa II was always referred to as the Kabaka or as Sir Edward.

5. Accounts of this remarkable incident, which fueled Ganda resentment against British rule, may be found in Mutesa (1967), Low (1971a), and Kavuma (1979).

6. On this political movement, see Hancock (1970).

7. Mutesa (1967) relates his dramatic escape under fire.

8. The pathologist's report states that Mutesa died of acute alcoholic poisoning (*The Times* 29 November 1969). This finding notwithstanding, royalist Baganda have told me that he was poisoned by an agent sent by Obote.

9. A variety of books describe Idi Amin's rise to power and his brutal regime. Among them are Martin (1978), Mittleman (1975), and Kyemba (1977). Kiwanuka (1979) chronicles Amin's ascendancy and rule from the Ganda vantage point.

10. Recent anthropological discussion of the ethnographer as an interpreter of culture may be found in Marcus and Fisher (1986) and Clifford (1988).

11. Eliade, who himself combined imagination with scholarship, might have followed this suggestion more closely, especially in regard to ethnographic materials. A case in point is his well-known interpretation of an Australian myth about the broken ancestral pole of the Tjilpa people. According to Eliade, the myth tells about the loss of an *axis mundi*, a sky-oriented sacred center, whereas in fact it tells about the termination of the wanderings of the Tjilpa ancestors, their death,

211

and their return to earth. The broken pole marks the place where these events occurred and where the ancestor's sacred *tjuringas* are to be found; it did not sever "communication with the sky" and cause the Tjilpa ancestors to die (Eliade 1959: 32ff). According to Smith, who has examined Eliade's interpretation of this myth in the context of Baldwin Spencer and Francis J. Gillen's ethnography, the "horizon of the Tjilpa myth is not celestial, it is relentlessly terrestrial and chthonic." Here, "it is anthropology, not cosmology, that is to the fore" (1987: 10, 11).

12. My criticism of the ontological role of the concept of the Sacred in the history of religions is similar to that which others have made against foundationalism in other academic disciplines. In the context of Anglo-American philosophy, the underpinnings of this critique have been formulated at length by Rorty (1979; 1989).

13. As Penner rightly points out, "the structure of religion is not to be confused with the empirical and historical facts of religion," nor is it to be found in the "immediate experience of the world" (1986b: 250–51). Structure in this sense is the product of interpretation; it is a theoretical construction of the relationships of parts within a system.

14. Sullivan correctly indicates that such comparative religionists as James Frazer, Raffaele Pettazzoni, Gerhardus van der Leeuw, and Mircea Eliade "knew that understanding any particular instance of a religious expression would require a total hermeneutics of the religious condition of humankind" (1988: 15). Unlike Sullivan, I am not emboldened by this method of interpretation, especially in relation to ethnographic materials whose specific linguistic and cultural meanings must first of all be carefully understood in their own context.

Chapter 1

1. For a general history of British overrule, see Low (1971a).

2. Kaggwa's full name was Kalibaala Gulemye Apolo Kaggwa. He was knighted (K.C.M.G.) on May 24, 1905, for his services to the British Crown. He held the office of Katikkiro from 1889 to 1926.

3. In his important study, Smith (1969) evaluates Frazer's theory of divine kingship in relation to African ethnography. Smith passes over Roscoe's Ganda ethnography because the Kabaka was not a clear-cut example of Frazer's divine king. For Frazer's concept of "divine king," see pp. 40–41.

4. Ackerman's (1987) excellent biography touches only briefly on Frazer's relationship with Roscoe.

5. Among these works, the following are the most significant: Ashe ([1889] 1970), Wilson and Felkin (1882), Johnston (1902), and Cunningham (1905).

6. The comings and goings of CMS personnel were recorded annually in *CMS Proceedings for Africa and the East*. The Roscoes are said to have been at home in 1897, a date that may have included the latter months of 1896. Ackerman

suggests a date of 1896 based on Frazer's notes of a conversation with Roscoe on November 15, 1896 (1987: 210).

7. W. A. Crabtree, a CMS missionary and linguistic scholar, confirms that elderly informants would have been "quite unapproachable and in some degree also unintelligible, without the Katikkiro [Kaggwa]" (1914: 46–47).

8. Cf. Rowe 1967: 165. Kiwanuka, however, notes that Kaggwa's papers and manuscript drafts do not indicate how he collected his information (1971b: xxxv).

9. Audrey Richards confirmed in an interview with Ham Mukasa, Kaggwa's loyal assistant, that Roscoe "knew Luganda very well" ("Interview with Ham Mukasa," 1 July 1956, Fallers' Collection, University of Chicago).

10. Ackerman comments that "given that JGF lived so deeply in his books, that he allowed Roscoe to make the catalogue is an index of their closeness" (personal communication). Ackerman also points out that Frazer signed his letters to Roscoe "Yours affectionately," a form he never used with anyone else (1987: 210).

11. The obituary notice in *The Times* referred to Roscoe as an "anthropologist of distinction and perhaps the greatest authority on the ancient manners and customs of the Baganda and kindred tribes" (5 December 1932).

12. The table of contents of *The Baganda* follows the subject headings and contents of Frazer's *Questions* almost exactly.

13. Unfortunately, nothing else is known about this exchange between James and Frazer; it is not even certain that it took place (see Smith 1969: 439, n. 55). Thus it is impossible to say whether Frazer's purported remark reveals a personal repulsion toward fieldwork or expresses his scholarly conviction about the separation between the armchair theorist and the fieldworking ethnographer. In any case, Frazer did have the occasion to become acquainted with one of colonial Africa's most distinguished native informants, Sir Apolo Kaggwa (see p. 26).

14. This notebook, which is not written in Roscoe's hand, appears to be a verbatim copy of some of Roscoe's interviews. Unfortunately, a thorough investigation by John Rowe has failed to turn up any of Roscoe's original fieldnotes, except a few brief entries in an early notebook (Roscoe n.d.).

15. So enamored was Frazer with the questionnaire method that he failed to notice the revolutionary significance of Malinowski's observational approach in *Argonauts of the Western Pacific* ([1922] 1967). In that book's preface, which Frazer wrote, he pointed out that *Argonauts* was devoted to an analysis of the system of ceremonial exchange and that its main contribution lay in the discussion of magical practices. This, Frazer asserted, furnished "fresh proof of the extraordinary strength and tenacity of the hold which this world-wide delusion has had, and still has, upon the human mind" ([1922b] 1967: xiv). Frazer entirely missed the point of Malinowski's functionalist argument, which was to show how magic (and mythology) made psychological and sociological sense in the lives of the Trobrianders. Although Malinowski was originally inspired to study anthropology by reading *The Golden Bough*, he came to reject Frazer's notion of anthropology as a science of origins and turned away from his blatant ethnocen-

trism. Instead, Malinowski developed a functional analysis of culture and embraced the norm of cultural relativism. By virtue of its impact, *Argonauts* constituted a methodological revolution in anthropology of Copernican proportions, a change that was utterly lost on Frazer.

16. Roscoe also confused the name of the shrines (*masiro*) with that of the body tombs (*malaalo*) (1911: 183).

17. The only writer to claim that the Kabakaship was divine is Gale (1954), who argues that Mutesa's superior attitude toward religion is evidence that he thought himself divine. But most scholars attribute Mutesa's haughtiness to his efforts at political control over the competing religious forces in his kingdom. For an evaluation of Frazer's concept of divine kingship for the rest of Africa, see Smith (1969). Smith carefully examines Frazer's use of African ethnography in *The Golden Bough* and investigates his theory of divine kingship in relation to more recent African ethnography. In view of Smith's general condemnation of Frazer's handling of his sources (cf. Note 20), he concludes surprisingly that "Frazer has treated his evidence on the whole judiciously and that 'Divine Kingship' and 'sacral kingship' are useful categories in treating African materials" (1969: 330). The same cannot be said of Frazer's handling of Roscoe's Ganda materials.

18. The CMS missionary Robert Pickering Ashe, who was much less well acquainted with the kingship than Roscoe, stated erroneously that "the king is always surrounded by his wives; and, when he is old and feeble, it is suspected that they give him his *coup de grace*" ([1889] 1970: 86).

19. Cf. Wilson's statement, "The former kings of the country appear also to be regarded as demi-gods, and their graves are kept with religious care" (Wilson and Felkin 1882 I: 208).

20. This was only one of several instances in which Frazer did not hesitate to impose his theories on Roscoe's ethnography. Despite the scrupulous care with which Frazer recorded ethnographic materials (he sometimes wrote to ethnographers in order to clarify points of fact), he was not above asserting his own hypotheses in the face of the evidence. In this respect, R. A. Downie, Frazer's personal secretary and scholarly scribe in the 1930s, is quite wrong in defending Frazer's methods: "[A]n 'armchair anthropologist' he may have been, but no one ever took more pains to make his hypotheses agree with the facts on which they were based" (1970: 114). See Smith (1969) for a thorough examination of Frazer's tendency to manipulate the data in *The Golden Bough*. Commenting on Frazer's first anthropological study, written in 1885, Smith writes that Frazer "misused his data either by adding details, burlesquing it, misunderstanding what his source has said, or deliberately falsifying what has been said. This sort of cavalier procedure is also all too typical of Frazer throughout his long career" (1969: 34). For the same assessment, see Leach (1966).

21. Irstam wrote confidently that "the king [of Buganda] was the high priest of his country" ([1944] 1970: 30). He based his assertion on Roscoe (1911) and Jonveaux (1884). The latter work is a fictional description of travels in East Africa, consisting of paraphrased accounts drawn from the writings of Speke and other European explorers.

22. In Mair's view, the Kabaka was "a secular monarch responsible for the upkeep of an established church" (1964: 221; cf. Rowe 1966: 62).

23. Irstam also picked up Roscoe's error. Irstam noted that the rites at Nankere's estate made sense only if they occurred at the conclusion of the installation process, when Nankere told the Queen Mother that she could no longer see the new king and that she had to build a separate palace of her own. These instructions would have been meaningless three years after the king had been installed (Irstam [1944] 1970: 23). Roscoe apparently missed this obvious point in his eagerness to interpret the rites as Frazerian revitalization ceremonies held some years after the king's enthronement. In 1907, when Roscoe sent Frazer a brief description of this rite, he did not know that it was part of the installation pattern and explained to Frazer that it was performed "when the king wishes to extend his life indefinitely and retain his powers" (8 February 1907). He went on to say that he had received his information from an old man in 1904 and that he intended to obtain a fuller description from Kaggwa. Kaggwa's account, which Roscoe apparently did not consult, makes it clear that the Nankere rites constituted the last part of the installation ceremonies.

24. Welbourn has rightly questioned whether these were, in fact, Kibuuka's actual remains (assuming that Kibuuka was a historical figure), since they would have to have been four centuries old (1962a: 17).

25. Downie, undoubtedly reflecting Frazer's own views, felt that Frazer's hypothesis about the killing of kings was "greatly strengthened" by the African examples provided by Roscoe and Seligman and later by C. H. Meek, H. R. Palmer, and P. A. Talbot. These, he noted, were "anthropologists of the Frazerian persuasion" (1970: 50, 113). Hence it was important for Frazer to incorporate their material in the relevant chapters of *Aftermath* (1936), almost all of which consists of African examples of ritual regicide.

Chapter 2

1. Ttanda is the name of a hill located about thirty-nine miles west of Kampala near Mityana in Ssingo county. It is riddled with over fifty prehistoric pit shafts of varying lengths, from ten to thirty feet deep. They are said to have been the places where Kayiikuuzi dug into the ground to catch Walumbe and where Walumbe tried to emerge again (Williams 1946: 65). Examination of the shafts has revealed that they were originally excavated for the purpose of extracting kaolin (Lanning 1956: 216–17; 1958: 188–89). It was the Kabaka's responsibility to send offerings to Walumbe's shrine at Ttanda to prevent his coming out of the ground and killing people wholesale (Roscoe 1911: 315; Kaggwa [1907] 1934: 209–10).

2. Dr. Aloysius M. Lugira, viewing Kintu's story from a Christian perspective, has commented that "the lesson of this story according to the traditions of the Baganda is not so much about disobedience as it is about *obuntubulamu* or humaneness" (personal communication). For a theological interpretation of the East African Bantu concept of *obuntu* as the "quintessence of human existence," see Twesigye (1987: 109–13, 150–51).

3. Another version says that Ggulu sent a figure named Mpobe to capture Walumbe and that he failed when children raised the alarm and scared Walumbe, who then fled into the ground (S. Byekwaso Mayanja, personal communication).

4. Chickens (and eggs) are still regarded as men's food, and women believe that if they eat them they will grow "beards" (like a chicken's crop) and that they will become barren.

5. Mair explains that the noun *kojja* comes from the verb *kulobola*, "to take one's share." "It is used of a chief taking his share of taxation, fines, or spoils of war, and its *raison d'être* was said to be 'to thank him [the *kojja*] for giving the woman who bore the children' and 'because the children are a sort of profit'" (1934: 62). Kojja, although referring specifically to the brother who arranged a woman's marriage, may also include all her classificatory brothers (*mwanyina*). Hence, kojja generally means "male of mother's lineage." Although Walumbe is never explicitly referred to as kojja in Kaggwa's text, he is described as one of Nnambi's brothers, and he implicitly performs the role of kojja by insisting on accompanying Nnambi to her new place of residence after her marriage. In Mulira's version, Walumbe's relationship to Kintu's children is explicit, and he is referred to as *kojjaabwe*, "their mother's brother" ([1951] 1970: 17). Welbourn has informed me that some Baganda with whom he discussed the story in the 1950s assumed that Walumbe was kojja and pointed out that Kintu was therefore wrong to refuse Walumbe's request for a child. Kaggwa's incomplete and simplified version of the story at the beginning of *Basekabaka* ([1901] 1971: 1) refers to Walumbe incorrectly as Kintu's brother (*muganda*). In this version, blood and clan relationships are not important, nor is the motive for Walumbe's killing Kintu's children. Roscoe recorded the same version, probably from Kaggwa's text, in his initial articles (1901; 1902), but later got Walumbe's relationship to Kintu right in *The Baganda* (1911: 460–64).

Chapter 3

1. The date of Kintu's founding of the Kabakaship can be only roughly approximated. The dynastic chronology of the Interlacustrine kingdoms is very complex and does not require full discussion here. For an explanation of the generally accepted chronological system, see Cohen (1970). The flaws in this dating scheme have been identified and explained by Henige (1974). A more recent and somewhat balanced view of the matter is presented by Oliver (1977). The present discussion demands only the most general chronology, based on the dynastic generations of the Ganda kinglist. For an examination of the accuracy of Kaggwa and Roscoe's kinglist, see the Appendix. There are strong reasons to accept this kinglist, which claims a generational depth of nineteen kings, from Kimera to Mutesa I (d. 1884). If we estimate twenty-seven years to a generation (cf. Oliver 1977), Kimera's reign may be placed in the mid-fourteenth century (around A.D. 1370). The arrival of the founder Kintu (Kimera's alleged great-grandfather) might therefore be placed in the late thirteenth century. Here I am in

agreement with Oliver and with Kiwanuka's calculations (1971b: 284–86). Although it must be recognized that the earliest parts of the genealogy are the least reliable, genealogical tie-ins with the kinglist of Bunyoro make this date, at least, a reasonable guess.

2. On the "Hamitic" question, see pp. 189–90.

3. Accounts of funerary rites and clan installation ceremonies can be found in Kaggwa ([1907] 1934: 196–209), Roscoe (1911: 116–24), Mair (1934: 205–22), Nsimbi (1956a: 32–33), and Mutebi (1971).

4. The full sequence of royal installation rites is described in Kaggwa ([1907] 1934: 4–26, 89–96, 111–17), Roscoe (1911: 104–14, 189–214), and Nsimbi (1956b: 45–48, 154).

5. The story of Kintu's conquest of Bbemba at Buddo Hill appears in somewhat different versions. See Kaggwa ([1901] 1971: 5–7; [1912] 1949: 41), Cunningham (1905: 170–78), "Kintu ne Bemba," *Munno* (1915: 93–95), Nsimbi (1956b: 153–54, 184–85), Kakoma, Ntate, and Serukaga (1959: 3–4), and Kabuga (1963).

6. For a list of sources, see Notes 4 and 9.

7. The same may be said of the structuralist studies of Luc de Heusch. At the beginning of *The Drunken King*, de Heusch asserts that in Africa "history is ensnared by myth, which imposes its own sovereignty on the kings" (1982: 2). Then he asks, "Do the foundation myths of African kingdoms provide us with the keys to their histories?" (1982: 8). Unfortunately, although de Heusch answers this question in the affirmative, his purpose is not historical but analytic: the laying bare of the "Bantu" mythical mind. The mythic symbols and topics that de Heusch selects for study — for example, the raw and the cooked, honey and tobacco, noise and silence — are those that were selected by Lévi-Strauss in *Mythologiques* for Amerindian myths. Satisfied that by examining such symbolisms he has found the mythic "key" to Bantu royal traditions, de Heusch ends his study; we never get to the historical issue of the reconstruction of early Kongo states.

8. See, for example, "Sesota" in Kaggwa ([1902] 1951: 77–88) and "Sesota, the Large Snake" in Roscoe (1911: 475–77).

9. Accounts of the ceremonies at Buddo Hill appear in Kaggwa ([1907] 1934: 4–14), Roscoe (1911: 191–96), *Okutikira Engule* (1914), "Ebye Buddo," *Munno* (October–November 1915), Zimbe (1939: 79–82), Snoxall (1937), Williams (1940), Nsimbi (1956b: 154–55), Richards (1966: 35–45), and "Olusozi Buddo" (n.d.).

10. The story of Kimera's birth and return to Buganda is found in Stanley (1878 I: 348–49; 1893: 126–60), Kaggwa ([1901] 1971: 10–17), Le Veux ([1882] 1914: 53–57), Mukasa (1946b), and Nsimbi (1956b: 38–43, 156–61).

Chapter 4

1. Previous accounts of the installation ceremonies are mostly descriptive and give little attention to questions of symbolic meaning and historical change. The relevant sources are listed under Chapter 3, Notes 4 and 9.

2. Although Mutesa died on October 9, Zimbe incorrectly wrote that he died on October 5 (Rowe 1966: 185; *CMS Intelligencer* April 1885: 250). This means that Zimbe's date of October 15 for Mwanga's accession (1939: 84), which was tied to Mutesa's funeral, may therefore be incorrect. Nevertheless, Zimbe's day-by-day account of the installation process indicates that it was completed within two weeks of Mutesa's death. After the accession, Zimbe says, Mwanga spent forty days in seclusion in the king's mourning "stockade" (*kakomera*) before founding his new capital at Bubeja (1939: 87). This, too, was an innovation, as Mwanga had already ended mourning before his accession.

3. Mwanga was reinstated on the throne by the Christian faction in 1889 but was subsequently ousted by the Christians in alliance with the British in 1897.

4. Since this part of the rite was a repetition of the abbreviated installation ceremony performed by Kaggwa in 1897, when Chwa was but an infant, the performance in 1910 was a tacit admission that the earlier rite was invalid.

5. A copy of "The Uganda Agreement of 1900" appears in Kiwanuka (1971a: 288–301).

6. Roscoe says that Kintu's jawbone was removed and preserved at Magonga (1911: 214), while Kaggwa says that the custom of preserving the royal jawbone was believed to have begun with the death of Prince Kalemeera ([1907] 1934: 18). Kaggwa himself reports that he discovered two jawbones tied together at Magonga and that the shrine keepers knew nothing about them. He supposed that they belonged to Kintu and Nnambi or to Chwa I ([1907] 1934: 18). Gorju says that this "discovery" occurred in 1894 when permission was sought from Kabaka Mwanga to investigate Kintu's shrine at Magonga (1920: 101–2).

7. It should be noted that Louis XIV himself probably never uttered this expression, although it aptly expresses his view of the relationship between him and the kingdom of France.

8. George Pilkington, a CMS missionary, wrote that after Mutesa died someone claimed to be possessed by Mutesa's spirit, but when he tried to read an Arabic book and failed, he was "well beaten for his pains" (Harford-Battersby 1898: 220).

9. The Roscoe ethnographic collection in the University Museum of Archaeology and Ethnology at Cambridge contains three egg-shaped Twins (nos. 20.369, 08.624, and 11.397) and two cylinder-and-handle ones (nos. 08.625 and 08.626), Roscoe, who wrote the identification cards for this collection, noted that the largest and most decorated of the egg-shaped Twins (no. 20.369) may have belonged to Kabaka Kamaanya (d. ca. 1824).

Chapter 5

1. Kaggwa ([1907] 1934: chap. 11) describes the capital in detail. Roscoe (1911: 523–25) gives "explanatory notes" to Kaggwa's diagram. Several articles in the Catholic newsletter *Munno* also contain descriptions of the court in Mutesa's

time (1933: 51–53, 71–74, 151–52, 217–20). See also a brief description of the capital by A. Sebbowa Pokino (*Munno* 1912: 90–92, 102–3).

2. I am grateful to Robert J. Thornton, who, in an excellent paper (1974), pointed out the significance of the right–left division within the capital.

3. The title "Kabaka" is in fact a gender-neutral term. In addition to the king, it applied to three women: the Queen Mother, the Queen Sister, and the Kaddulu-baale or Chief Wife, who had charge of the king's charms. Both the Queen Mother and the Queen Sister were high-ranking, chiefly authorities who paid no taxes or tribute, not even to the king; they lived in their own palaces and "ruled over" (*kufuga*) their own officials and county estates with absolute powers of life and death, which they exercised in their own courts, exactly like the king. Even though they ranked below the king, they held the title of Kabaka in view of their unusual power and autonomy in the kingdom (cf. Roscoe 1911: 232, 236–37). Roscoe also points out that peasants often used the term *Kabaka* in reference to any person freed of state labor and taxation (1921: 168). Ganda princesses were also regarded as socially male; they had to be addressed by the male title "Sir" (*Ssebo*), not "Lady" or "Madame" (*Nnyabo*). They were forbidden to marry and were prohibited from having children on penalty of death. In this way, the line of succession was secured through the males. Today, princesses still are addressed in this fashion out of respect, even though they are permitted to marry and have children.

4. The county of Busiro, I was told, took its name from the fact that most of the royal shrines, called *masiro*, were located within the county (*bu* being the locative prefix added to the stem *siro* [cf. Roscoe 1911: 252]). According to Kagg-wa, Obusiro was originally the name of a small hill in Busiro county where Kabaka Ttembo, Kimera's successor, founded his capital. Thereafter, Kaggwa says, the name *obusiro* referred to the place where the king resided, and it became synonymous with the king's palace, especially his court where he met his chiefs. Hence, chiefs said they went to see the king at Busiro. By extension, Kaggwa suggests, *obusiro* came to refer to the county where the deceased kings were buried and where their shrines were located [1907] 1934: 170). In its broadest sense, *busiro* may refer both to the king and to the kingdom as a whole. Hence, the expression *obusiro buladde*, which means that "the king and the kingdom are well and at peace."

5. Stanley refers to a side door that led to the rear of the audience hall (1878 I: 399).

6. Roscoe, too, refers to the platform as a "throne" (1901: 130; 1911: 284). The term *mwaliiro* is also translated as "shrine in heathen temple" (Snoxall 1967: 233) because the lubaale temples contain similar platforms of beaten earth on which the mediums sit when possessed. Such earthen platforms are called *kituuti*—literally, "mud platform" (Rigby and Lule 1973: 73, n. 13). Kaggwa explains that the royal kituuti in the king's audience hall measured five feet long, four feet wide, and three feet high ([1907] 1934: 169). In 1862, Speke gave Mutesa

a metal chair, which was placed on top of the royal platform and thereafter used as the throne.

7. Although the term "new moon" refers to the lunar phase when the moon is invisible, I use this expression (like other authors) to translate the Luganda verb *okuboneka*, "to be new," in reference to the first appearance of the crescent moon.

8. Lush refers to the "end of the moon" as *okuwabya olumbe*—literally, the "end of mourning" (1937: 19). Although I have never heard this expression used to refer to the dark phase of the moon, it aptly suggests that the moon was thought to die at the end of its monthly cycle.

9. A few of the songs sung at twin ceremonies are recorded in Kaggwa ([1907] 1934: 193), and Mutebi (1972).

10. Taylor confirms that royal mediums are sometimes drawn from far away. He also describes an interesting case of a Christian woman who was possessed by the spirit of Prince Luyidde, son of Kabaka Mulondo, and went to live at Mulondo's shrine (1958: 211).

11. Both Taylor (1958: 211–15) and Orley (1970: 18, 64) describe this nonroyal perspective, in which the spirits of dead kings and princes are regarded as lubaale.

12. Ezera Musoke, the chief of this area (Mumyuka district) in Busiro, attested to the fact that there were no lubaale temples in the vicinity of the royal shrines (1935). An earlier list published in *Munno* (October 1922: 152–53) also made clear that the divination practices associated with the lubaale did not occur in the royal shrines.

Chapter 6

1. There is no evidence for Yoder's claim that Sabadu and his fellow chiefs invented the story of the benevolent Kintu and his wicked sons "to voice their discontent against his [Mutesa's] violence and tyranny by circulating a boldly revised version of the sacred Kintu myth" (1988: 367).

2. Throwing out the grass floor covering of the deceased's house is also called *okutwala olumbe ebwera*, "to take death outside" (Mutebi 1971: 4).

Chapter 7

1. The current edition of Oliver and Fage (2nd rev. ed.: 1970) contains the same statement.

2. Shinnie misunderstood Seligman's statement about the identity between the Egyptian falcon and the Ganda royal eagle and assumed that Seligman was referring to Bunyoro instead of Buganda.

3. This passage was removed from the 1938 revised edition of *The Conquest of Civilization*.

4. Luc de Heusch, in examining the question of royal incest in Buganda, fails to note that the lubuga is not a uniquely royal office but part of the general clan succession pattern. The purpose of the clan lubuga is to provide the newly installed chief with a clan "wife" who "will never leave him" (Nsimbi 1956a: 33). The royal Lubuga, or Queen Sister, is an extension of this idea, the woman being the king's faithful half-sister who later becomes the ritual official (*Nnaalinnya*) in charge of her brother's jawbone shrine. Although the sources do not say it, the symbolism of the royal Lubuga would make sense only if she belonged to the same totemic clan as the king — that of his mother. (It is possible that Mutesa II, in choosing a Lubuga who did not belong to his mother's clan, departed from custom.) When seen in context, then, the royal Lubuga is not a mark of "sacral kingship" nor of "secret hierogamy" related to ritual fertility, nor is it a sign of ancient royal matrilineality (de Heusch 1987: 77–78, 94, 127).

Appendix

1. Prince Kalemeera, son of Kabaka Chwa Nabakka, and Prince Wampamba, son of Kabaka Kiggala, both have shrines that contain their jawbones and Twin symbols. Kalemeera's is located at Serinya and Wampamba's at Nsekwa in Busiro county (cf. Musoke 1935).

BIBLIOGRAPHY

Ackerman, Robert. 1987. *J. G. Frazer: His Life and Work*. Cambridge: Cambridge University Press.

Alpers, Edward A. 1964. Charles Chaillé-Long's mission to Mutesa of Buganda. *Uganda Journal* 29: 1–11.

Alston, William P. 1967. Religion. In *Encyclopedia of Philosophy*. Vol. 7: 140–45. Edited by Paul Edwards. New York: Macmillan.

Apter, D. E. 1961. *The Political Kingdom in Uganda*. Princeton, N.J.: Princeton University Press.

Arkell, A. J. 1961. *A History of the Sudan from Earliest Times to 1821*. 2nd ed. London: University of London, Athlone Press.

Ashe, Robert Pickering. [1889] 1970. *Two Kings of Uganda*. London: Cass.

_____. 1895. *Chronicles of Uganda*. New York: Randolf.

Atkinson, Ronald R. 1975. The traditions of the early kings of Buganda: Myth, history, and structural analysis. *History in Africa* 1: 17–57.

Baines, John. 1987. Practical religion and piety. *Journal of Egyptian Archaeology* 73: 79–98.

_____. n.d. The origins of kingship in Egypt. Unpublished paper.

Baskerville, Mrs. George. [1925] 1969. *The Flame Tree and Other Folk-Lore Stories from Uganda*. New York: Negro Universities Press.

Baumann, H., D. Westermann, and H. Thurnwald. 1940. *Volkerkunde von Afrika*. Essen: Essener Verlagsanstalt.

Beattie, John. 1968. Kingship. In *International Encyclopedia of the Social Sciences*. Vol. 8: 386–89. Edited by David L. Sills. New York: Macmillan.

_____. 1971. *The Nyoro State*. Oxford: Clarendon Press.

Beidelman, T. O. 1966. Swazi royal ritual. *Africa* 36: 373–405.

Bellefonds, Ernest Linant de. 1876–1877. Itinéraire et notes de E. Linant de Bellefonds voyage de service fait entre le poste militaire de Fatiko et la capitale de M'tesa, roi d'Ouganda (avec carte), février–juin 1875. *Bulletin Trimestriel de la Société Khédival de Géographie du Caire*, ser. 1: 1–104.

Belmont, Nicole. 1979. *Arnold Van Genep*. Translated by Derek Coltman. Chicago: University of Chicago Press.

Bernal, Martin. 1987. *Black Athena*. Vol. 1. London: Free Association Books.

Blackman, Aylward M. 1916. Some remarks on an emblem upon the head of an ancient Egyptian birth-goddess. *Journal of Egyptian Archaeology*: 235–49.

Blanc, Nicole. 1978. The peopling of the Nile Valley south of the twenty-third parallel. In *The Peopling of Ancient Egypt and the Deciphering of the Meroitic Script*, 37–63. Paris: UNESCO.

Brain, James L. 1973. Ancestors as elders — Further thoughts. *Africa* 43: 122–33.

Breasted, James Henry. 1926. *The Conquest of Civilization*. New York: Harper & Brothers.

———. 1938. *The Conquest of Civilization*. Edited by Edith Williams Ware. New York: Harper & Brothers.

Breckenridge, Carol A. 1978. From Protector to litigant: Changing relations between Hindu temples and the Raja of Ramnad. In *South Indian Temples*. Edited by Burton Stein, 72–106. Delhi: Vikas.

Budge, E. A. Wallis. 1911. *Osiris and the Egyptian Resurrection*. 2 vols. London: Philip Lee Warner.

Bulck, V. van. 1959. La place du roi divin dans les cercles culturels d'afrique noire. In *The Sacral Kingship*, 98–134. Leiden: Brill.

Buligwanga, Eriya M. 1916. *Ekitabo Ekitegeza Ekika Kye Mamba*. Kampala: Uganda Publishing.

Burton, Richard F. [1860] 1961. *The Lake Region of Central Africa*. 2 vols. New York: Horizon Press.

Cannadine, David, and Simon Price. 1987. *Rituals of Royalty*. Cambridge: Cambridge University Press.

Chaillé-Long, Charles. 1875. Colonel Long's mission to king M'tesa. *Proceedings of the Royal Geographical Society* 14: 107–10.

———. 1876. *Central Africa*. London: Sampson Low, Marston, Searle & Rivington.

Clifford, James. 1988. *The Predicament of Culture: Twentieth-Century Ethnography, Literature, and Art*. Cambridge, Mass.: Harvard University Press.

Cohen, David W. 1970. A survey of Interlacustrine chronology. *Journal of African History* 11: 177–99.

———. 1972. *The Historical Tradition of Busoga*. Oxford: Clarendon Press.

Coronation of King Daudi. 1949. *Uganda Journal* 13: 225–28. (Originally published in *Uganda Notes* [September 1910])

Cox, A. H. 1950. The growth and expansion of Buganda. *Uganda Journal* 14: 153–59.

Crabtree, W. A. 1914. Review of *The Baganda*. *Man*: 46–47.

Cunningham, J. F. 1905. *Uganda and Its Peoples*. London: Hutchinson.

Curtin, Philip, et al. 1978. *African History*. Boston: Little, Brown.

Curto, Silvio. 1959. Ricerche sulla natura e significato dei caratteri geroglifici di forma circolare. *Aegyptus* 39: 227–79.

de Heusch, Luc. 1982. *The Drunken King*. Translated by Roy Willis. Bloomington: Indiana University Press.

———. 1985. *Sacrifice in Africa*. Translated by Linda O'Brien and Alice Morton. Bloomington: Indiana University Press.

———. 1987. *Ecrits sur la royauté sacrée*. Brussels: Université de Bruxelles.

Diop, Cheikh Anta. 1974. *The African Origin of Civilization: Myth or Reality?* Translated by Mercer Cook. New York: Lawrence Hill.

Doornbos, Martin R. 1975. *Regalia Galore: The Decline and Eclipse of Ankole Kingship.* Nairobi: East African Literature Bureau.

Douglas, Mary. 1966. *Purity and Danger.* London: Routledge and Kegan Paul.

Downie, R. Angus. 1970. *Frazer and the Golden Bough.* London: Gollancz.

Drake, St. Clair. 1987. *Black Folk Here and There.* Vol. 1. Los Angeles: University of California Press.

Ebifa Mu Buganda (Events in Buganda). Mmengo: Church Missionary Society in Buganda.

Ekika kye Mpologoma (The Lion Clan). 1956. Namirembe, Uganda.

Ekitabo ky'Ekika Kye Mpewo (The Book of the Oribi Antelope Clan). n.d.

Eliade, Mircea. 1959. *Cosmos and History.* Translated by Willard R. Trask. New York: Harper & Row.

––––––. 1961. *The Sacred and the Profane.* Translated by Willard R. Trask. New York: Harper & Row.

––––––. 1963. *Myth and Reality.* Translated by Willard R. Trask. New York: Harper & Row.

––––––. 1969. *Yoga.* Translated by Willard R. Trask. Princeton, N.J.: Princeton University Press.

Evans-Pritchard, E. E. [1948] 1962. The divine kingship of the Shilluk of the Nilotic Sudan [Frazer Lecture 1948]. In *Social Anthropology and Other Essays*, 192–212. New York: Free Press.

––––––. 1965. *Theories of Primitive Religion.* Oxford: Oxford University Press.

––––––. 1971. Sources with particular reference to the southern Sudan. *Cahiers d'Études Africaine* 11: 129–79.

Fallers, L. A. 1959. Despotism, status culture and social mobility in an African kingdom. *Comparative Studies in Society and History* 2: 11–32.

––––––, ed. 1964. *The King's Men.* London: Oxford University Press.

Faulkner, R. O. 1969. *The Ancient Egyptian Pyramid Texts Translated into English.* Oxford: Clarendon Press.

––––––. 1985. *The Ancient Egyptian Book of the Dead.* London: British Museum.

Faupel, J. F. 1962. *African Holocaust.* London: Geoffrey Chapman.

Feeley-Harnik, Gillian. 1985. Issues in divine kingship. *Annual Review of Anthropology* 14: 273–313.

Felkin, Robert W. 1885–1886. Notes on the Waganda tribe. *Proceedings of the Royal Society of Edinburgh* 13: 699–770.

Foucault, Michel. 1979. *Discipline and Punish.* Translated by Alan Sheridan. New York: Vintage Books.

Frankfort, Henri. [1948] 1978. *Kingship and the Gods.* Chicago: University of Chicago Press.

––––––. 1949. Ancient Egyptians and the Hamites. *Man*: 95–96.

Frazer, James G. [1887] 1889. Questions on the manners, customs, religion, superstitions, &c. of uncivilized or semi-civilized peoples. *Journal*

    of the Anthropological Institute of Great Britain and Ireland 18: 431–
    39.
_____. 1907. *Questions on the Customs, Beliefs, and Languages of Savages*.
    Cambridge: Cambridge University Press.
_____. 1907–1922. Unpublished letters to John Roscoe. Trinity College Library,
    Cambridge University.
_____. 1910. *Totemism and Exogamy*. 4 vols. London: Macmillan.
_____. 1911–1915. *The Golden Bough*. 12 vols. London: Macmillan.
_____. 1922a. *The Golden Bough*. 1 vol. abridged ed. New York: Macmillan.
_____. [1922b] 1967. Preface to *Argonauts of the Western Pacific*, by Bronislaw
    Malinowski. New York: Dutton.
_____. 1931. *Garnered Sheaves*. London: Macmillan.
_____. [1935] 1968. Canon John Roscoe. In *Creation and Evolution in Primitive
    Cosmogonies*, 73–79. London: Dawson's of Pall Mall.
_____. 1936. *Aftermath: A Supplement to the Golden Bough*. London: Macmillan.
Funeral of the Late King Mwanga. 1949. *Uganda Journal* 13: 224–25. (Originally
    published in *Uganda Notes* [September 1910])
Gale, H. P. 1954. Mutesa I – Was he a god? *Uganda Journal* 20: 72–87.
Geertz, Clifford. 1973. Religion as a cultural system. In *The Interpretation of
    Cultures*, 87–125. New York: Basic Books.
_____. 1980. *Negara: The Theatre State in Nineteenth-Century Bali*. Princeton,
    N.J.: Princeton University Press.
_____. 1983a. Centers, kings, and charisma: Reflections on the symbolics of
    power. In *Local Knowledge*, 121–46. New York: Basic Books.
_____. 1983b. From the native's point of view: On the nature of anthropological
    understanding. In *Local Knowledge*, 55–70. New York: Basic Books.
_____. 1988. *Works and Lives*. Stanford, Calif.: Stanford University Press.
Gennep, Arnold van. [1911] 1967. The questionnaire: Or, ethnographic enquiries.
    In *The Semi-Scholars*. Edited and translated by Rodney Needham. London: Routledge and Kegan Paul.
Ggomotoka, J. T. K. 1934. *Magezi Ntakke* (The Wisdom of the Termites [proverb]). Bukalasa, Uganda: White Fathers' Printing Press.
Giesey, Ralph E. 1960. *The Royal Funeral Ceremony*. Geneva: Librairie Droz.
Girard, René. 1977. *Violence and the Sacred*. Translated from the French. Baltimore: Johns Hopkins University Press.
Gluckman, Max. 1960. Rituals of rebellion in South-East Africa. In *Order and
    Rebellion in Tribal Africa*, 110–36. New York: Free Press.
Goody, Jack. 1961. Religion and ritual: The definitional problem. *British Journal
    of Sociology* 12: 148–52.
Gorju, Julien. 1920. *Entre le Victoria, L'Albert et L'Edouard*. Rennes: Oberthur.
Grant, James A. 1862. "Journals of James A. Grant." MS. 17915, National
    Library of Scotland.

———. 1864. *A Walk Across Africa*. Edinburgh: Blackwood & Sons.

———. 1872. Summary of observations on the geography, climate, and natural history of the Lake Regions of Equatorial Africa made by the Speke and Grant Expedition, 1860–63. *Journal of the Royal Geographical Society* 42: 243–342.

Gray, John Milner. 1934. Mutesa of Buganda. *Uganda Journal* 1: 22–133.

———. 1935. Early history of Buganda. *Uganda Journal* 2: 259–71.

———. 1947. Ahmed Bin Ibrahim—The first Arab to reach Buganda. *Uganda Journal* 11: 80–97.

———. 1956. Kibuuka. *Uganda Journal* 20: 52–71.

———. 1964. Ernest Linant de Bellefonds. *Uganda Journal* 28: 31–54.

Griffiths, J. Gwyn. 1980. *The Origins of Osiris and His Cult*. Leiden: Brill.

Grottanelli, Cristiano. 1987. Kingship: An overview. *The Encyclopedia of Religion*. Vol. 8: 313–17. Edited by Mircea Eliade. New York: Macmillan.

Gutkind, Peter C. W. 1963. *The Royal Capital of Buganda*. The Hague: Mouton.

Haddon, A. C. 1933. Canon John Roscoe. *Man*: 52–53.

Hadfield, P. [1949] 1979. *Traits of Divine Kingship in Africa*. Westport, Conn.: Greenwood Press.

Hancock, I. R. 1970. Patriotism and neo-traditionalism in Buganda: The Kabaka Yekka ("The King Alone") Movement, 1961–1962. *Journal of African History* 11: 419–34.

Harford-Battersby, Charles F. 1898. *Pilkington of Uganda*. London: Marshall Brothers.

Hattersley, C. W. [1908] 1968. *The Baganda at Home*. London: Cass.

Haydon, E. S. 1960. *Law and Justice in Buganda*. London: Butterworth.

Henige, David. 1974. Reflections on early Interlacustrine chronology. *Journal of African History* 15: 27–46.

———. 1980. "The disease of writing": Ganda and Nyoro kinglists in a newly literate world. In *The African Past Speaks*. Edited by Joseph C. Miller, 240–61. Folkestone: Dawson.

Herbert, J. S. 1943. The coronation in Uganda. *C.M.S. Outlook*, no. 34.

Hobsbawm, Eric, and Terence Ranger, eds. 1983. *The Invention of Tradition*. Cambridge: Cambridge University Press.

Hyman, Stanley Edgar. 1959. *The Tangled Bank*. New York: Atheneum.

Irstam, Tor. [1944] 1970. *The King of Ganda*. Westport, Conn.: Negro Universities Press.

Johnston, H. H. 1902. *The Uganda Protectorate*. 2 vols. London: Hutchinson.

Jonveaux, Emile. 1884. *Deux ans dans l'Afrique oriental*. Tours: Mame.

Kabuga, Charles E. S. 1963. The genealogy of Kabaka Kintu and the early Bakabaka of Buganda. *Uganda Journal* 27: 205–16.

Kaggwa, Apolo. [1901] 1971. *Basekabaka be Buganda*. [2nd ed., 1912; 3rd ed., 1927. Reprinted 1953, 1971]. Kampala: Uganda Bookshop. Translated by

M. S. M. Kiwanuka under the title *The Kings of Buganda*. Nairobi: East African Publishing House.

————. [1902] 1951. *Engero za Baganda* (Folktales of the Baganda). London: Sheldon Press. Partially translated by F. Rowling under the title *The Tales of Sir Apolo*. London: Religious Tract Society, n.d.

————. [1907]. 1934. *Empisa za Baganda*. [2nd ed., 1911; 3rd ed., 1918. Reprinted 1927, 1934, 1952]. Kampala: Uganda Bookshop. Partially translated by Ernest B. Kalibala under the title *The Customs of the Baganda*. Edited by May Mandelbaum. Columbia University Contributions to Anthropology, no. 22. New York: Columbia University Press, 1934.

————. [1912]. 1949. *Ebika bya Baganda* (The Clans of the Baganda). Kampala: Uganda Bookshop. Translation, Department of History, Makerere University, n.d.

Kakoma, S. K. L., A. M. Ntate, and M. Serukaga. 1959. *Ekitabo Eky'Abakyanjove Ab'e Mmamba Mu Siiga Lya Nankere e'Bukerekere* (Book of the Kyanjove Members of the Lungfish Clan, the Lineage of Nankere at Bukerekere). Kampala: E.A.I.S.R.

Kakooza, J. M. N. 1967. The evolution of juridical control in Buganda. Ph.D. diss., Oxford University.

Kalibala, Ernest B. 1946. The social structure of the Buganda tribe of East Africa. Ph.D. diss., Harvard University.

Kantorowicz, Ernst. 1957. *The King's Two Bodies*. Princeton, N.J.: Princeton University Press.

Karugire, Samwiri Rubaraza. 1971. *A History of the Kingdom of Nkore*. Oxford: Clarendon Press.

Kasirye, J. S. 1971. *Abataregga ku Nnamulondo ya Buganda* (Princes of the Throne of Buganda). London: Macmillan.

Kavuma, Paulo. 1979. *Crisis in Buganda 1953-55*. London: Rex Collings.

Kenny, Michael G. 1988. Mutesa's crime: Hubris and the control of African kings. *Comparative Studies in Society and History* 30: 595-612.

Kibuuka, G. B. 1974. The rituals of twins amongst the society of the Baganda. Conference for Research on African Religious History in East Africa. Limuru, Kenya.

Kiwanuka, Semakula. 1971a. *A History of Buganda*. London: Longman.

————, trans. 1971b. *The Kings of Buganda*, by Apolo Kaggwa. Nairobi: East African Publishing House.

————. 1979. *Amin and the Tragedy of Uganda*. Munich: Weltforum Verlag.

Knappert, Jan. 1970. *Myths and Legends of the Swahili*. London: Heinemann.

Kopytoff, Igor. 1971. Ancestors as elders in Africa. *Africa* 41: 129-41.

Kulubya, Owekitibwa S. W. 1942. Some aspects of Baganda customs. *Uganda Journal* 9: 49-56.

K. W. 1935. The kings of Bunyoro-Kitara. *Uganda Journal* 3: 155-60.

————. 1936. The kings of Bunyoro-Kitara: Part II. *Uganda Journal* 4: 75-83.

————. 1937a. The kings of Bunyoro-Kitara: Part III. *Uganda Journal* 5: 53-67.

_____. 1937b. The procedure in accession to the throne of a nominated king in the kingdom of Bunyoro-Kitara. *Uganda Journal* 4: 289–99.

Kyemba, Henry. 1977. *State of Blood*. New York: Ace Books.

Kyomya, E. 1960. *Ebyafaayo bya Kabaka* (History of the Kabakas). Nakivubo, Uganda: Mutundwe Commercial College.

Lagercrantz, Sture. 1944. The sacral king in Africa. *Ethnos* 9: 118–40.

Lanning, E. C. 1956. Shafts in Buganda and Toro. *Uganda Journal* 20: 216–17.

_____. 1958. Shafts in Buganda and Toro. *Uganda Journal* 22: 188–89.

Leach, Edmund, 1966. On the "Founding Fathers." *Current Anthropology* 7: 560–75.

LeBlond, G. 1912. *Le Père August Achte*. Algiers: Maison-Carrée.

Leeuw, Gerhardus, van der. [1932] 1963. *Religion in Essence and Manifestation*. Translated by J. E. Turner. Appendices by Hans H. Penner. 2 vols. New York: Harper & Row.

Le Veux, R. P. [1882] 1914. *Manuel de Langue Luganda*. Algiers: Maison-Carrée.

_____. 1917. *Vocabulaire Luganda-Français*. 2nd ed. Algiers: Maison-Carrée.

Lévi-Strauss, Claude. 1966. *The Savage Mind*. Translated from the French. Chicago: University of Chicago Press.

Low, D. A. 1971a. *Buganda in Modern History*. London: Cox & Wyman.

_____. 1971b. *The Mind of Buganda*. London: Heinemann.

Lugira, A. M. 1968. Redemption in Ganda traditional belief. *Uganda Journal* 32: 199–203.

_____. 1970. *Ganda Art*. Kampala: Osasa.

Lukongwa, P. M. 1961. *Ebintu Ebisaanidde Okumanyibwa Abalangira n'Abambejja Be Buganda* (Things Fitting to Be Known About the Princes and Princesses of Buganda). Kampala: Uganda Argus Press.

Lush, Allan J. 1937. Kiganda drums. *Uganda Journal* 1: 7–25.

Macdonald, J. R. L. [1897] 1973. *Soldering and Surveying in British East Africa, 1891–1894*. Folkestone: Dawson.

MacGaffey, Wyatt. 1970. Concepts of race in the historiography of Northeast Africa. In *African Prehistory*. Edited by J. D. Fage and R. A. Oliver, 99–115. Cambridge: Cambridge University Press.

Mackay, A. M. 1890. *A. M. Mackay*. Letters compiled by J. W. Harrison. London: Hodder and Staughton.

The MacKie Expedition. 1922. *The Eagle* 42: 70–71.

Mair, Lucy. 1934. *An African People in the Twentieth Century*. London: Routledge and Kegan Paul.

_____. 1964. *Primitive Government*. Harmondsworth: Penguin Books.

Malinowski, Bronislaw. [1922] 1967. *Argonauts of the Western Pacific*. New York: Dutton.

_____. [1925] 1954. Myth in primitive psychology [Frazer Lecture 1925]. In *Magic, Science and Religion*, 93–148. New York: Doubleday.

Mandelbaum, May. 1934. Preface to *The Customs of the Baganda*, by Apolo Kaggwa. Translated by Ernest B. Kalibala. Columbia University Contributions to Anthropology, no. 22. New York: Columbia University Press.

Marcus, George E., and Michael M. J. Fisher. 1986. *Anthropology as Cultural Critique*. Chicago: University of Chicago Press.

Martin, D. 1978. *General Amin*. Rev. ed. London: Sphere.

Martin, K. 1984. Sedfest. In *Lexikon der Agyptologie*. Vol. 5: 782–90. Edited by Wolfgang Helk and Wolfhart Westendorf. Wiesbaden: Otto Harrassowitz.

Mitchell, Philip. *Diaries 1927–59*. 33 vols. Rhodes House Library, Oxford.

Miti, James. n.d. A short history of Buganda. Translation of manuscript, Makerere University Library. CAMP microfilm.

Mittleman, James H. 1975. *Ideology and Politics in Uganda: From Obote to Amin*. Ithaca, N.Y.: Cornell University Press.

Montagu, Ashley. 1964. *The Concept of Race*. New York: Free Press.

Mukasa, Ham. 1904. *Uganda's Katikiro in England*. Translated by Ernest Millar. London: Hutchinson.

————. 1938. *Simuda Nyuma—Ebiro Mutesa* (Do Not Look Back [proverb]—The Reign of Mutesa). Vol. 1. Translated by John Rowe. London: S.P.C.K. CAMP microfilm.

————. 1946a. The rule of the kings of Buganda. *Uganda Journal* 10: 136–43.

————. 1946b. The reason for the creation of the post of Mugema in Buganda. *Uganda Journal* 10: 150.

Mulira, Enoch E. K. 1945. *Thoughts of a Young African*. London: Lutterworth Press.

————. [1951] 1965. *Olugero lwa Kintu* (The Story of Kintu). Vol. 1. [2nd ed., 1955]. London: Oxford University Press.

————. [1951] 1959. *Olugero lwa Kintu* (The Story of Kintu). Vol. 2. [2nd ed., 1955]. Nairobi: East African Literature Bureau.

————. [1951] 1970. *Olugero lwa Kintu* (The Story of Kintu). Vol. 2. [2nd ed., 1955; 3rd ed., 1965]. London: Oxford University Press.

Mullins, Joseph V. 1904. *The Wonderful Story of Uganda*. London: Church Missionary Society.

Musoke, Ezra. 1935, 1 May. Letter giving burial places of Kabakas, princes, princesses, and Queen Mothers. L. A. Fallers Collection, University of Chicago.

Mutebi, Wilson. 1971. Okwabya olumbe among Baganda, no. 27. In *Occasional Papers in African Traditional Religion and Philosophy*. Vol. 3. Edited by A. B. T. Byaruhanga-Akiiki. Kampala: Department of Religious Studies and Philosophy, Makerere University.

————. 1972. Abalongo: Twins—Buganda Uganda, no. 35. In *Occasional Papers in African Traditional Religion and Philosophy*. Vol. 4. Edited by A. B. T. Byaruhanga-Akiiki. Kampala: Department of Religious Studies and Philosophy, Makerere University.

Mutesa II, Edward Frederick. 1967. *Desecration of My Kingdom*. London: Constable.

Nabasuta, Helen K. 1974. Creative expression in Kiganda folk narrative. B.A. thesis, Makerere University.

Nsimbi, M. B. 1950. Baganda traditional personal names. *Uganda Journal* 14: 204–14.

_____. [1952] 1971. *Waggumbulizi* (Your Intimate Friend [proverb]). Kampala: Uganda Bookshop.

_____. 1956a. Village life and customs in Buganda. *Uganda Journal* 20: 27–36.

_____. 1956b. *Amannya Amaganda n'Ennono Zaago* (Ganda Names and Their Origins). Kampala: East African Literature Bureau.

_____. 1964. The clan system in Buganda. *Uganda Journal* 28: 25–30.

_____. 1968. *Omweso, a Game People Play in Uganda*. Occasional Paper, no. 6. Los Angeles: African Studies Center, University of California.

Nyakatura, J. W. 1973. *Anatomy of an African Kingdom*. Translated by Teopista Muganwa. Edited by Godfrey N. Uzoigwe. New York: Anchor Books.

Oded, Arye. 1974. *Islam in Uganda*. Jerusalem: Israel Universities Press.

Oden, R. A., Jr. 1979. Method in the study of Near Eastern myths. *Religion* 9: 182–96.

Okutikira Engule (The Coronation) *His Highness Daudi Chwa II*. 1914. Budo.

Oliver, Roland. 1955. The traditional histories of Buganda, Bunyoro, and Nkole. *Journal of the Royal Anthropological Institute* 85: 111–17.

_____. 1959. The royal tombs of Buganda. *Uganda Journal* 23: 124–33.

_____. 1977. The East African interior. In *The Cambridge History of Africa*. Edited by Roland Oliver, 621–69. Cambridge: Cambridge University Press.

Oliver, Roland, and J. D. Fage. 1966. *A Short History of Africa*. 2nd ed. Harmondsworth: Penguin Books.

"Olusozi Buddo" (Buddo Hill). n.d. MS F. 6 Busiro. L. A. Fallers Collection, University of Chicago.

Orley, John H. 1970. *Culture and Mental Illness*. Nairobi: East African Publishing House.

Otto, Rudolf. [1910] 1963. *The Idea of the Holy*. Translated by John W. Harvey. London: Oxford University Press.

Penner, Hans. 1971. The poverty of functionalism. *History of Religions* 11: 91–97.

_____. 1986a. Criticism and the development of a science of religion. *Studies in Religion* 15: 165–75.

_____. 1986b. Structure and religion. *History of Religions* 25: 236–54.

Pettazzoni, Raffaele. 1967. *Essays on the History of Religions*. Translated by H. J. Rose. Leiden: Brill.

Pillai, T. K. Velu. 1940. *The Travancore State Manual*. Trivandrum: Government of Travancore.

Posener, G. 1965. Le nom de l'enseigne appelée "Khons." *Révue d'Egyptologie* 17: 193–95.

Posnansky, Merrick. 1966. Kingship, archaeology and historical myth. *Uganda Journal* 30: 1–12.

Ray, Benjamin C. 1972. Royal shrines and ceremonies of Buganda. *Uganda Journal* 36: 35–48.

———. 1976. *African Religions*. Englewood Cliffs, N.J.: Prentice-Hall.

———. 1977a. Sacred space and royal shrines in Buganda. *History of Religions* 16: 363–73.

———. 1977b. Death and kingship in Buganda. In *Religious Encounters with Death*. Edited by Earle H. Waugh and Frank E. Reynolds, 56–69. University Park: Pennsylvania State University Press.

———. 1981. The story of Kintu: Myth, death, and ontology in Buganda. In *Explorations in African Systems of Thought*. Edited by Ivan Karp and Charles S. Bird, 60–79. Bloomington: Indiana University Press.

Richards, Audrey I., ed. 1959. *East African Chiefs*. London: Faber & Faber.

———. 1964. Authority patterns in traditional Buganda. In *The King's Men*. Edited by L. A. Fallers, 256–93. London: Oxford University Press.

———. 1966. *The Changing Structure of a Ganda Village*. Nairobi: East African Publishing House.

———. 1969. Keeping the king divine. *Proceedings of the Royal Anthropological Institute 1968*: 23–35.

Ricoeur, Paul. 1970. *Freud and Philosophy: An Essay on Interpretation*. Translated by Denis Savage. New Haven, Conn.: Yale University Press.

Rigby, Peter, and Fred Lule. 1973. Divination and healing in peri-urban Kampala, Uganda. *Nkanga*, no. 7: 67–92.

Rorty, Richard. 1979. *Philosophy and the Mirror of Nature*. Princeton, N.J.: Princeton University Press.

———. 1989. *Contingency, Irony, and Solidarity*. Cambridge: Cambridge University Press.

Roscoe, John. 1901. Notes on the manners and customs of the Baganda. *Journal of the Anthropological Institute of Great Britain and Ireland* 31: 117–30.

———. 1902. Further notes on the manners and customs of the Baganda. *Journal of the Anthropological Institute of Great Britain and Ireland* 32: 25–80.

———. 1907a. Kibuuka, the war god of the Baganda. *Man*: 161–66.

———. 1907b. Worship of the dead as practiced by some African tribes. In *Varia Africana*. Edited by Oric Bates, 33–47. Harvard African Studies Series, vol. 1. Cambridge, Mass.: Peabody Museum of Harvard University.

———. 1908. Nantuba, the female fetish of the king of Uganda. *Man*: 132–33.

———. 1909. Python worship in Buganda. *Man*: 88–90.

———. 1911. *The Baganda: An Account of Their Native Customs and Beliefs*. London: Macmillan.

———. 1915. *The Northern Bantu*. Cambridge: Cambridge University Press.

———. 1921. *Twenty-Five Years in East Africa*. Cambridge: Cambridge University Press.

———. 1922. *The Soul of Central Africa*. London: Cassell.

———. 1923a. *The Bakitara of Banyoro*. Cambridge: Cambridge University Press.

———. 1923b. *The Banyankole.* Cambridge: Cambridge University Press.

———. 1924a. *The Bagesu and Other Tribes of the Uganda Protectorate.* Cambridge: Cambridge University Press.

———. [1924b] 1932. Immigrants and their influence in the Lake Region of Central Africa. In *The Frazer Lectures 1922-32.* Edited by Warren R. Dawson, 25-47. London: Macmillan.

———. n.d. Notebook. [In the possession of John Rowe, lent by Veronica Little, St. Alban's, England].

Roscoe, John, and Apolo Kaggwa. 1906. Enquiry into native land tenure in the Uganda Protectorate. R.H. MSS Afr. s. 17. Bodleian Library, Oxford University.

Rowe, John. 1966. Revolution in Buganda 1856-1900. Part One: The reign of Mukabya Mutesa, 1856-1884. Ph.D. diss., University of Wisconsin.

———. 1967. Roscoe's and Kagwa's Baganda. *Journal of African History* 8: 163-66.

———. 1969. Myth, memoir and moral admonition: Luganda historical writing, 1893-1969. *Uganda Journal* 33: 17-40; 34: 217-19.

Seligman, Charles G. 1913. Some aspects of the Hamitic problem in the Anglo-Egyptian Sudan. *Journal of the Royal Anthropological Institute of Great Britain and Ireland* 43: 593-683.

———. [1930] 1966. *The Races of Africa.* London: Oxford University Press.

———. 1934. *Egypt and Negro Africa: A Study of Divine Kingship.* London: George Routledge and Sons.

Seligman, C. G., and Margaret A. Murray. 1911. Notes upon an early Egyptian standard. *Man* 11: 165-71.

Shils, Edward. 1975. *Center and Periphery: Essays in Macro-Sociology.* Chicago: University of Chicago Press.

Shinnie, P. L. 1971. The legacy of Egypt. In *The Legacy of Egypt.* 2nd ed. Edited by J. R. Harris, 434-55. Oxford: Clarendon Press.

Smart, Ninian. 1973. *The Science of Religion and the Sociology of Knowledge.* Princeton, N.J.: Princeton University Press.

———. 1985. *Concept and Empathy.* Edited by Donald Wiebe. London: Macmillan.

Smith, Jonathan Z. 1969. The glory, jest and riddle: James George Frazer and *The Golden Bough.* Ph.D. diss., Yale University.

———. 1971. Adde Parvum Parvo Magnus Acervus Erit. *History of Religions* 11: 67-90.

———. 1973. When the bough breaks. *History of Religions* 12: 342-71.

———. 1982. *Imagining Religion.* Chicago: University of Chicago Press.

———. 1987. *To Take Place.* Chicago: University of Chicago Press.

Snoxall, R. A. 1937. The coronation ritual and customs of Buganda. *Uganda Journal* 4: 277-88.

———. 1967. *Luganda-English Dictionary.* Oxford: Clarendon Press.

Southwold, Martin M. 1961. *Bureaucracy and Chiefship in Buganda.* East African Studies, no. 14. Kampala: East African Institute of Social Research.

_____. 1967. Was the kingdom sacred? *Mawazo* 1: 17–23.

_____. 1968. The history of a history: Royal succession in Buganda. In *History and Social Anthropology*. Edited by I. M. Lewis, 127–51. London: Tavistock.

_____. 1973. The "mother's brother" and other problems of meaning in Buganda. *Nkanga*, no. 7: 51–57.

Speke, John Hanning. 1863. *Journey of the Discovery of the Source of the Nile*. Edinburgh: Blackwood & Sons.

Stanley, Henry M. 1878. *Through the Dark Continent*. 2 vols. London: Sampson Low, Marston, Searle & Rivington.

_____. 1893. How Kimera became king of Uganda. In *My Dark Companions and Their Strange Stories*, 126–60. London: Sampson Low, Marston.

Stanner, W. E. H. 1967. Reflections on Durkheim and aboriginal religion. In *Social Organization: Essays Presented to Raymond Firth*. Edited by Maurice Freedman, 217–40. Chicago: Aldine.

Stocking, George W., Jr. 1968. *Race, Culture, and Evolution*. New York: Free Press.

Sullivan, Lawrence E. 1988. *Icanchu's Drum*. New York: Macmillan.

Taylor, John A. 1958. *The Growth of the Church in Buganda*. London: SCM Press.

Thornton, Robert J. 1974. The kibuga: Traditional capital of the Baganda. M.A. thesis, University of Chicago.

Tucker, A. R. 1908. *Eighteen Years in Uganda and East Africa*. 2 vols. London: Edwin Arnold.

Turner, Victor. 1969. *The Ritual Process*. Chicago: Aldine.

_____. 1974. *Dramas, Fields, and Metaphors*. Ithaca, N.Y.: Cornell University Press.

_____. 1982. *From Ritual to Theatre*. New York: Performing Arts Journal Publications.

Twaddle, Michael. 1969. The Bakungu chiefs of Buganda under British colonial rule. *Journal of African History* 10: 309–22.

_____. 1974. On Ganda historiography. *History in Africa* 1: 85–99.

Twesigye, Emmanuel K. 1987. *Common Ground: Christianity, African Religion and Philosophy*. New York: Peter Lang.

Valeri, Valerio. 1985. *Kingship and Sacrifice*. Translated by Paula Wissing. Chicago: University of Chicago Press.

Vaughn, James H. 1980. A reconsideration of divine kingship. In *Explorations in African Systems of Thought*. Edited by Ivan Karp and Charles S. Bird, 120–42. Bloomington: Indiana University Press.

Waller, Horace, ed. 1874. *The Last Journals of David Livingston*. London: John Murray.

Welbourn, Fred B. 1962a. Kibuuka comes home. *Transition* 2: 15–17.

_____. 1962b. Some aspects of Kiganda religion. *Uganda Journal* 26: 171–82.

_____. 1965. *Religion and Politics in Uganda, 1952–1962*. Nairobi: East African Publishing House.

Wiebe, Donald. 1984. The failure of nerve in the academic study of religion. *Studies in Religion* 13: 401–22.

Williams, Bruce. 1984. The lost pharoahs of Nubia. Nile Valley Civilizations. *Journal of African Civilizations* 6: 29–43.

Williams, F. Lukyn. 1940. The Kabaka of Buganda: Death of His Highness Sir Daudi Chwa K. G. M. G., K. B. E. and accession of Edward Mutesa II. *Uganda Journal* 7: 176–87.

_____. 1946. Myth, legend and lore in Uganda. *Uganda Journal* 10: 64–75.

Wilson, C. T., and R. W. Felkin. 1882. *Uganda and the Egyptian Sudan*. 2 vols. London: Sampson Low, Marston, Searle & Rivington.

Wright, Michael. 1971. *Buganda in the Heroic Age*. Nairobi: Oxford University Press.

Wrigley, Christopher C. 1958. Some thoughts on the Bacwezi. *Uganda Journal* 22: 11–21.

_____. 1959. Kimera. *Uganda Journal* 23: 38–43.

_____. 1964. The changing economic structure of Buganda. In *The King's Men*. Edited by L. A. Fallers, 17–48. London: Oxford University Press.

_____. 1965. Sir Apolo Kagwa. *Tarikh* 1: 14–25.

_____. 1974. The kinglists of Buganda. *History in Africa* 1: 129–39.

Yoder, John. 1988. The quest for Kintu and the search for peace: Mythology and morality in nineteenth-century Buganda. *History in Africa* 15: 363–76.

Young, Michael W. 1966. The divine kingship of the Jukun: A re-evaluation of some theories. *Africa* 36: 135–53.

Zimbe, Bartolomayo M. 1939. *Buganda ne Kabaka*. Mengo, Uganda: Gambuze.

Index

DATE DUE